"The authors have done a superb job making the case for the importance of intergenerational ministry in our churches. And the practical suggestions make it doable for every church. This book belongs on every pastor's bookshelf."

Ivy Beckwith, Ph.D., author of *Postmodern Children's Ministry*

"Holly Allen and Christine Ross make a strong case for the importance of intergenerational ministry. They then follow this up with stories, examples and specific ideas for how to make intergenerational ministry happen in churches large or small. This book is a valuable resource for anyone in ministry."

Robert J. Keeley, professor of education, Calvin College, and author of *Helping Our Children Grow in Faith*

"It is most encouraging to read Holly Allen and Christine Ross's new take on this focus in their *Intergenerational Christian Formation*. Whether readers are those who sense that God's heartbeat for his special community is about inclusiveness in how Christians express their lives together—and indeed, the corporate life of the faith communities themselves—or skeptics willing to come to the topic with an open mind, this book is likely to be a life-giver, as it draws together broad insights to reinforce that the intergenerational perspective can be held with integrity, and also as it provides a wide range of examples and practical ideas to enable effective practice."

Allan Harkness, dean of AGST Alliance, a postgraduate theological education venture in Southeast Asia

"Christine Ross and Holly Allen genuinely believe in the intergenerational nature of the church, the people of God at every age together. They lay out an excellent vision for rebuilding that intergenerational nature in contemporary congregational life. Segmentation of a church's membership and age segregation have almost no place in their vision. They lay out the scriptural basis for the multigenerational church and review an amazing amount of literature in a concise and cogent way, and their writing is engaging and reader-friendly. Being a big fan of generational history, I really liked their presentation of it and how it works in the church. Read this book and intergenerational ministry seems so obvious."

Terry Dittmer, director of youth ministry, the Lutheran Church—Missouri Synod

"Families are complex; family ministry even more so. Allen and Ross explain how the best of intentions brought about the separation of generations in the church with serious unintended consequences. Now the question is: How do we bring the generations back together again into the one body that is the church?

In *Intergenerational Christian Formation* this question is scrutinized from every possible angle, with input from every possible source. Allen and Ross conclude by offering more than enough activities to get the generations mixing again. Pastors, directors of Christian education and lay ministers will be pulling this book off their shelves for advice and inspiration over and over again."

Dr. John W. Oberdeck, professor of theology and director for lay ministry, Concordia University Wisconsin

"Thought-provoking—and refreshing! Allen and Ross present a perfect blend of the biblical principles, academic inquiries and practical solutions surrounding one of the most significant, yet uncharted, areas in today's church communities. A must-read for all who desire to pass along a lasting Christian faith from generation to generation."

Jessica Stollings Strang, generational speaker and founder of re:Generations

"In *Intergenerational Christian Formation* Holly Allen and Christine Ross give us thorough, powerful and practical approaches to growing Christ-followers of all generations. Pastors, church leaders and all believers can greatly benefit from their wise insights into how Christians grow and mature when the different generations learn that we are better together. I highly recommend this book."

Peter Menconi, author of *The Intergenerational Church: Understanding Congregations from WWII to www.com*

"Allen and Ross have opened up a critical issue for thoughtful ministry leaders to consider. We have recognized for some time the strengths and limitations of age-segregated ministry but not had strong advocates to help us consider ways to strengthen our ministry efforts through intergenerational approaches. This book is a welcome guide to show us the needs, consider the biblical foundations for intergenerational ministry and learn from recent research about how people grow in their interactions with others from different generations. The final section on intergenerational Christian formation practices is worth the price of the whole book. If you care about the Christian formation of children, youth and adults in your church, you have to read this book and begin to put into practice what you have learned!"

Dr. Kevin E. Lawson, director, Ph.D. and Ed.D. programs in educational studies at Talbot School of Theology, Biola University, and editor of the *Christian Education Journal*

INTERGENERATIONAL CHRISTIAN FORMATION

Bringing the Whole Church Together
in Ministry, Community and Worship

Holly Catterton Allen
and Christine Lawton Ross

IVP Academic

An imprint of InterVarsity Press
Downers Grove, Illinois

InterVarsity Press
P.O. Box 1400, Downers Grove, IL 60515-1426
World Wide Web: www.ivpress.com
E-mail: email@ivpress.com

InterVarsity Press® is the book-publishing division of InterVarsity Christian Fellowship/USA®, a movement of students and faculty active on campus at hundreds of universities, colleges and schools of nursing in the United States of America, and a member movement of the International Fellowship of Evangelical Students. For information about local and regional activities, write Public Relations Dept., InterVarsity Christian Fellowship/USA, 6400 Schroeder Rd., P.O. Box 7895, Madison, WI 53707-7895, or visit the IVCF website at <www.intervarsity.org>.

All Scripture quotations, unless otherwise indicated, are taken from the THE HOLY BIBLE, NEW INTERNATIONAL VERSION®, NIV® *Copyright © 1973, 1978, 1984, 2011 by Biblica, Inc.™ Used by permission. All rights reserved worldwide.*

While all stories in this book are true, some names and identifying information in this book have been changed to protect the privacy of the individuals involved.

Some parts of this book were adapted from or previously published in "Bringing the Generations Back Together: Introduction to Intergenerationality," an introductory article by Holly Catterton Allen in Christian Education Journal *(series 3), Volume 9, Issue 1, (Spring 2012), pp. 101-4. Published by Talbot School of Theology in Cooperation with the North American Professors of Christian Education, www.biola.edu/cej. This material is copyrighted and is reprinted here by permission.*

Some parts of this book were adapted from or previously published in "Four Congregations That Practice Intergenerationality," an article by Christine Ross in Christian Education Journal *(series 3), Volume 9, Issue 1 (Spring 2012), pp. 135-47. Published by Talbot School of Theology in Cooperation with the North American Professors of Christian Education, www.biola.edu/cej. This material is copyrighted and is reprinted here by permission.*

Some parts of this book were previously published in "No Better Place: Fostering Intergenerational Christian Community," a chapter in Shaped by God: Twelve Essentials for Nurturing Faith in Children, Youth and Adults, *edited by Robert Keeley, published in 2010 by Faith Alive Christian Resources in Grand Rapids, Michigan. Used by permission of Faith Alive Christian Resources. To order a copy of* Shaped by God, *please call 1-800-333-8300 or visit www.faithaliveresources.org.*

Some parts of this book were adapted from or previously published in "Bringing the Generations Together: Support from Learning Theory," an article by Holly Catterton Allen in Lifelong Faith: The Theory and Practice of Lifelong Faith Formation, *Spring 2009, pp. 3-11. Used by permission of Lifelong Faith.*

Some parts of this book were adapted from or previously published in "Bringing the Generations Together: Support from Learning Theory," an article by Holly Catterton Allen in Christian Education Journal *(series 3), Volume 2, Issue 2 (Fall 2005), pp. 319-33. Published by Talbot School of Theology in Cooperation with the North American Professors of Christian Education, www.biola.edu/cej. This material is copyrighted and is reprinted here by permission.*

Some parts of this book were adapted from or previously published in "Nurturing Children's Spirituality in Intergenerational Settings," a chapter by Holly Catterton Allen in Children's Spirituality: Christian Perspectives, Research, and Applications, *edited by Donald Ratcliff, published in 2004 by Wipf & Stock/Cascade in Eugene, Oregon. Used by permission of Wipf & Stock. www.wipfandstock.com.*

Some parts of this book were adapted from or previously published in "Nurturing Child's Spirituality in Intergenerational Settings," an article by Holly Catterton Allen in the Lutheran Education Journal, *Volume 139, Number 2 (Winter 2003), pp. 111-24. Published by Concordia University, River Forest, Illinois. Used by permission.*

Lyrics to "There Is a Redeemer" by Melody Green: Copyright © 1982 Birdwing Music (ASCAP) BMG Songs (ASCAP) Ears To Hear Music (ASCAP) (adm. at EMICMGPublishing.com) All rights reserved. Used by permission.

Cover design: Cindy Kiple
Images: Michael Hitoshi/Getty Images
Interior design: Beth Hagenberg

ISBN 978-0-8308-3981-0

Printed in the United States of America ∞

Library of Congress Cataloging-in-Publication Data

Allen, Holly Catterton.
Intergenerational Christian formation: bringing the whole church together in ministry, community and worship / Holly Catterton Allen and Christine Lawton Ross.
      p. cm.
Includes bibliographical references and index.
ISBN 978-0-8308-3981-0 (pbk. : alk. paper)
1. Church. 2. Intergenerational relations—Religious aspects—Christianity. I. Ross, Christine Lawton, 1962- II. Title.
BV640.A55 2012
253—dc23

                                                                                            2012027650

P   24   23   22   21   20   19   18   17   16   15   14   13   12   11   10   9   8   7

Y   33   32   31   30   29   28   27   26   25   24   23   22   21   20

CONTENTS

ACKNOWLEDGMENTS

HOLLY

I must first acknowledge the support I have received from John Brown University, where I have taught for nine years. Over those years, I have received internal grants and course releases for research and writing, and in the fall of 2009 I was awarded a sabbatical for the explicit purpose of writing the proposal for this book. It took the whole semester to conceptualize, organize and outline the frame of the book; I could not have done it without that semester-long period of concentrated effort. Also a recent course release, granted by my division chair, David Brisben, allowed for additional editing and revisions in the writing process.

Several colleagues have encouraged me in my professional life and the writing of this book—among them are Joyce Hood Boettcher, Colleen Durrington, David Wray, Holbert Rideout, Kevin Lawson, Don Ratcliff, Jason Lanker, Robbie Castleman and Gloria Gale. Women in my decade-long Bible study/prayer group who have listened to these ideas over the years are Diana Bland, Marilyn Holliday and Cindi Siemens. Current and recently graduated students continue to ask about this manuscript and offer warm words of support. A cadre of lifelong friends has shared some of the journey that is described in this book, as well as the joys and setbacks of writing about it; they are Melanie Savage, Carla McDonald, Martha Smallwood, Kim Fries McMillin and my sister, Judy Thomas. Also, Al Hsu with IVP has been an excellent editor; he has offered insightful suggestions to hone, illustrate and clarify key points in the book.

Several other unique acknowledgments are needed:

Thanks to Mack Ed and Sharon Swindle, gracious friends of ours, who during my sabbatical gave me the opportunity to isolate and focus by inviting me to stay in their newly purchased country home before they moved in. Those two weeks were the minutes, hours and days during which the ideas for this book coalesced and the actual proposal was hammered out.

Special thanks to the managers and staff at Panera Bread on 71B in Fayetteville, Arkansas. For eighteen months, while I composed basic sections of the manuscript and ate black bean soup and tomato-mozzarella paninis, these men and women were consistently warm, welcoming and thoughtful.

To Christine: From the time we first met at a conference in 2003, Christine and I recognized in each other a common passion for bringing the generations together. Since that time, we have enjoyed a collegial and supportive relationship as we envisioned and conceptualized the scope of this book, and later as we sorted out specific sections to tackle and processed our ideas into a seamless whole.

To my husband: for unfailing support, for his deep belief in me, and for every delicious dinner he prepared—each one was "my favorite."

And finally, to the God of hope: When the beloved faith community that I describe in this book broke up, I was deeply wounded. It was my dark night of the soul. My prayer at the time was that God would use this deep grief for good. And he has, more than I could have asked or imagined. Therefore, this book at its most basic level is a tribute to a God who brings good out of the most desolate places, who can use all things for his glory, and who is able to redeem seemingly hopeless situations.

CHRISTINE

Most of the people who played a part in the content of this book are mentioned within the following chapters. I must thank Josee Jordon, director of my BA in Christian education major for introducing me to intergenerational education. I'm thankful for dedicated professors at St. Louis University, primarily Dr. Mary Stephen, Dr. Michael Grady, Dr. Mary "Rina" Chittooran and Dr. Douglas Pettinelli, who guided my studies and expressed enthusiasm for intergenerational ministry. Thanks goes to Dr. Jim Gambone, Pastor Don Smidt and the intergenerational ministry leaders of my dissertation research churches who took time to teach me the intricacies of establishing intergenerational Christian relationships. I'm thankful for Concordia University Irvine's administrators who provided encouragement and sabbaticals for writing and to my students who were patient when I was forced (by deadlines) to spend more time writing than grading papers. I greatly appreciate everyone who played a direct part in the writing—our editor, Al Hsu; Pete Menconi; Michael Bridges; Robert Sundquist; Key Han; and especially Holly Allen, whom I was privileged to have as a writing partner.

I am particularly grateful that members, especially the youth, of churches I was blessed to serve were willing to attempt new ministry ideas. My final acknowledgments are of my family, for whom "intergenerational" is a daily action, and to Richard, whose encouragement and willingness to eat canned soup dinners enabled my writing. May the Lord bless each of you, and may he receive the glory, honor and praise due his name.

*To all Christians who enjoy the
intergenerational household of God.*

VENTURING INTO INTERGENERATIONALITY

Our Stories

HOLLY'S STORY

For four years my family worshiped with a nondenominational church that was intentionally intergenerational. Every Sunday evening we met in homes in cross-generational small groups; on a weekly basis, I participated in these small intimate settings where children, teens, college students, young families, middle-age adults and older adults sang, prayed, listened, laughed, shared, played, cried, ate and hoped together—and blessed one another.

My experiences in those intergenerational groups changed my understanding of children and my understanding of Christian spiritual formation for children *and* adults. Ultimately these new understandings led me to change my career. The work I do now has grown out of those life-changing intergenerational small groups and is the work that I believe God has called me to do in this season of my life.

During those years, God began to grow in me a passion for looking deeply at intergenerational issues—to explore these issues, to study them, to research them. I had observed (and experienced) multiple spiritual blessings, as had the children, teens and other adults in our setting, but I wanted to *understand* what I had seen and experienced; I wanted to grasp the phenomenon biblically, theoretically, empirically, developmentally and holistically in order to *explain* to others why it was such a blessing.

With a master's degree in educational psychology (reading disabilities specialization) from the University of Iowa, fifteen years teaching reading courses in the education departments of two Christian universities, and twenty-one graduate hours of theology and Christian education, I entered the doctoral program at Talbot School of Theology with one burning question: What can explain the profound spiritual effects I and my family had observed and experienced in those intergenerational small groups? Related questions that emerged from that central query included:

- What biblical and theological insights inform what I experienced in those intergenerational small groups?
- What can learning theory contribute to this inquiry?
- Are developmental theory and intergenerational theory inherently incompatible? Can they be integrated?
- Is there empirical support for correlations between spiritual growth and intergenerationality?
- Are there other intergenerational practices that promote spiritual formation as small groups do?

My doctoral dissertation plunged me deeply into spiritual formation, learning theory and intergenerational conceptualizations in sociological literature as well as the biblical and theological realm.

Though the dissertation was completed in 2002, it did not fully answer all my questions, and thus, for the past decade, I have followed the literature that tracks the growing interest in intergenerationality. Besides fifty-four doctoral dissertations on the topic (2000–2012), a few books representing various theological perspectives have been published since 2001, and Christine and I have combined our experience, knowledge and passion for intergenerationality to write another.

CHRISTINE'S STORY

I became interested in intentional intergenerational interactions several years ago while on staff as the Director of Christian Education (DCE) in a large Lutheran church. The youth of the congregation expressed feelings of alienation from other church members, especially adults. They saw themselves, and the church-sponsored activities they were involved in, as separate from the larger church community. Desiring to help the youth both understand and experience the church as the "body of Christ" (1 Cor

12:27; Eph 4:12), the "family of God" and the "community of faith,"[1] I began considering how I could integrate the generations and build positive relationships among them.

During this time I read a few curriculum resources regarding family-night activities and subsequently modified this material to include all members of the congregation. I utilized the term *faith family* and adapted ideas from *Funtastic Family Nights*.[2] The first activity was a Reformation Family Night in which everyone in the congregation was invited to eat dinner and to learn about Martin Luther. I assigned people to tables to ensure a mix of generations in each table group. Activities were structured so that everyone at the table talked and worked together, and the teaching about Luther occurred through skits and movie clips. This experiment yielded such positive reviews from the participants and pastors that by the time I left the church two years later, these Faith Family Nights occurred for Reformation, Advent and Lent. Sunday school also became less age segregated as the age-graded classes evolved into three grades (or more) interacting together for crafts, music and teaching. Ages were separated only for fifteen minutes for discussion of the theme of the day, and prayer took place in these smaller group settings as well. Other small changes took place: the church music director incorporated youth into his choirs; a retired adult joined the youth committee and began attending youth activities; and congregational service projects became intergenerational—for example, the youngest member on a mission trip to teach Vacation Bible School in Alaska was seven years old, while the oldest member was seventy. Finally, a faith family committee was formed to guide the various activities, teach the intergenerational philosophy to the congregation and continue intergenerational activities after my departure from the congregation.

These experiences primed my interest to investigate intergenerational literature while studying for a Ph.D. in Curriculum and Instruction at Saint Louis University. As I discovered and read literature that espoused intergenerationality in both the secular and religious realms, I became

---

[1]Dietrich Bonhoeffer, *The Communion of Saints: A Dogmatic Inquiry into the Sociology of the Church*, trans. R. Gregor Smith (New York: Harper and Row, 1963).
[2]Kurt Bickel, *Funtastic Family Nights* (St. Louis: Concordia, 1998).

even more intrigued by the subject. I began to believe that an intergenerational educational methodology is inherently more aligned with Christian theology than an age-segregated educational model is, that intergenerational ministry intrinsically stems from and teaches the essence of the biblical understanding of the body of Christ, and that intergenerationality capitalizes upon the natural multigenerational quality of a congregation. While at Saint Louis University I completed two small qualitative studies on different intergenerational activities and wrote a research paper on intergenerational Christian education to ascertain if it was a subject worthy of a dissertation. After completing this research, I set my energies toward pursuing a qualitative research dissertation that would explore intergenerational ministry participants' perceptions of the benefits of intentional intergenerational activities.

Reflecting upon experiences with intergenerational activities, I have realized that the groundwork for my interest was laid prior to the church experience mentioned above. Why was I so open to explore and so able to creatively implement a ministry model that was relatively uncharted? First, I grew up in a small rural congregation that practiced intergenerationality as a matter of course. Children were encouraged to read Scripture during worship or to usher, and youth were encouraged to sing in the choir or be on committees. Since there were no Bible studies or Sunday school classes specific to high school youth (we were expected to teach the younger grades), I attended the adult Bible study on Sunday evenings. The members of my congregation were my extended family; I thought of them as aunts or grandfathers. Even now, after twenty-five years away from the congregation, I am saddened by the deaths of these members of my first faith family and feel a sense of loss.

Second, I was recently reminded that the director of the Christian Education undergraduate program under whom I studied wrote intergenerational curriculum. As I now look back on the books she asked students to read, I see the philosophy (and theology) of the body of Christ emerging,[3] and I appreciate more fully why my career philosophy statement for the last twenty years has read: "To utilize education and administrative skills

---

[3]For example, Lawrence O. Richards, *A Theology of Christian Education* (Grand Rapids: Zondervan, 1975).

in a Christian setting for the building up of Christ's body."

Finally, for eight years in inner-city Philadelphia my husband and I lived in a house with anywhere from one to six other Christian singles or married couples. This stemmed from a desire to act upon what we believe is a biblical model of Christian community.

As the director of the Christian Education program at Concordia University in Irvine, California, I quite often receive e-mails from ministry leaders who ask me to share resources that will help them understand or foster intergenerational ministry within their congregations, and I have heard students make comments such as, "I understand the philosophy behind intergenerationality, and I agree with it. I can see the benefits of integrating an intergenerational mindset into the congregation, but I have no idea how to do it! I've never seen an intergenerational ministry model put into practice in a congregation." Such requests and comments provided the motivation to work with Holly in creating this book, with the hope that it will provide growth in understanding and in fostering intergenerational Christian formation.

▩   ▩   ▩

And that is our prayer—that the biblical, theological, theoretical, empirical, developmental, sociological and practical support for intergenerationality in this text will foster a renewed commitment to bringing the generations back together again in our communities of faith.

Holly Catterton Allen and Christine Lawton Ross

INTRODUCTION

The best way to be formed in Christ is to sit among the elders, listen to their stories, break bread with them, and drink from the same cup, observing how these earlier generations of saints ran the race, fought the fight, and survived in grace.

James Frazier, in *Across the Generations: Incorporating All Ages in Ministry*

INTERGENERATIONAL MINISTRY OCCURS when a congregation intentionally brings the generations together in mutual serving, sharing or learning within the core activities of the church in order to live out being the body of Christ to each other and the greater community.[1] Throughout much of Christian history, the whole body of Christ—that is, all the generations—met together for ministry and worship as well as most other gatherings; intergenerationality was the norm. However, in the last several decades, all but the smallest congregations have tended to separate the generations regularly for learning, frequently for fellowship and service, and sometimes (or always) for worship.

RESEARCH CONGREGATION: SOUTHWEST CHURCH[2]

If a congregation today decides to practice intergenerationality, it must be

---

[1]Christine M. Ross, "A Qualitative Study Exploring Churches Committed to Intergenerational Ministry" (doctoral dissertation, Saint Louis University, St. Louis, MO, 2006), p. 127.

[2]Ibid. The Southwest faith community described here is one of four research congregations in Christine's dissertation research on churches committed to implementing an intergenerational philosophy of ministry. Her field research included interviews with fifteen ministry leaders; observations of worship and intergenerational activities; and reading of promotional materials at the four congregations in the United States and Canada. The congregations' membership and staffing ranged from a small Lutheran church of a hundred members with one full-time pastor, to a 2600-member Presbyterian congregation led by fifteen paid ministry staff members. The one commonality among the four churches was that each purported to integrate intergenerationality into the congregation's mission and vision.

intentional. One such faith community is a congregation in the southwestern United States that began in 1980 as a mission plant in a retirement community. In the 1990s a pastor with a strong mission and outreach vision came to the church; he enabled members to understand that they needed to be concerned about the families who lived outside of their retirement community. After six years and work with an outside consultant, the leaders created a vision statement that began, "We welcome and encourage visitors of all ages, cultures, and ethnic backgrounds," and they purchased property in a nearby community of young families. As leaders developed plans for a new building, the needs of all generations were taken into consideration as they planned structures for a preschool, elementary school and adult daycare, with the vision that the children and senior adults would interact on a regular basis. A few couples could not accept the new vision and left for other congregations; however, simultaneously adult children and grandchildren of members began attending and started children's ministry activities. Nine years after the senior pastor arrived, the congregation held its first worship service in the new church building.

When Christine visited six years later, three blended worship services hosted nearly a thousand people of all ages. All ages assisted in ushering, banner processing, candle lighting, Scripture reading and musical accompaniment. During the week, school children and older adults met together in the adult daycare center for an activity that all could enjoy together—most often guests teaching music, art or even animal care skills, although sometimes they simply played games or read a story together. Christine observed positive dynamics during all of these events, as well as a seventh- and eighth-grade confirmation class that included youths' parents or an older adult church member as mentor for youth whose parents did not attend the church.

INTERGENERATIONAL CHRISTIAN FORMATION: DEFINING TERMS

The term *intergenerational* has been defined and applied in congregational ministry in various ways over the past few decades. For example, in its earliest use, "intergenerational ministry" described only an acknowledgment that the church remained one of the few institutions where people of all generations assembled. To distinguish themselves from this broad understanding of intergenerationality, some practitioners began to use "intentional intergenerational ministry."[3] The term *intentional* indicated a commitment to a philosophy of ministry that purposefully brought various generations together in meaningful dialogue. Currently *intergenerational* most often describes a church that intentionally cultivates meaningful interaction between generations.

Another current word faith communities employ is *multigenerational;* this term, however, may not reflect intentional cross-age experiences. *Multigenerational* may simply mean that the church honors all generations and has programming for all generations. Multigenerational resources do not assume increased interaction between the generations, but rather use generational theory to understand how to serve each generation within one congregation. The book *The Multigenerational Congregation: Meeting the Leadership Challenge*[4] is one such resource, providing solid ideas regarding how leaders must understand themselves and their congregational demographics in light of generational theory; however, the focus of the book is learning how to do ministry with each age group[5] rather than how to enable the various generations to unite together in intergenerational faith formation. A church that describes itself as multigenerational will most likely provide ministries for children, youth, young adults, middle adults and older adults while offering few opportunities for cross-generational contact. Peter Menconi, a long-term proponent of ministry that initiates intergenerational understanding and communication among church members, writes: "While many churches are *multigenerational* and seemingly healthy on the surface, in reality, the generations act like ships in the night that pass by one another but rarely have meaningful contact and interaction. This lack of significant communication and relations between generations must be addressed if churches are to thrive—not merely survive—now and in the future."[6]

At the time of this writing, *transgenerational* is the newest term some

---

[3]James V. Gambone, *All Are Welcome: A Primer for Intentional Intergenerational Ministry and Dialogue* (Crystal Bay, MN: Elder Eye Press, 1998).
[4]Gil Rendle, *The Multigenerational Congregation: Meeting the Leadership Challenge* (Bethesda, MD: Alban Institute, 2002).
[5]Ibid, p. 9.
[6]Peter Menconi, *The Intergenerational Church: Understanding Congregations from WWII to www.com* (Littleton, CO: Mt. Sage Publishing, 2010), p. 13.

faith communities are utilizing to indicate their awareness of the many generations in the body of Christ. In perusing the websites of the first twenty churches that appeared with an Internet search of the phrase "transgenerational church," we found that about half of these churches noted ways they were bringing generations together, while the other half offered detailed information regarding special programs for babies, children, teens, college-age students, singles, men's ministry and women's ministry, with little information regarding how they integrate generations. Therefore, when a congregation is described as *transgenerational*, it *may* or *may not* reflect intentional cross-age experiences.

What is meant by the term **intergenerational** *in this book?* We are building our understanding primarily on James White's and Allan Harkness's definitions. James White defines intergenerational religious experience as "two or more different age groups of people in a religious community together learning/growing/living in faith through in-common experiences, parallel learning, contributive-occasions, and interactive sharing."[7] Allan Harkness says that "intentional intergenerational strategies are those in which an integral part of the process of faith communities encourages interpersonal interactions across generational boundaries, and in which a sense of mutuality and equality is encouraged between participants."[8] We also draw on descriptions of intentional intergenerational ministry[9] and intergenerational faith formation.[10]

To convey our understanding of intergenerationality we will unpack three phrases: *intergenerational outlook, intergenerational ministry* and *intergenerational experiences.* An intergenerational outlook acknowledges that the gifts every generation brings to the spiritual formation of the other generations strengthen the whole church.[11] A faith com-

---

[7]James W. White, *Intergenerational Religious Education: Models, Theories, and Prescription for Inter-age Life and Learning in the Faith Community* (Birmingham, AL: Religious Education Press, 1988), p. 18.

[8]Allan G. Harkness, "Intergenerational and Homogeneous-Age Education: Mutually Exclusive Strategies for Faith Communities?" *Religious Education* 95 (2000): 52.

[9]Gambone, *All Are Welcome.*

[10]Mariette Martineau, Joan Weber and Lief Kehrwald, *Intergenerational Faith Formation: All Ages Learning Together* (New London, CT: Twenty-Third Publications, 2008).

[11]Jane Rogers Vann, foreword to *The Church of All Ages: Generations Worshiping Together*, ed. Howard Vanderwell (Herndon, VA: The Alban Institute, 2008), pp. xiii-xvi.

munity that practices intergenerational ministry will use these gifts, creating frequent opportunities for various generations to communicate in meaningful ways, to interact on a regular basis, and to minister, worship and serve together regularly.[12] And intergenerational experiences are experiences in which multiple representatives of two or more generations are present, and those present are engaged in *mutual* activities.

What is meant by* Christian formation *in this book? We use *Christian formation* to refer to the process of Christians being formed, transformed and conformed to the image of Christ. Biblical passages such as 2 Corinthians 3:18 indicate that the Spirit is the instrument of change: "we . . . are being transformed into his image with ever-increasing glory, which comes from the Lord, who is the Spirit." Other passages indicate that the person also has a role in this transformation; Romans 12:2 says "do not conform to the pattern of this world, but be transformed by the *renewing of your mind*" (emphasis ours). And beyond this personal agency, Paul indicates that being formed into the image of Christ is also a process in which other believers are involved: "My dear children, for whom I am again in the pains of childbirth until Christ is formed in you" (Gal 4:19). Among other implications of this verse, we want to emphasize that Paul recognizes that his influence with these believers—his prayer for and presence with them—will in some way affect the forming of Christ in them. Therefore we believe that while Christians are in the process of being formed, conformed and transformed into the image of Christ by the Holy Spirit, they are actively involved in that process both personally and, significantly for this book, *communally.*

Though we unequivocally acknowledge that "the Spirit of God is the primary force in moving persons toward maturity and in forming Christ in them,"[13] we maintain that the believing community is a key locus of the Spirit's activity. The believing community does not supplant the work of the Spirit; it is a channel through which the Spirit works. We build closely on Ephesians 4:11-16:

---

[12]Christine Ross, "Being an Intergenerational Congregation," *Issues* 41, no. 2 (2007): 24-32.

[13]Julie Gorman, "Christian Formation," in *The Evangelical Dictionary of Christian Education,* ed. Michael Anthony (Grand Rapids: Baker Academic, 2001), p. 135.

So Christ himself gave the apostles, the prophets, the evangelists, the pastors and teachers, to equip his people for works of service, so that the body of Christ may be built up until we all reach unity in the faith and in the knowledge of the Son of God and become mature, *attaining to the whole measure of the fullness of Christ.*

Then we will no longer be infants, tossed back and forth by the waves, and blown here and there by every wind of teaching and by the cunning and craftiness of people in their deceitful scheming. Instead, speaking the truth in love, we will grow to become in every respect the mature body of him who is the head, that is, Christ. *From him the whole body, joined and held together by every supporting ligament, grows and builds itself up in love, as each part does its work.* (emphasis ours)

Many definitions or descriptions of Christian spiritual formation embrace the importance of a believing community to that process. James Wilhoit defines Christian spiritual formation as "the *intentional communal process* of growing in our relationship with God and becoming conformed to Christ through the power of the Holy Spirit" (emphasis ours).[14] The Mennonite World Conference website describes Christian formation as "those efforts of the church to help one another grow as disciples of Jesus and to be formed more and more into the likeness of Christ."[15] Julie Gorman, in her article titled "Christian Formation" in *The Evangelical Dictionary of Christian Education,* affirms strongly that "Christian community plays a *powerful* role in formation" (emphasis ours).[16]

For this book, we are focusing particularly on the *intergenerational* nature of the Christian community. We believe that the Spirit of God is at work formatively—through the community's worship, through the teaching, through modeling and mentoring relationships, and through spiritually empowered and gifted roles—in special and unique ways when believers across the life span are present and participating *together.*

---

[14]James C. Wilhoit, *Spiritual Formation As If the Church Mattered: Growing in Christ Through Community* (Grand Rapids: Baker Academic, 2008), p. 23.

[15]"Christian Formation," Mennonite World Conference, <franconiaconference.org/vision/definitions-of-missional-terms>.

[16]Gorman, "Christian Formation," p. 135.

SETTING *INTERGENERATIONAL CHRISTIAN FORMATION* IN CONTEXT

James White's 1988 *Intergenerational Religious Education*[17] was the only widely read book on intergenerationality and Christian settings published before 2000. However, due to growing awareness of the unintended consequences of generational segregation as well as renewed interest in the possibility of unique cross-age blessings, other books on intergenerationality have been published in the past decade, including books from the Reformed,[18] Lutheran[19] and Catholic[20] perspectives. Three other recent books consider intergenerational issues by exploring the unique characteristics of the generational cohorts (e.g., Boomer, Gen X, Millennial) that currently populate faith communities,[21] and several other books from the United Kingdom (not widely circulated in the States) also strongly endorse more intentional intergenerationality in faith communities.[22] Annotated descriptions of each of these books can be found in appendix B, "Intergenerational Ministry Resources."[23]

The publication of nearly a dozen books in the last decade endorsing intergenerationality in Christian contexts is evidence that it is a current topic garnering keen interest among virtually all Christian faith communities. Leaders in evangelical churches, emerging churches, mainline churches, missional churches, charismatic churches, Catholic churches—all types of Christian communities—are asking the same question: "How

---

[17]White, *Intergenerational Religious Education*.

[18]Howard Vanderwell, ed., *The Church of All Ages: Generations Worshiping Together* (Herndon, VA: The Alban Institute, 2008).

[19]Vicky Goplin, Jeffrey Nelson, Mark Gardner and Eileen Zahn, eds., *Across the Generations: Incorporating All Ages in Ministry: The Why and How* (Minneapolis: Augsburg Fortress, 2001).

[20]Martineau, Weber and Kehrwald, *Intergenerational Faith Formation*.

[21]Jackson W. Carroll and Wade Clark Roof, *Bridging Divided Worlds: Congregational Cultures in Congregations* (San Francisco: Jossey-Bass, 2002); Gary McIntosh, *One Church, Four Generations: Understanding and Reaching All Ages in Your Church* (Grand Rapids: Baker, 2002); Menconi, *The Intergenerational Church*.

[22]Jason Gardner, *Mend the Gap: Can the Church Reconnect the Generations?* (Nottingham, UK: InterVarsity Press, 2008); David Hilborn and Matthew Bird, *God and the Generations: Youth, Age and the Church Today* (Carlisle, UK: Paternoster Press, 2003); Philip Mounstephen and Kelly Martin, *Body Beautiful? Recapturing a Vision for All-Age Church* (Cambridge: Grove Books, 2004).

[23]For a fuller discussion of recent books on intergenerational faith formation, see Faye Chechowich, "Intergenerational Ministry: A Review of Selected Publications Since 2001," *Christian Educational Journal* (NS 3) 9 (Spring 2012): 182-93.

can we bring the generations back together?" This text, *Intergenerational Christian Formation*, proposes to respond to that basic question in a variety of ways for faith communities seeking to transition toward a more intergenerational perspective in their practices.

THIS BOOK'S FORMAT AND BASIC PREMISE

This book is divided into four parts. The first three parts of the book are research based and academic, though accessible to church leaders, youth and family ministers, and undergraduate students, while offering adequate substance for graduate students. The fourth part is very practical and anecdotal.

Part One: Generational Realities

Part one describes the late twentieth-century trend to separate the generations, explains a variety of factors that have led to this trend, and introduces the book's premise that intergenerational faith experiences uniquely nurture spiritual growth and development in both adults and children. Part one also traces various iterations of intergenerationality from the last four decades, drawing from the conceptual work of Christian educational leaders such as John Westerhoff and C. E. Nelson. Further, it notes the changing terminology for the concept from James White's "intergenerational religious education" to the current popular phrase "intergenerational faith formation."

Part Two: Biblical, Theological and Theoretical Foundations

Part two, the heart of the book, provides biblical, theological and theoretical support for the main premise introduced in part one. After offering biblical directives regarding the interrelatedness of the generations and outlining the pervasive presence of intergenerational community throughout Scripture, this section offers insights from developmental theory, social learning theory and ecological systems theory that connect to intergenerationality. And last, part two introduces and develops the situative-sociocultural perspective as the fundamental learning theory undergirding intergenerationality, making key connections between this perspective and theological principles regarding Christian formation in community.

Part Three: Social Science Foundations

This section unpacks research that supports intergenerational approaches to learning and growing. One chapter outlines the findings of sociologists of religion; for example, Christian Smith's important recent research is examined. Other chapters offer insights from gerontology and generational theory. The concluding chapter describes research that focuses directly on intergenerational Christian experiences and their impact on children, adolescents and adults, and on congregations that practice intentional intergenerationality.

Part Four: Intergenerational Christian Formation Practices

Part four offers spiritual insights and practical recommendations for the process of *initiating* and *nurturing* an intergenerational culture within a faith community. The bulk of this section describes and explores dozens of ways to bring the generations together; it is very practical, full of anecdotal material, guidelines, stories and recommendations.

In addition, three appendices include the very practical "Forty Intergenerational Ideas," "Intergenerational Ministry Resources" and "Biblical Passages that Reflect an Intergenerational Outlook."

For a variety of reasons, the church has increasingly moved toward segregation of people by ages and life stages. However, our research indicates that frequent cross-generational experiences are essential to Christian formation and the development of mature faith. Further, we are convinced that *perennially* segregating the various generations inherently hinders spiritual growth and development. We recognize that reversing the trend toward segregation of ages is a daunting enterprise. Therefore, this book offers biblical, theological, empirical, sociological, theoretical, developmental and practical support to equip, inform and inspire ministry leaders with courage for the journey ahead.

Part One

■ ■ ■

GENERATIONAL REALITIES

1

WHAT IS THE PROBLEM?

Life in modern society is often divided into three parts: children and youth spend much of their time in daycare and school, adults make up the workforce, and older persons are expected to live a retired life of leisure.

Dagmar Grefe, "Combating Ageism with Narrative and Intergroup Contact"

The church is the only agency in Western civilization which has all the members of the family as part of its clientele . . . through the complete life cycle from birth to death.

Margaret Sawin, *Family Enrichment with Family Clusters*

IN A RECENT UNDERGRADUATE COURSE ON MINISTRY across the life span, the class was contrasting ministry for seniors of the Silent generation (those currently about 65-85 years old) with the anticipated ministry changes for the next generation, the Boomers, as they age. Initially the students chatted through a discussion about Boomers—their active lifestyles, their workaholism, their amusing refusal to admit that they are growing old— and how ministry to this age cohort might look different from recent approaches to senior ministry. Then Holly asked these students what the senior adult ministry in their home congregations looked like. A few activities were mentioned—potlucks, game night in the church activity center, shuttle service to the building on Sundays. There was a pause in the discussion, then another student offered hesitantly: "Well, I think it's important to say that . . . *I don't know;* I don't have any idea what they do.

I was in the youth group; I don't know what happened with the seniors in my church."

This young man was acknowledging to the class the dawning realization that his unawareness of the seniors of his home church was a perfect illustration of a problem we had alluded to regularly throughout the semester—that ministering by age cohorts can yield unintended consequences: generational fragmentation, silo mentality[1] and an involuntary ignorance of all others not in one's own age group. His verbalized realization was a keen *aha* moment for the class.

THE PROBLEM OF AGE SEGREGATION

During the last hundred years, steady changes have occurred in society that have separated families and segregated age groups, not only in educational settings but in life in general. "There are less regular and structured interactions between old and young . . . than ever before. Not only families but also other institutions in modern society have reduced the chance for old and young to share activities in meaningful ways."[2] Examples of this pervasive age segregation include the ubiquity of age-graded public education, the geographical mobility of families, the movement from extended to nuclear family, the rise of divorce and single-parent families, and the prevalence of retirement and nursing homes for older persons and preschools for the young.

Faith communities are perhaps the only places where families, singles, couples, children, teens, grandparents—all generations—come together on a regular interacting basis. Yet the societal trend toward generational fragmentation has moved into churches also. Though church leaders endorse intergenerationality in general whenever they cite biblical metaphors such as "the body of Christ" or "the family of God," in practice American mainline and evangelical churches generally conduct many of their ser-

---

[1]"Silo ministries" is a current catchphrase for ministry approaches that segment by age or stage (for example, children's ministry, youth ministry, singles ministry, etc). It references the image of the tall, free-standing grain silos on Midwestern farms, and thus a "silo mentality" would suggest a stand-alone, age-segregated outlook.

[2]Peter N. Stearns, "Historical Trends in Intergenerational Contacts," in *Intergenerational Programs: Imperatives, Strategies, Impacts, Trends*, ed. Sally Newman and S. W. Brummel (Binghamton, NY: Haworth Press, 1989), p. 30.

vices and activities (worship, Sunday school, fellowship, outreach, service, etc.) in age-segregated settings. Consequently, in the second decade of twenty-first-century America, all generations of the faith community—babies through nonagenarians—are seldom together.

Holly experienced firsthand this sea change in the way churches do business. Her family moved from Texas to California in 2000 and observed there a phenomenon they had not yet experienced in Texas. They found that some churches, besides having age-specific children's and teen worship services, were offering Gen X worship services as well as traditional worship services at 8:00 or 8:30 and contemporary worship services at 10:30 or 11:00, thus in effect dividing the church into five generations. Those who grew up in these church settings could experience the community of Christ as age-segregated silos their whole lives; it would be possible, even probable, for a whole cohort to know only those their own age, never experiencing opportunities to worship with, minister with or even *know* those older and younger.[3]

Separating the generations may seem efficacious, practical and desirable, especially when excellent age- or stage-focused programs exist. Perhaps one might ask, what would be wrong with persons experiencing life in the body of Christ as an age-specific journey? What indeed? While the chief purpose of this book is to offer biblical, theological, developmental, empirical, sociological and practical support for intergenerationality, along the way the intrinsic limitations of a pervasively, perennially age-segregated Christianity will emerge.

One of Holly's colleagues attended the funeral of a much-loved, elderly matriarch of her church. She noticed a college student at the funeral and afterward spoke with the young woman: "I didn't know you knew Mrs. Ellison."

"Oh, I don't. I just wanted to come to a funeral. I've never been to one

---

[3]An even more radical version of the age-segregated phenomenon appeared in the middle of the 2000s; some churches began to re-vision their mission, to focus on a specific target demographic, for example, young thirtysomethings and their families. What this meant was that worship, the educational ministry, outreach events, sermon topics and illustrations would be targeted for this particular demographic. Church growth gurus were recommending such an approach at the time, but teens, single twentysomethings, middle adults and older adults (in this example) could be relegated to the periphery with such an approach.

before. I've been coming to this church for a few months, and they have been praying for Mrs. Ellison ever since I've been coming, so I wanted to come."

"We're glad you came."

"You know, I've never been part of a church where there are old people who die. It changes the way you see life."

RECONSIDERING AGE SEGREGATION

Singles' ministers, youth ministers, children's ministers and others who have played a part in separating the generations are beginning to have second thoughts about age segregation. Joseph Hellerman says: "I spent the first 15 years of vocational Christian service involved in specialized ministry to single adults. Now I find myself with increasing reservations about the wisdom of compartmentalizing God's family into separate fellowship groups according to life stages."[4]

After a couple of decades as a youth minister, Mark DeVries recognized that youth ministry was failing in its goal to foster spiritual growth and mature faith in teens. His diagnosis of the problem was that in typical youth ministries, teens had been systematically separated from adults, isolating them "from the very relationships that are most likely to lead them to maturity."[5]

Ivy Beckwith, a longtime children's minister, claims in *Postmodern Children's Ministry* that children's ministry is broken. She came to see that the systematic separation of children from all other cohorts of the church was detrimental to them. Beckwith advocates regular opportunities for children to worship with the full body of Christ, to be received and welcomed fully as contributing participants in faith community. Beckwith says, "A church program can't spiritually form a child, but a family living in an intergenerational community of faith can."[6]

A Christian leader tells a story of parents who were talking together

---

[4]Joseph Hellerman, *When the Church Was a Family: Recapturing Jesus' Vision for Authentic Christian Community* (Nashville: B & H Academic, 2009), p. 161.

[5]Mark DeVries, *Family-Based Youth Ministry*, rev. ed. (Downers Grove, IL: InterVarsity Press, 2004), p. 36.

[6]Ivy Beckwith, *Postmodern Children's Ministry: Ministry to Children in the 21st Century* (Grand Rapids: Zondervan, 2004), p. 14.

about the church being the family of God. Their young son, Abe, over-hearing the conversation, asked, "If our church is a family, how come we don't do more things together?"[7] Perhaps the time has come to reconsider the pervasive age segregation that has characterized faith communities over the past few decades. This book joins a growing body of literature that advocates just such a shift.

FAITH COMMUNITIES AS OLDER AND YOUNGER SIBLINGS IN A FAMILY

Christine's understanding of the family of God was formed through visual and auditory catechesis. After an infant baptism in her church, the pastor presented the child to the congregation by holding her for the whole con-gregation to see her face and by walking her down the aisle so that ev-eryone could greet her directly with these words: "We welcome you into the Lord's family. We receive you as a fellow member of the body of Christ, and a child of the same heavenly Father, to work with us in his kingdom."[8] The pastor's actions and the congregation's words made the family of God very real to Christine. As she looked around and saw the gentle and joyous expressions on the usually rough and weathered faces of her agrarian "faith family," she realized how even an infant has a God-given role to play within his family.

When Holly was four and five, she spent two summers with her grand-mother while her mother completed her college degree. She has vivid memories of those weeks, "helping" her grandmother wash clothes in the wringer washer, hanging heavy, wet clothes on the line outside, feeding the chickens, gathering the eggs, packing an enormous lunch for her grandfather to take into the cotton fields, and weeding the big vegetable garden. She also has layered memories of worshiping in the small rural church with all ages together. She remembers particularly the quaint way her grandmother referred to the men and women of the church: "Sister Markham's been ill—we'll take her some soup," or "We'll just take some of these apples over to the McFaddens—you know Brother McFadden has lost his job." Holly found this practice of addressing everyone at church as

---

[7]Charles Nichols, "If We're a Family, Let's Learn Together!" *The Messenger* 41, no. 1 (2003), p. 4.
[8]*Lutheran Worship* (St. Louis: Concordia, 1982), p. 204.

"Sister" or "Brother" quite curious—though she doesn't recall asking her grandmother about it.

Holly has thought only occasionally about this practice over the last few decades. Yet last year when one of the preteens at church was baptized, Holly hugged her afterward and whispered in her ear, "Now you are my sister too." The girl looked at Holly with wonder in her eyes, not sure how to respond, but she was clearly intrigued.

Joseph Hellerman offers an in-depth and fascinating description of the first-century family culture as a way of understanding the richness of Paul's analogy of church as family—especially the relationships as brothers and sisters among Christians.[9] Hellerman's book assumes an intergenerational church, where the older, wiser sisters and brothers know their younger siblings well, and advise, guide and accompany them on their journeys, while the younger siblings work with, care for and join their older siblings on their journeys. It is a powerful, inviting image, reflective of Paul's admonitions in 1 Timothy 5:1-2 regarding cross-generational relationships in the early church.

Why have churches in North America moved past this image, this picture of familial intergenerationality that so characterized first-century faith communities? Why did twentieth-century churches embrace so wholeheartedly an age-segregated version of life in Christ? What cultural, ecclesial, developmental, theological, philosophical or practical rationales have been used to support such a fundamental departure from the historical practices of the communal body of Christ through the ages? Chapter two addresses these questions.

---

[9]Hellerman, *When the Church Was a Family*.

2

HOW DID WE GET HERE?

*Why Churches Tended
to Separate the Generations*

*I appeal to you, brothers and sisters, in the name of our Lord Jesus Christ,
that all of you agree with one another in what you say and that there be no
divisions among you, but that you be perfectly united in mind and thought.*
1 Corinthians 1:10

*The easiest thing to do in the local church is to divide up the various ages
and do separate ministry. It is not as messy [as cross-age ministry]. It takes
more time, energy and effort to do intergenerational ministry.*
Research participant, in Brenda Snailum, "Implementing Intergenerational Youth
Ministry Within Existing Evangelical Church Congregations"

❧

HOUSE CHURCHES OF THE FIRST CENTURY were places in which all
generations were present (see chapter five for a fuller explanation of house
churches). The generations remained integrated throughout much of
Christian history until fairly recently. Several diverse factors have contributed to the age segregation that characterizes many Christian faith
communities in the twenty-first century. As described in the first chapter,
when believers today gather for worship, service, ministry or simply for
fellowship, they tend to gather in age- or stage-segregated silos. The
question this chapter addresses is, "Why?" That is, "Why has the body of

Christ (at least in North America) embraced an age-segregated approach to community in the last several decades?"

Harkness[1] traces the decline of cross-generational Christian practices to the Protestant Reformation, particularly in its role in the development of modern public schooling. Prior to the Reformation only the elite were schooled; the masses were taught their fathers' trade and learned of life and faith through home, church and community. The Reformers' focus on *everyone* being able to read Scripture for themselves ultimately ushered in mandated schooling for all. Brian Hill[2] also points out that universal age-segregated schooling as we know it began with the biblical reading focus of the Reformation. Harkness notes that "the development of the highly age-graded approach to educational activities within congregations arose out of this milieu, concurrent with the development of a widespread assumption of the schooling model as the appropriate one for Christian faith communities."[3] Harkness does acknowledge, however, that other factors besides age-graded Sunday schools have contributed to the decline of intergenerationality in Christian faith communities. Among those factors are modern and postmodern tendencies toward individualism and dependence on psychological, therapeutic or secular educational models rather than theological models.

Martinson and Shallue[4] attribute the movement toward age segregation to shifting core values, fast-paced lifestyles and the high value of individualism. Vanderwell[5] indicates that one factor has been the pressure to tailor Christian activities and practices to meet expectations of particular generational cohorts, for example, Boomers or Millennials. Kara Powell[6] suggests that the trend toward age segregation among churches

[1]Allan G. Harkness, "Intergenerational Christian Education: An Imperative for Effective Education in Local Churches (Part 2)," *Journal of Christian Education* 42, no. 1 (1998): 37-50.

[2]Brian Hill, "Is It Time We Deschooled Christianity?" *Journal of Christian Education* 63 (November 1978): 5-21.

[3]Allan G. Harkness, "Intergenerational Christian Education: An Imperative for Effective Education in Local Churches (Part 1)," *Journal of Christian Education* 41, no. 2 (1998): 7.

[4]Roland Martinson and Diane Shallue, "Foundations for Cross-Generational Ministry," in *Across the Generations: Incorporating All Ages in Ministry: The Why and How*, ed. Vicky Goplin, Jeffrey Nelson, Mark Gardner and Eileen Zahn (Minneapolis: Augsburg, 2001), pp. 4-10.

[5]Howard Vanderwell, foreword to *The Church of All Ages: Generations Worshiping Together*, ed. Howard Vanderwell (Herndon, VA: The Alban Institute, 2008), pp. xiii-xvi.

[6]Kara Powell, "Is the Era of Age Segregation Over?" *Leadership* 30 (Summer 2009): 43-48.

began in the 1940s and post–World War II when parachurch organizations such as Young Life, InterVarsity and Youth for Christ focused so
successfully on teenagers and young adults[7]; because of the success of
these specialized ministries aimed at a specific age group, church leaders
came to believe that churches should adopt similar specialized ministry
approaches, especially with youth.

This chapter explores the age-segregating influence of developmental
concerns and rampant individualism as well as other factors, noting along
the way how these factors have become barriers that tend to undermine
intergenerational faith practices.

THE INFLUENCE OF AMERICAN CULTURE

As mentioned in chapter one, the move toward age segregation in society
in general is one factor that has contributed to age segregation in
American churches. Mary Pipher offers this insight regarding the issues
surrounding this age-separating phenomenon: "A great deal of America's
social sickness comes from age segregation. If ten fourteen-year-olds are
grouped together, they will form a *Lord of the Flies* culture with its com-
petitiveness and meanness. But if ten people ages 2 to 80 are grouped
together, they will fall into a natural age hierarchy that nurtures and
teaches them all. For our own mental and societal health, we need to
reconnect the age groups."[8]

Hagestad and Uhlenberg argue that children/youth, working adults
and older adults have been systematically separated institutionally, socially
and spatially. They call this age-based separation the "tripartition of the
life course," which "emerged as the state adopted rules using chronological
age to require children's school attendance, while excluding them from
the workplace, and entitling older persons to pensions. Children and
youth are channeled into daycare and schools where they spend most of
the day with a narrow band of age peers. For adults, days are anchored in

---

[7]Mark Senter's book indicates that a number of earlier specialized youth organizations existed before World War II. Senter points to the advent of Robert Raikes's Sunday school (1780s), the
Young Men's Christian Association (1851), Francis Clark's Society of Christian Endeavor (1881)
and the United Christian Youth Movement (1933). In *When God Shows Up: A History of Protestant
Youth Ministry in America* (Grand Rapids: Baker Academic, 2010).
[8]Mary Pipher, "The New Generation Gap," *USA Weekend*, March 19-21, 1999, p. 12.

work settings that exclude the young and the old. And older people, who have limited access to school and work sites, are expected to live retired lives of leisure."[9]

Throughout the ages Christians have tended to emulate—often unintentionally or unthinkingly—the culture around them, and as American culture has become more and more generationally fragmented over the last hundred years, churches have followed that same trend. Beyond this general trend to reflect the surrounding culture, churches have embraced other pieces of the cultural outlook that have ultimately contributed to the pervasive age segregation that characterizes American Christianity.

One such influence on the onset of age segregation in church life is the dominant cultural ideology of individualism (as noted above by Harkness as well as Martinson and Shallue), evidence of which is seen in worship wars between generations, but is also revealed in an individualistic soteriological stance that diminishes the communal aspect of salvation.

Another cultural influence since the mid-twentieth century is evident in church leaders' recognition of the importance of cognitive developmental differences as well as differing life-stage needs,[10] prompting the use of age-graded curriculum and the formation of small groups based on age or stage. The enormous Boomer generation with its particular outlook and its members' demands for doing things their way has enormously influenced decisions in faith communities. In their seminal work regarding generations, Strauss and Howe describe Boomers as a generation with very strong opinions regarding the inner life (spiritual) and outer life (moral, political) and with little care for the opinions of the other generations.[11]

---

[9]Gunhild O. Hagestad and Peter Uhlenberg, "The Social Separation of Old and Young: A Root of Ageism," *Journal of Social Issues* [serial online] 61 (June 2005): 346.

[10]For example, Carter and McGoldrick's life stages are: leaving home, the new couple, families with young children, families with adolescents, launching children, and families in later life. Elizabeth A. Carter and Monica McGoldrick, *The Changing Family Life Cycle: A Framework for Family Therapy* (New York: Allyn & Bacon, 1989), p. 15.

Life stages are sometimes called the family career or life phases. Because of the diverse forms of families, the typical life stages don't fit the majority of families now, but churches still often form classes or ministry opportunities around these typical stages.

[11]William Strauss and Neil Howe, *Generations: The History of America's Future, 1584 to 2069* (New York: Quill, William Morrow, 1991), pp. 299-316.

DEVELOPMENTAL AND LIFE-STAGE CONCERNS

Twentieth-century developmental theorists have outlined ways that children, teens, younger adults and older adults typically progress cognitively (Piaget[12]), psychosocially (Erikson[13]), morally (Kohlberg[14] and Gilligan[15]) and in faith development (Fowler[16]), and life-span specialists such as Levinson[17] have highlighted the differences among adults of various ages regarding the life issues they encounter and tasks that they must undertake. Informed and diligent ministry leaders have become more aware of the developmental differences from infants to octogenarians in the faith communities they oversee, and have desired to create learning, worship and service opportunities that meet a wide range of cognitive, psychosocial, spiritual and life-stage needs.

Piaget's work in cognitive development—the way persons of various ages think—revolutionized preschool and elementary education in public schools in the 1960s and 1970s, and eventually Sunday schools as well. Christian educators began to implement teaching-learning approaches that were more age appropriate for children, such as the use of the five senses, body movement, visual aids, active involvement—all excellent ideas. Eventually developmentalist concerns were applied to the worship hour, especially since churches at this time were moving toward the understanding of the worship gathering as a primary teaching service for adults, according to Glassford,[18] and some faith communities began to offer "children's church" options in the late 1960s and early 1970s.[19]

In children's church settings, sometimes an entire alternative worship service was offered, following the general format or liturgy of the adult

---

[12]Jean Piaget and Bärbel Inhelder, *The Psychology of the Child*, trans. Helen Weaver (New York: Basic Books, 1969).

[13]Erik Erikson, *Childhood and Society*, 2nd ed. (New York: Norton, 1963).

[14]Lawrence Kohlberg, *Essays on Moral Development*, vol. 2, *The Psychology of Moral Development* (San Francisco: Harper & Row, 1984).

[15]Carol Gilligan, *In a Different Voice: Psychological Theory and Women's Development* (Cambridge, MA: Harvard University Press, 1982).

[16]James Fowler, *Stages of Faith: The Psychology of Human Development and the Quest for Meaning* (San Francisco: Harper, 1981).

[17]Daniel Levinson, *The Seasons of a Man's Life* (New York: Ballantine Press, 1978).

[18]Darwin Glassford, "Fostering an Intergenerational Culture," in *The Church of All Ages: Generations Worshiping Together*, ed. Howard Vanderwell (Herndon, VA: The Alban Institute, 2008), pp. 71-93.

[19]Ibid.

worship service; in these cases, children's church was seen as a training ground for children to participate at their own developmental levels in the basic forms of adult worship. In other settings, children were released from the worship hour only during the sermon time, and children's songs, puppets and games were employed to make this time engaging and enjoyable—also in keeping with developmental concerns. With both types of children's church, it was simply deemed age inappropriate for children to sit through "boring" hymns, prayers and/or sermons when they could be more actively involved in teaching and activities that accommodated shorter attention spans and more body movement. Thus, churches moving toward a more educational model of worship (and away from a spiritual model) viewed separating children from the adults during the worship service as a benefit for the children. The practice seemed to be based on a pedagogically sound rationale.

Strictly age-graded Sunday school classes in recent decades have been formulated around established cognitive (and, to some degree, social) developmental concerns of children.[20] Youth ministry was (and is), in part, a response to the unique psychological/emotional/social needs of teens, such as differentiation issues, identity development and distinctive doubt/faith concerns. And with adults, ministry leaders have become keenly aware that single twentysomethings adjusting to the adult work world, coping with financial responsibility and navigating a sexually charged environment face vastly different concerns than Boomers who are adjusting to retirement, coping with health worries, and navigating a world in which they are marginalized and far less powerful than in their prime. A sensitive leadership deeply aware of the broad spectrum of these cognitive, social and life-stage needs would understandably perceive dividing by age or generational cohort as a sensible, even laudable, means of meeting those needs.

CHURCH GROWTH STRATEGIES

Church growth experts have been offering "how to build a bigger church"

---

[20]Ted Ward says, "As a field of academic study, Christian education has gradually come to accept developmentalism at its theoretical base." Ted Ward, foreword to *Nurture That Is Christian: Developmental Perspectives in Christian Education*, ed. James Wilhoit and John Dettoni (Grand Rapids: Baker, 1995), p. 7.

advice for several decades. The unintended consequence of some of these recommendations has been the systematic separation of congregations into generational cohorts. For example, building on Donald McGavran's Homogeneous Units Principle (HUP),[21] some church growth specialists in the 1970s and 1980s began to promote homogeneity (around ages or stages of life) at the small group level and even at the macrochurch level.[22] Though age- or stage-defined small groups can provide empathy and social comfort, ultimately they have had the effect of sorting faith communities by generation.[23]

In church growth literature, numerical growth is typically seen to be tied directly to attracting families with children. Offering an exciting, entertaining hour of children's church can be a big draw for those who are church shopping. One children's minister says he wants children to leave church thinking, "That was the funnest hour I had all week."[24] And if the children enjoy children's church (and if their parents do not need to tend to their children), more families will place membership. It is simply good church growth strategy. This strategy is also reinforced by the fact that some growing congregations may lack worship space for families to worship together. When determining whether to add another worship time or separate children and youth from adults, the fact that the latter corresponds more

---

[21]Donald A. McGavran, *Understanding Church Growth* (Grand Rapids: Eerdmans, 1970). McGavran was a missionary in India and the founder of Fuller Theological Seminary's School of World Missions. McGavran derived his Homogeneous Units Principle (HUP) from his experiences in India. Homogeneous units are people who share the same language, culture, or economic or other characteristic that makes them a unique group from others (easily illustrated in the Indian caste system). McGavran's well-known statement is that people "like to become Christians without crossing racial, linguistic or class barriers" (p. 198). McGavran taught that the missionary evangelist should identify with a specific homogeneous unit and contextualize the gospel in such a way that it communicates to them. As a result, congregations that desire to reach out must become sufficiently like their target homogeneous unit that this people group will not need to cross cultural boundaries to hear about Jesus, but rather will feel at home in the church setting. Of course, recent church growth specialists have modified HUP for use beyond Indian culture.

[22]For example, Donald A. McGavran with Win C. Arn, *How to Grow a Church* (Glendale, CA: Regal, 1973); Kennon Callahan, *Twelve Keys to an Effective Church* (New York: Harper & Row, 1983); George Barna, *Marketing the Church* (Colorado Springs: NavPress, 1988).

[23]We are not denouncing all age- or stage-defined small group gatherings; indeed they can be spiritually enriching and powerful life journey tools. However, perennially forming small groups around ages or stages promotes generational fragmentation.

[24]"A 1-2 Punch Church's Kids' Program Entertains As It Educates," *Daily Herald*, Arlington Heights, IL, July 21, 2006. Retrieved from <http://business.highbeam.com/5444/article-1G1 -148587528/12-punch-church-kids-program-entertains-educates>.

directly to some tenets of church growth theory resolves the problem.

In conference or seminar settings, when we ask participants why some churches do everything intergenerationally, a common response we both hear is, "Because they are too small for age-segmented grouping." Although this perception may be true, we believe that all churches regardless of size are more faithful to the scriptural theme of unity and are more likely to foster faith maturity when they intentionally integrate various generations for 50 to 80 percent of congregational activities.[25]

INDIVIDUALISM

As churches have faced increasingly unpleasant generational conflict, one solution that seems to ameliorate the problem is to offer separate-but-equal opportunities. For example, in regard to the worship wars, churches might provide separate worship hours, encouraging each generation to shape its own worship hour to suit its tastes. Thus, the youth group can enjoy loud music, flashing lights and cool videos; the Millennials can pull into their intimate settings; Gen Xers can have their contemplative yet technologically savvy style; Boomers can choose old rock-style praise tunes using guitars and drums; the older generations can sing traditional hymns; and the children get to sing "Father Abraham" as often as they wish.[26] All in all, a very amenable solution—except it is a perfect recipe for generational isolation. This solution arises from an individualistic outlook that emphasizes personal needs, rather than communal needs. And "when the needs of the individual are preeminent, generational fragmentation is inevitable."[27] Surprisingly, it isn't always the youngest members of the community who most adamantly and vociferously claim their rights.[28]

---

[25]In Christine Ross's research with fifteen leaders in intentionally intergenerational congregations, comments regarding how much of a congregation's ministry should be intergenerational varied from 50 to 80 percent. Unpublished data from her dissertation research. See Christine M. Ross, "A Qualitative Study Exploring Churches Committed to Intergenerational Ministry" (doctoral dissertation, Saint Louis University, St. Louis, MO, 2006).

[26]Generational music descriptions provided by Jen Edwards, instructor of worship ministries at John Brown University.

[27]Darwin Glassford and Lynn Barger-Elliot, "Toward Intergenerational Ministry in a Post-Christian Era," *Christian Education Journal* (series 3) 8, no. 2 (Fall 2011): 366.

[28]In Christine Ross's dissertation research, the only characteristic that all four churches agreed upon was that changing adult members' mindset was a problem for the implementation of intergenerational ministry. In each congregation, there were adults who didn't want to be around noisy

Soong-Chan Rah connects the dots regarding individualism, Western culture and religion. He states that "from the earliest stages of American history, individualism has been the defining attribute in understanding our nation's ethos. . . . The American church, in taking its cues from Western, white culture, has placed at the center of its theology and ecclesiology the primacy of the individual."[29] William Dinges critiques the excessive individualism that pervades religion in America, saying that evangelical churches in particular "emphasize *individual* spiritual empowerment," and are growing because of their attention to individual needs.[30] And when individual needs are considered paramount, churches tend to offer special programs for children, teens, and young, middle, and older adults, so that these individual needs can be met more conveniently.

Hellerman frames this rampant individualism theologically. He makes a powerful (and controversial) point about evangelical Christianity's "fixation upon Jesus as personal Savior."[31] This accusation may sound almost heretical to evangelicals, but Hellerman convincingly argues that this fixation has in essence "privatized" the Christian faith as an accommodation to "culture's unbiblical obsession with individual determinism and personal subjective experience."[32] Hellerman argues that this individualization of the gospel message has severely diminished the crucial importance of the faith *community* in the spiritual formation of believers: "Framing conversion to Christ in solely individualistic terms has left us with little social capital to draw on in our churches as we try to encourage our people to stay in community and grow together as brothers and sisters in Christ."[33]

The excessive individualism of secular Western culture is fundamentally incompatible with the life of community as depicted in Scripture. The central events of the Old Testament—the deliverance of the Israelites

---

children or didn't want to alter the worship service to honor requests of other generations. See Ross, "A Qualitative Study Exploring Churches."

[29]Soong-Chan Rah, *The Next Evangelicalism: Freeing the Church from Western Cultural Captivity* (Downers Grove, IL: InterVarsity Press, 2009), p. 29.

[30]William Dinges, "Faith, Hope, and (Excessive) Individualism," in *Handing on the Faith: The Church's Mission and Challenge,* ed. Robert P. Imbelli (New York: Crossroad, 2006), p. 36.

[31]Joseph Hellerman, *When the Church Was a Family: Recapturing Jesus' Vision for Authentic Christian Community* (Nashville: B & H Academic, 2009), p. 143.

[32]Ibid.

[33]Ibid.

BOX 2.1

Adopted into Community

After the birth of their fourth child, Carin and her husband, Jared, adopted Songju, a seven-year-old Korean girl. Carin flew to Korea for the final adoption process; it took six weeks to complete all the paperwork and bring Songju back to the States. Carin and Songju spent the last three weeks of that time getting to know one another and preparing for the transition from the orphanage to a new home and a new family.

During those three weeks Carin showed Songju pictures of Jared and of their other four children, explaining through an interpreter that these children would be Songju's new brothers and sisters. However, when Songju and Carin flew into Charlotte, North Carolina, and Jared and the children met them at the airport, Songju became fearful and even angry. She clung to Carin ferociously and would not make eye contact with Jared or any of the children, even Rebekah, her new eight-year-old sister. Over the next several weeks, Songju remained devoted to Carin and alienated from other members of the family. As she began to learn more English, she began to tell the other children that Carin was her mother, not their mother—that Jared was their father, not hers.

Over the next several months, Carin painstakingly fostered the relationships between Songju and Jared and between Songju and each of her new siblings. It was an arduous journey for the whole family, but especially for Songju. Her new siblings were not always loving and forgiving toward her; they sometimes didn't want to include Songju in their activities; they sometimes were selfish and argued among themselves.

The conflict came to a head one afternoon when Songju wanted to help Carin prepare dinner, but it was Rebekah's turn. Carin asked Songju to do her other chores while Rebekah helped with dinner. As Songju flounced out of the kitchen to the basement to fold clothes, she hissed to Rebekah that she didn't like her or want her for a sister. Re-

bekah shouted back: "I don't want you either—you mess everything up." Carin, utterly distraught, broke into tears, sobbing that she wanted all of her children to love each other, support each other and help each other. Both Rebekah and Songju stared open-mouthed at Carin in alarm. Then they looked at each other; Songju slowly lifted a hand to Rebekah. Rebekah took her hand, then reached out and embraced her, saying, "I'm sorry. I didn't really mean that. I do want you for a sister, but sometimes it's just really hard."

This vignette illustrates Hellerman's points well: "We are saved to community. Salvation involves adoption into the family of God. Indeed, salvation is becoming a member of God's family—a family that includes both a new Father and a new set of brothers and sisters." [a]

---

[a]Ibid., p. 221.

from Egypt, crossing the Red Sea and the giving of the Law at Sinai—were community-creating events. Some scholars argue that before these events, the Israelites, though acknowledging that they were descendants of Abraham, Isaac and Jacob, did not identify themselves as God's people. When he delivered, rescued and formed them through the law and in the desert, they truly became his people and he became their God.[34]

In a similar fashion, Pentecost too was a community-creating event: "Those who accepted his message were baptized, and about three thousand were added to their number that day" (Acts 2:41); "the disciples were called Christians first at Antioch." (Acts 11:26). As Hellerman says, "In the New Testament era, a person was saved not solely to enjoy a personal relationship with Jesus. A person was saved to community. Our truncated evangelical conception of Jesus as personal Savior turns out to be an unfortunate distortion of radical American individualism, not a holistic reflection of biblical soteriology."[35]

---

[34]Ibid., pp. 125-28.
[35]Ibid., p. 220.

WHY INTERGENERATIONALITY?

Given the power of the factors described in this chapter—the general societal acceptance of age segregation in American culture, diverse developmental and life-stage needs, recommendations of church growth experts,
and entrenched individualism—why should church leaders even consider
moving toward a more interage approach to Christian spiritual formation?
The response to that question is to be found in chapter three.

3

WHY BRING THE GENERATIONS BACK TOGETHER?

The Benefits of Intergenerationality

When generations collide, the ensuing conflict reminds everyone, Church is not just about me. Who knew that church could be the cure to narcissism?

Chad Hall, *"All in the Family* Is Now *Grey's Anatomy"*

THIS CHAPTER PRESENTS SUPPORT for the basic premise of this book—that intergenerational faith experiences uniquely nurture spiritual growth and development in both adults and children. We must clarify here that we are not recommending that *all* activities of a faith community be conducted with all ages present. There are powerful, valid and important reasons to gather by age or stage or interest; spiritual growth and development can and indeed does happen when teens gather separately, when the seniors meet for mutual support and care, and when the preschoolers join together and learn. We are rather proposing that frequent and regular cross-generational opportunities for worship, learning, outreach, service and fellowship offer distinctive spiritual benefits and blessings.

When Christine asked her research interviewees why they believed intergenerational faith formation was a valid church ministry model, the most common response was that it is scriptural. Intergenerationality enables the whole church to benefit from each individual's God-given gifts and enables believers to fully live out being the body of Christ and the family of faith. Among the many benefits for both adults and children are a sense of belonging, support for troubled families, better use of resources, character growth and sharing each other's spiritual journeys. Additionally, this chapter will highlight special benefits for particular age cohorts—children, teens, emerging adults, young adults, middle adults and older adults.

BELONGING

"Belongingness" is the third in Maslow's hierarchy of needs.[1] After physiological needs and safety needs are met, human beings seek—and need—places to belong. Sandage, Aubrey and Ohland identify five aspects that characterize healthy community.[2] The first one—belongingness—is particularly important in the realm of spiritual care and formation. Healthy belongingness offers support for people in difficult situations, release from shame through forgiving grace and opportunity for authenticity. Intergenerational faith communities provide experiences that foster this deep sense of belonging in children, teens and adults; all feel welcome and received.

Children especially need to feel a deep sense of belonging, and they know if they are welcome or not. One of Lawrence Richards's five processes for guiding the spiritual development of children is that they must feel like they *belong* in the faith community.[3] Ivy Beckwith agrees: "This belonging needs to be demonstrated through the policies and practices of the community. Forming relationships with children is the responsibility of all members of the community, not just those who work with them in educational programs."[4]

In her chapter on intergenerational ministry, coauthored with her mother (Carol Rask), Karen Rask Behling describes several poignant intergenerational memories (sharing stories, celebrating advent, delivering

---

[1] Abraham Maslow, *Motivation and Personality* (New York: Harper & Brothers, 1954).
[2] Steven Sandage, Carol Aubrey and Tammy Ohland, "Weaving the Fabric of Faith," *Marriage and Family: A Christian Journal* 2, no. 4 (1999): 381-98.
[3] Lawrence Richards, *Theology of Children's Ministry* (Grand Rapids: Zondervan, 1984).
[4] Ivy Beckwith, *Postmodern Children's Ministry: Ministry to Children in the 21st Century* (Grand Rapids: Zondervan, 2004), p. 66.

BOX 3.1

Emerging Adults and Belonging

Abbie Smith says that emerging adults especially need to belong: "College-aged people don't cut themselves, suffer from eating disorders, change majors seven times, change churches ten times or abandon church altogether because they're flighty. They do so because they don't know where they belong."[a] Smith describes the care and influence of three women—an eighty-year-old nun, a mom who was also a campus minister, and an older single woman—who invited her into their spiritual journeys during her college years. She says, "I got to be the one whose dreams were listened to and whose doubts were held. And in the most practical of terms I got to be cared for in my adolescence while being caringly invited into adulthood. I got to belong."[b]

---

[a]Reggie Joiner, Chuck Bomar and Abbie Smith, *The Slow Fade* (Colorado Springs: David C. Cook, 2010), p. 41.
[b]Ibid.

meals to the elderly, worship) from her childhood and youth.[5] Rask concludes the chapter saying, "It was significant to be known. I knew I belonged in that community of believers; I knew that my life mattered to others."[6] To be received by a multigenerational body of believers is to belong at a deeply satisfying level.

SUPPORT FOR TROUBLED FAMILIES

All faith communities have families who are facing severe difficulties. How does bringing the generations together uniquely benefit these families? Sharon Koh, senior associate pastor of Evergreen Baptist Church–Los Angeles in Rosemead, California, says: "When our church is intentional about cross-generational interactions, it expands the concept of family beyond the

---

[5]Karen Rask Behling and Carol Rask, "Ordinary Time: Intergenerational Ministry," in *Ordinary Ministry, Extraordinary Challenge: Women and the Roles of Ministry,* ed. Norma Cook Everist (Nashville: Abingdon Press, 2000), pp. 73-79.
[6]Ibid., p. 75.

nuclear family alone. . . . Because of this new concept of family, many inadequacies in the nuclear family can be made up for, in Christ's name."[7]

David Fraze with Fuller Youth Institute notes that youth ministry in general has done a pretty good job with young people who come from "strong, intact and engaged" families, but the real question is how to nurture students whose families are scattered, unsupportive and disengaged.[8] His answer is to implement intergenerational strategies, that is, "practices designed to create opportunities for spiritual growth across generational lines."[9] These strategies call the community of faith to offer hope not only to youth, but also single parents, divorced persons and others who have been hurt by family relationships, "by providing a family in which healing and acceptance are found."[10]

Pentecostal Tabernacle in Cambridge, Massachusetts, began in 1927, but attendance was down in the 1980s to only forty—mostly older—people. Senior pastor Brian Greene says that at that point the church began to focus on its multicultural neighborhood, and now there are over three hundred attendees, half under the age of thirty. Though the church wanted to welcome this influx of young people, the older generations at first did not know how. By way of background, Greene notes that "only 0.5 out of every ten African-American children will be raised in a home with both parents, compared with four out of every ten Caucasian children."[11] According to Greene, Pentecostal Tabernacle has now become a fathering church—a parenting church. "Many in our church have not been properly parented. But now, by being in our church, they don't have just one mother. They have eight or ten. That's a fruit of being a cross-generational church."[12]

BETTER USE OF RESOURCES

Chad Hall decries the trend toward churches that appeal to or draw only a narrow age range. He has ministered in churches that are primarily

---

[7]Helen Lee, "Age-Old Divide: How Do You Integrate the Generations and Life Stages at Your Church? Five Church Leaders Respond," *Leadership* 27 (Fall 2006): 43-44.

[8]David Fraze, "Something Is Not Right: Revisiting Our Definition of Family," Fuller Youth Institute, 2009, <fulleryouthinstitute.org/2009/01/something-is-not-right/>.

[9]Ibid., p. 1.

[10]Ibid., p. 3.

[11]Lee, "Age-Old Divide," p. 44.

[12]Ibid., p. 46.

young and others that are predominantly older. "While many established churches struggle to attract and retain young adult members, newer churches are attracting nothing but."[13] Hall offers several reasons to avoid age segregation in faith communities, one of which is the uneven distribution of resources: "Both young and old have resources to share. Generational homogenization results in an overabundance of one type of resources in certain congregations. Many older generation churches have plenty of money and facilities, but lack the energy and fresh vision young congregations have aplenty."[14] A growing Gen Xer church in Covina, California, struggles with one aspect of this imbalance: "Raising sufficient money to pay for the ministries, let alone a new building, is a special challenge facing a congregation of young Xers."[15] One minister at this church notes that many in their twenties and thirties are in debt and give only five or ten dollars a week. On the other hand, this minister says that a great strength of this church is that the leaders as well as the members are always asking, "How can we be fresh? How can we do things differently? How can we adapt our approach?"[16]

While thirty- and fortysomething leaders of younger churches may have a plethora of fresh ideas and plenty of energy, they lack the experience and deep spiritual resources of more seasoned leaders who have navigated repeatedly the multifarious, often troubled waters of a rapidly growing faith community. Young leaders sometimes flame out in the absence of older, wiser heads who can hold the course and traverse tricky terrain. Intergenerational faith communities bring together the young, fresh thinkers with the older, wiser veterans, creating an integrated profusion of resources.

CHARACTER GROWTH

Mike Breaux, teaching pastor at Heartland Community Church in Illinois, says that when he moved from youth ministry to senior ministry

---

[13]Chad Hall, *"All in the Family* Is Now *Grey's Anatomy:* Today's Segregation Is by Age," *Leadership* 27 (Fall 2006): 33.
[14]Ibid., p. 33.
[15]Jackson Carroll and Wade Roof, *Bridging Divided Worlds: Congregational Cultures in Congregations* (San Francisco: Jossey-Bass, 2002), p. 190.
[16]Ibid., p. 192.

he "envisioned a church with young and old and in-between learning from one another, *deferring*, serving, praying, working, worshiping together—one heart, one mind, one church (Acts 4:32)."[17] Breaux says that "while each generation maintains its uniqueness and offers different strengths, the heartbeat of God is for one church. So many forces drive generations apart, but moderns and postmoderns can coexist. It requires *humility, mutual submission,* and respect for different strengths and passions. Those virtues don't happen easily. They emerge as we teach them and model them."[18]

Chad Hall also believes that bringing all the generations together yields unique opportunities for character growth. He has experienced the particular type of conflict that intergenerational churches encounter, and says that negotiating contradictory generational priorities can breed godliness.

> Churches who value their young and their old will have to deal with clashing perspectives, which may slow things down, make decisions harder to come by, force compromise on difficult matters, and automatically elevate the value of relationship over that of task.
>
> But when generations collide, the ensuing conflict reminds everyone, Church is not just about me. Who knew that church could be the cure to narcissism?[19]

UNIQUE BENEFITS BY AGE AND STAGE

Children. Over a period of years, Lance Armstrong, a Christian educator in Australia, asked participants in his workshops what led them to faith.[20] Their answers included evangelistic rallies, life crises, family influence, significant persons, church camp and Sunday school. Armstrong notes that family influence always received the most votes, but that other relationships (e.g., a significant person or people at church camp) always came in next. Armstrong further notes that what appears to be most important in people's growth to faith "is a loving, caring, close relationship with

---

[17]Mike Breaux, "A Mad, Multi-Gen Strategy That Works, Dude," *Leadership* 26 (Spring 2005): 44, emphasis ours.

[18]Ibid., p. 45, emphasis ours.

[19]Hall, *"All in the Family,"* p. 33.

[20]Lance Armstrong, *Children in Worship: The Road to Faith* (Melbourne, Australia: Joint Board of Christian Education, 1988).

other Christians."[21] Given this truth, Armstrong concludes that "in the nurturing process of our children, we must allow them to develop deep personal relationships with as many of the people of God as possible."[22]

Ivy Beckwith, longtime children's minister, agrees. She says that children need frequent, regular, ongoing opportunities to interact with people of faith "who struggle, who trust God, who make mistakes and are forgiven, who work for mercy and justice, who model kingdom values."[23] Beckwith says children will remember the stories and lives of people they have known in their faith communities more than Bible facts they may have learned.

Not long ago Holly reconnected with Paul, who as a middle schooler was part of a small cross-age VBS teaching team that she led in the 1980s. They chatted and caught up. Toward the end of the conversation, Paul said he had never forgotten the story she told about lying to her teacher when she was in the sixth grade, and how God had used that experience to enlighten her and teach her the importance of trust. He said her story had prompted him to ask God to use every experience of his life to teach him. Holly was surprised (and chagrined) that he remembered this particular incident. God uses unlikely tools, and by regularly interacting with adults of all ages, children will be nurtured in their faith journeys, even in unlikely ways.

Teens. Kara Powell with the Fuller Youth Institute led a recent study, the College Transition Project, that gathered data from five hundred youth group graduates regarding their faith journeys. The ultimate purpose of the study was to determine what elements of youth ministry were significantly related to higher faith maturity in teens transitioning to college.[24] One important finding of the study was that "high school and college students who experience more intergenerational worship tend to have higher faith maturity."[25]

---

[21]Ibid., p. 15.
[22]Ibid., p. 18.
[23]Beckwith, *Postmodern Children's Ministry,* p. 66.
[24]Kara E. Powell, Brad M. Griffin and Cheryl A. Crawford, *Sticky Faith: Youth Worker Edition: Practical Ideas to Nurture Long-Term Faith in Teenagers* (Grand Rapids: Zondervan, 2011).
[25]Ibid., p. 75.

Several youth ministry leaders in recent years have argued that teens benefit spiritually from nonparental mentors as well as from parents.[26] Jason Lanker's recent work on natural mentoring and teens offers strong support for the importance of intergenerational opportunities for teens because these opportunities yield multiple prospects for natural adult-teen mentorships to form.[27] An interesting finding for our purposes is that, at the time of the research, participants in Lanker's study had known their mentors for an average of 6.7 years. (Other studies have shown the average

---

BOX 3.2

For teens, intergenerational faith experiences offer

- *extended faith family ("aunts," "uncles," "grandparents") when blood family is distant*

- *support as they negotiate Erikson's identity vs. role confusion crisis[a]*

- *opportunities to mentor preadolescents*

- *opportunities to serve those outside their teen worlds*

- *wisdom and encouragement while navigating transitions from childhood to adolescence*

- *physical, emotional, psychological and spiritual support when life falls down: parental divorce, sibling illness or death, failure in school, being bullied, feelings of loneliness*

- *opportunity to find examples and mentors among emerging adults and older adults*

---

[a]Erik Erikson, *Childhood and Society,* 2nd ed. (New York: Norton, 1963).

---

[26]Chap Clark, *Hurt: Inside the World of Today's Teenagers* (Grand Rapids: Baker Academic, 2004); Mark DeVries, *Family-Based Youth Ministry,* rev. ed. (Downers Grove, IL: InterVarsity Press, 2004); Merton Strommen and Richard Hardel, *Passing on the Faith* (Winona, MN: St. Mary's Press, 2000); Peter Benson, *All Kids Are Our Kids* (San Francisco: Jossey-Bass, 1997).

[27]Jason Lanker, "The Relationship Between Natural Mentoring and Spirituality in Christian Adolescents," *Journal of Youth Ministry* 9 (Fall 2010): 93-109; Jason Lanker, "The Family of Faith: The Place of Natural Mentoring in the Church's Christian Formation of Adolescents," *Christian Education Journal* (series 3) 7, no. 2 (Fall 2010): 267-80.

time to be as much as 10 years.[28]) Since the average age of participants in Lanker's study was 18.2 years, these participants were, on average, 11 years old when they met their mentors. In today's highly segregated church environments, the benefits of the mentoring process are not available to teens unless they have had opportunities to come to know those who are further ahead of them on the journey. No better setting for those opportunities exists than in intergenerational small groups, mission trips, service projects, musical or dramatic productions, age-integrated Sunday schools, and worship.

Emerging adults. Joiner, Bomar and Smith acknowledge in their book, *The Slow Fade,* that eighteen- to twenty-five-year-olds who were active, fervent Christians during their childhood and teen years often become disconnected from their communities of faith during their young adult years.[29] The authors say these older teens fade out after high school [the "finish line"] and then fade back later, and "for a few years we just assume they are transforming into mature adults."[30] These authors castigate churches that are passively waiting for these young adults to return after they mature, marry and have children. Precisely because these are the critical years when emerging adults are choosing careers and a spouse, churches should move the "finish line" to early or mid-twenties rather than high school graduation. Of course, the question is, how? The suggestion Joiner, Bomar and Smith offer is that emerging adults need other, older adults to come alongside them to listen to their stories, validate their search for identity and join them "as they journey toward God and adulthood."[31]

The teens in Christian Smith's 2005 national study reported that their parents were the primary influence on their spiritual lives.[32] Smith has continued to follow these teens as they have entered what is now being

[28]Jean Rhodes, *Stand by Me: The Risks and Rewards of Mentoring Today's Youth* (Cambridge, MA: Harvard University Press, 2004); John E. Harrison, "Forming Connections: A Study of Adolescent Faith Development as Perceived by Adult Christians" (doctoral dissertation, Princeton Theological Seminary, *Dissertation Abstracts International, 60,* 07A, 1999).

[29]Joiner, Bomar and Smith, *Slow Fade.*

[30]Ibid., p. 21.

[31]Ibid., p. 44.

[32]Christian Smith with Melinda Denton, *Soul Searching: The Religious and Spiritual Lives of American Teenagers* (Oxford: Oxford University Press, 2005).

called "emerging adulthood." Smith found that for these twentysomethings, parents are still the primary influence, but also as with teens, it is
not only parents who matter in forming the religion of emerging adults.[33]
Nonparental adults in their lives are also important—those in their faith
communities who have reached out to them and built meaningful personal relationships with them.

> The empirical evidence tells us that it does in fact matter for emerging
> adult religious outcomes whether or not [the participants] have had non-
> parental adults in their religious congregation to whom they could turn for
> help and support. It matters whether or not [they] have belonged to con-
> gregations offering youth groups that they actually liked and wanted to be
> part of. It matters whether or not [they] have participated in adult-taught
> religious education classes, such as Sunday school. Adult engagement with,
> role modeling for, and formation of youth simply matters a great deal for
> how they turn out after they leave the teenage years.[34]

Joseph Hellerman, who was a singles' minister for fifteen years, says
emerging adults are asking profound life questions during these years:
"What am I going to do with my life? Who am I going to spend my life
with? And where am I going to live?"[35] They are also seeking community
and are looking for ways to pour their lives into the hurting people of the
world. Perhaps more than at any other time period in their lives, they need
input, feedback, insight and wisdom from those who are further ahead on
the journey. Intentionally intergenerational communities of faith can
provide especially well for those entering the adult world.

Adults. Allan Harkness, a Christian educator and dean of Asia Graduate
School of Theology in Singapore, has been writing about intergenerational issues since 1996.[36] In one of his articles Harkness states that inter-

---

[33]Christian Smith with Patricia Snell, *Souls in Transition: The Religious and Spiritual Lives of Emerging Adults* (Oxford: Oxford University Press, 2009).

[34]Ibid., p. 285.

[35]Joseph Hellerman, *When the Church Was a Family: Recapturing Jesus' Vision for Authentic Christian
Community* (Nashville: B & H Academic, 2009), p. 169.

[36]Allan Harkness, "Intergenerational Christian Education: Reclaiming a Significant Educational
Strategy in Christian Faith Communities" (doctoral dissertation, Murdoch University, Perth,
Australia, 1996); Allan Harkness, "Intergenerational Education for an Intergenerational Church?"
Religious Education 93 (1998a): 431-47; Allan Harkness, "Intergenerational Christian Education:
An Imperative for Effective Education in Local Churches (Part 1)," *Journal of Christian Education*

BOX 3.3

For emerging adults, intergenerational faith experiences offer

- *much-needed community*
- *support for lingering issues regarding identity development*
- *opportunities to mentor teens*
- *opportunities to serve outside their bubble*
- *wisdom and encouragement while negotiating central life issues: job/career choices and marriage partners*
- *physical, emotional, psychological and spiritual support when facing difficult situations: faith doubts, addictions, financial instability, unwed pregnancy, poor choices*
- *opportunity to find examples and mentors among those further ahead on the journey*

generational Christian experiences "enhance personal faith development."[37] Interestingly, Harkness's main point here is that *adult* faith development will be enhanced when adults are allowed to participate with children in intergenerational activities: "[Intergenerational Christian experience] provides a setting in which adults can be both challenged by, and assisted to reflect upon, the childlike attitude of discipleship which Jesus urged on this followers. This is done by working through issues with younger people who are demonstrating the ability to learn new, or adapt old, concepts as a natural part of their search for reality and meaning."[38] Basically Harkness's argument is that children (and younger adults) often question givens and traditions that older adults may have accepted uncritically. The young are perhaps more willing to consider alternate ways of seeing things.

41, no. 2 (1998b): 5-14; Allan Harkness, "Intergenerational Christian Education: An Imperative for Effective Education in Local Churches (Part 2)," *Journal of Christian Education* 42, no. 1 (1998c): 37-50; Allan Harkness, "Intergenerational and Homogeneous-Age Education: Mutually Exclusive Strategies for Faith Communities?" *Religious Education* 95 (2000): 51-63; Allan Harkness, "Intergenerational Corporate Worship as a Significant Educational Activity," *Christian Education Journal* 7NS (Spring 2003): 5-21.

[37]Harkness, "Intergenerational Christian Education (Part 2)," p. 41.

[38]Ibid., pp. 42-43.

Harkness does indicate that intergenerational experiences will also contribute to the faith maturity of the younger participants, but his focus in this article is on the importance of intergenerational experiences for adult faith development.

Young adults. As emerging adults settle into career paths, they often feel ill prepared to navigate the politics of the workplace, the responsibility for their financial futures, the weight of adult decisions. In strong intergenerational faith communities, there are others to whom a young adult can turn for encouragement, advice, insight or for simply a listening ear—someone who has perspective on career choices, ethical dilemmas or financial difficulties.

In addition to learning to carry their own weight, many men and women of Generation X (the cohort now in their thirties and forties) are currently buried in the arduous tasks of rearing young children. Married couples with small children are typically at a very stressful time in their lives as they learn to juggle their spouse's needs, their children's needs, work responsibilities and personal needs. This season of life can be exhausting; perhaps moms and dads should not be attempting to juggle all these responsibilities without the love and support from those who have faced these same struggles and survived.

In his discussion of first-century mores, Hellerman describes a world of

---

BOX 3.4

"I can't do it all!" thirty-four-year-old Lanae wailed.

"I read about these supermoms who use organic diapers, feed the birds in the winter, take cupcakes to school, present a case at court between breastfeedings, keep spotless homes, scrapbook, prepare gourmet dinners, preserve an hour of quiet devotional time each morning, chair the worship planning team, discuss the three branches of the government over home-cooked Sunday dinner, make their own greeting cards, go canoeing with their families over the weekend, visit the nursing home with their children, recycle every bottle and bag, and put on a sexy nightie every evening. Are you kidding me! I can't even stay awake!" (recent conversation with a friend, used by permission)

BOX 3.5

Intentional intergenerational faith communities offer young adults

- *support for transition into responsibilities of adulthood*
- *support for early years of marriage*
- *physical, emotional, psychological and spiritual support for the stress and weight of parenting young children*
- *opportunity to find examples and mentors among those further ahead on the journey*
- *encouragement of living among those who have survived and thrived past the early parenting years*
- *physical, emotional, psychological and spiritual support when hardship comes: divorce, miscarriage, infertility, illness, job loss*
- *opportunity to anticipate the next life stage*

"extended family societies" where parenting was not such a lonely enterprise.[39] Hellerman indicates that intergenerational faith communities can emulate this "extended family society" so that young parents will not feel such isolation in the crucial tasks of parenting.

For his recent book, *After the Baby Boomers: How Twenty- and Thirty-Somethings Are Shaping the Future of American Religion*, Robert Wuthnow analyzed data collected from dozens of studies conducted both recently and over the past decades to assess how young adults are doing spiritually.[40] Wuthnow found that "young adults are currently less involved at houses of worship than young adults were a generation ago."[41] Furthermore, Wuthnow found that *all* Americans (both young adults and older adults) have fewer social relationships than their parents and grandparents did. He cites Putnam (of *Bowling Alone* fame) as saying that com-

[39]Hellerman, *When Church Was a Family*, p. 158.
[40]Robert Wuthnow, *After the Baby Boomers: How Twenty- and Thirty-Somethings Are Shaping the Future of American Religion* (Princeton, NJ: Princeton University Press, 2007).
[41]Ibid., p. 231.

munities are breaking down. Wuthnow's conclusion is that young adulthood lacks the institutional support it needs and deserves.

Middle adults. Common issues among forty- and fiftysomethings include grappling with the needs of aging parents, coping with unexpected career changes, accepting the loss or compromise of youthful dreams, and coming to terms with middle age.[42] According to Robert Kegan, many adults do not regularly participate in a genuine relational community that could support them as they face these important developmental issues.[43] Intergenerational faith communities can provide a plethora of people who have successfully negotiated some of these crises and could offer love and empathetic support to those coming along behind them.

Middle adults may also be parenting adolescents, which can be stressful and demanding; parents in this season of life sometimes feel overwhelmed and overburdened. DeVries notes that "our culture has put an incredible emotional weight on the shoulders of the nuclear family, a weight [he believes] God never intended for families to bear alone."[44] DeVries recommends that parents need the "rich support of the extended Christian family of the church."[45] Hellerman agrees, saying that "there are some tremendously practical and relational benefits to having more than one adult male and one adult female participating in the family unit."[46]

Many Christian families have at least one child who spends a period of time wandering from their childhood beliefs. These wanderings may range from a few months of doubt, to a dabbling in Eastern religions, to complete rebellion with forays into drugs, promiscuity and/or atheism. During these difficult times, parents desperately need a loving community to hold up their hands. "The faith community provides a perspective on staying true to our children, no matter how wayward they become."[47]

---

[42]Russell Haden Davis, "The Middle Years," in *Human Development and Faith: Life-Cycle Stages of Body, Mind, and Soul,* ed. Felicity B. Kelcourse (St. Louis: Chalice Press, 2004), pp. 251-58.

[43]Robert Kegan, *The Evolving Self: Problem and Process in Human Development* (Cambridge, MA: Harvard University Press, 1982).

[44]DeVries, *Family-Based Youth Ministry,* p. 17.

[45]Ibid.

[46]Hellerman, *When Church Was a Family,* p. 158.

[47]Stephen Post, "Preface: Love Begets Love," in *The Best Love of the Children: Being Loved and Being Taught to Love as the First Human Right,* ed. Timothy Jackson (Grand Rapids: Eerdmans, 2011), p. xviii.

And as parents enter their late forties and fifties, they begin to experience the "empty nest." The energies that these adults have been pouring into parenting can now be harnessed toward other forms of generativity (Erik Erikson's term for pouring the self into rising generations[48]); and if these middle adults are involved actively in intergenerational communities, both younger and older generations are readily available for their ministrations—the older population that is beginning to need help, younger adults swamped with parenting tasks, emerging adults navigating a new world, as well as teens and children.

BOX 3.6

Intentional intergenerational faith communities offer middle adults

- *support for transition into middle age*
- *support for the middle years of marriage*
- *physical, emotional, psychological and spiritual support for the stress and weight of parenting teen children and young adult children*
- *opportunity to find examples and mentors among those further ahead on the journey*
- *opportunity to be examples and mentors for those following on the journey*
- *physical, emotional, psychological and spiritual support when facing grief or loss: teen pregnancy, a child on drugs, divorce, job loss, disability, long-term or terminal illness*
- *hope from those who have survived parenting teens and emerging adults*
- *opportunities to begin pouring into the next generation of young parents*
- *opportunities to serve the older population*
- *opportunity to anticipate the next life stage*

[48]Erik Erikson, *Childhood and Society,* 2nd ed. (New York: Norton, 1963).

Older adults. Mary Pipher said in 1999 that "the old often save the young and the young save the old,"[49] but this mutual blessing is not possible if the young and old are never together. Older adults have much to offer the younger generations. "Like all people, they want to be needed and loved and often seek out opportunities to be in service to others."[50] However, older adults are often so marginalized in our society that they have little opportunity to bless those coming behind them. Pervasive segregation of the elderly has yielded negative stereotyping and discrimination against the older population, which is known as ageism. They can be perceived as inflexible, depressing, less competent, passive and senile.[51] Grefe notes that "intergenerational . . . groups, in which members have equal status, work together toward common goals, and meet over an extended period of time can reduce stereotypes toward the elderly."[52] Faith communities that intentionally and regularly draw older, middle and younger generations together provide opportunities for younger members to know the older and to move away from the negative perception that pervades American society toward seniors. These opportunities open the way for the older to pour their accumulated wisdom and insight into those coming along behind them, which, according to Gentzler, is a deep desire among those who are older.[53]

The older generations also need the younger particularly because of the many losses associated with older adulthood: loss of significant loved ones, independence, purpose, external jobs, and time to accomplish dreams and goals.[54] These losses are deep and abiding; the presence of the young and hopeful can be a salve, can provide new purpose for moving out of mourning and grief, and can refocus attention toward "the incredible calculus of old age—that as more is taken, there is more love for what remains."[55]

[49]Mary Pipher, "The New Generation Gap," *USA Weekend,* March 19-21, 1999, p. 12.
[50]Richard Gentzler, *Designing an Older Adult Ministry* (Nashville: Discipleship Resources, 1999), p. 25.
[51]Bill Bytheway, "Ageism and Age Categorization," *Journal of Social Issues* 61, no. 2 (2005): 361-74, doi:10.1111/j.1540-4560.2005.00410.x; Jon F. Nussbaum et al., "Ageism and Ageist Language Across the Life Span: Intimate Relationships and Non-Intimate Interactions," *Journal of Social Issues* 61, no. 2 (2005): 287-305, doi:10.1111/j.1540-4560.2005.00406.x.
[52]Dagmar Grefe, "Combating Ageism with Narrative and Intergroup Contact: Possibilities of Intergenerational Connections," *Pastoral Psychology* 60 (February 2011): 105.
[53]Gentzler, *Designing an Older Adult Ministry.*
[54]Ibid., p. 25.
[55]Pipher, "The New Generation Gap," p. 12.

BOX 3.7

Intentional intergenerational faith communities offer older adults

- *support for transition into older adulthood*

- *physical, emotional, psychological and spiritual support for the aging process*

- *opportunity to be examples and mentors for those following on the journey*

- *physical, emotional, psychological and spiritual support when facing hard transitions: illness, loss of spouse, death of adult child, Alzheimer's diagnosis, frailty*

- *opportunities to bless children and teens with unconditional love and acceptance*

- *opportunity to embrace the process of death and dying with faith and hope*

CONCLUSION

The Search Institute, which has been conducting global research on spiritual development for fifty years, notes that one fundamental aspect of spiritual development is *interconnecting*, that is, "linking oneself to narratives, communities, mentors, beliefs, traditions, and/or practices that remain significant over time."[56] The best way for the most people to link to the narratives, communities, mentors, traditions and practices of their faith communities is to participate actively in intentionally age-integrated experiences with others in those faith communities. Truly intergenerational communities welcome children, emerging adults, recovering addicts, single adults, widows, single parents, teens whose parents are not around, the elderly, those in crisis, empty nesters and struggling parents of young children into a safe but challenging place to be formed into the image of Christ.

---

[56]Eugene Roehlkepartain, "Engaging International Advisors in Creating a Shared Understanding of Spiritual Development: Seeking Common Ground in Understanding Spiritual Development: A Preliminary Theoretical Framework," Search Institute, 2012. Retrieved from <www.search-institute.org/csd/major-projects/definition-update>.

4

WHAT SHALL WE NAME THIS APPROACH?

What's in a name? That which we call a rose
By any other name would smell as sweet.
William Shakespeare, *Romeo and Juliet*

INTERGENERATIONALITY *AS A CONSTRUCT* has been embedded in the writings of prominent religious educationists and sociologists for decades, though the term *intergenerational* has not always been the operative term employed.[1] We will first examine the concepts promoted by C. Ellis Nelson, John Westerhoff III and Gabriel Moran; then we'll explore James Fowler's work from the 1990s and Joseph Hellerman's descriptive paradigm from his recent *When Church Was Family* (see figure 1).

The term *intergenerational*, though used descriptively in religious literature occasionally, was not a prominent term until James White's *Intergenerational Religious Education* was published in 1988. Since then the word has been cobbled with other terms to create several common phrases in use today, from Harkness's phrase *intergenerational Christian education* to Gambone's *intentional intergenerational ministry* to John Roberto's *intergenerational faith formation* (see figure 1).

CONCEPTUAL CONSTRUCTS

Throughout the twentieth century, leading Christian educationists have recognized the importance of the believing Christian community to the

---

[1]Parts of this chapter were adapted from Allen, "Bringing the Generations Together" (2005) and Allen, "Bringing the Generations Together" (2009). See permissions, page 4.

Intergenerational constructs	Phrases that employ the term *intergenerational*
"Community of believers" (Nelson, 1967)	Intergenerational religious education (White, 1988)
"Enculturation" (Westerhoff, 1976)	Intergenerational Christian education (Prest, 1993; Harkness, 2000)
"Interplay across the generations" (Moran, 1978)	Intentional intergenerational ministry (Gambone, 1997)
"Church as an ecology of faith nurture" (Fowler, 1991)	Intergenerational faith formation (Martineau, Weber & Kehrwald, 2008; Roberto, 2009)
"Strong-group entity" (Hellerman, 2009)	

Figure 1: A rose by any other name

spiritual growth of faith in children as well as adults. Though these scholars have used a variety of phrases to describe this process, the concept is the same—that it is in community that believers are formed, conformed, transformed into the image of Christ. And this idea, though it may not be stated expressly in "intergenerational" terms, provides foundational principles for intergenerational concepts with its emphasis on the importance of community for Christian life and spiritual growth.

Community of believers. The phrase that Nelson[2] uses to refer to the importance of the faith community is the "community of believers." Nelson summarizes his thesis, that "faith is communicated by a community of believers and that the meaning of faith is developed by its members out of their history, by their interaction with each other, and in relation to the events that take place in their lives."[3] Nelson develops this theme throughout his work *Where Faith Begins,* stating in myriad ways that coming to faith takes place in a community and that the character, theology and ethos of that community are crucial to the development of that faith.

According to Nelson faith begins in a community of believers, and it is in the community of believers that faith matures. In 1989, Nelson was sounding the same refrain: "A person's faith matures when life experiences

[2]C. Ellis Nelson, *Where Faith Begins* (Atlanta: John Knox Press, 1967).
[3]Ibid., p. 10.

are interpreted in the light of the Christian tradition in order to understand and do the will of God amid ongoing events in which that person is involved. Because a congregation is part of the body of Christ, it is the place where individuals receive guidance as they work out the meaning of their experiences, and support as they attempt to follow the leading of God's spirit."[4] Nelson's work is not directly linked to the term *intergenerational,* but his phrase *community of believers* carries intergenerational implications.

Enculturation. Westerhoff describes the process of coming to faith in Christian community as "enculturation."[5] He emphasizes that enculturation is not simply the idea that environment, experiences and actions of others have influence *upon* persons. Rather, he says, enculturation "emphasizes the process of interaction between and among persons of all ages. It focuses on the interactive experiences and environments within which persons act to acquire, sustain, change, and transmit their understandings and ways. In enculturation one person is not understood as the actor and another the acted upon, but rather both act, both initiate action, and both react. It is the nature, character, and quality of these interactive experiences among people of all ages within a community of faith that best describes the means of Christian education."[6]

In sociological terms this process is called "religious socialization" (see chapter nine for a fuller discussion of this construct). Westerhoff and Neville define religious socialization as "a process consisting of lifelong, formal and informal mechanisms through which persons sustain and transmit their faith (worldview, value system) and lifestyle, and this is accomplished through participation in the life of a tradition-bearing community with rites, rituals, myths, symbols, expressions of belief, attitudes and values, organizational patterns, and activities."[7]

For three decades Westerhoff has been encouraging faith communities to revisit the practice of corporate worship with all ages present, to question the schooling nature of Christian education programs and to seek other avenues for the whole body of believers to meet together in interactive

---

[4]C. Ellis Nelson, *How Faith Matures* (Louisville, KY: Westminster John Knox, 1989), p. 18.
[5]John H. Westerhoff III, *Will Our Children Have Faith?* rev. ed. (Toronto: Morehouse, 2000).
[6]Ibid., p. 80.
[7]John H. Westerhoff III and Gwen K. Neville, *Generation to Generation: Conversations on Religious Education and Culture* (Philadelphia: United Church Press, 1974), p. 47.

ways. Westerhoff utilizes the term *intergenerational* occasionally, but more frequently he embeds its tenets within his concept of enculturation.

Interplay across generations. Though Moran is not widely known for his intergenerational ideas, his comments on the subject are straightforward and quite comprehensive: "We need learning within families, learning between children and other adults, learning between the very old and the very young, learning between families and all of society's 'outsiders' (the divorced, widowed, homosexual, 'retarded,' etc.)." [8] In a later book, Moran adds that the more we can foster this "interplay across generations," the stronger will be the possibilities of spiritual growth and formation.[9]

Church as an ecology of faith nurture. James Fowler directly connects his faith development stages with the intergenerational life of the faith community.[10] In general, Fowler's stages can be characterized as preconventional (typically children), conventional (adolescents and many adults) and postconventional (some adults). Those with a conventional faith have adopted the beliefs and values of the surrounding faith community, but have done so uncritically and without deep reflection. Postconventional levels of faith reflect an owned faith that has weathered doubt and suffering. Though Fowler recognizes that churches will always have children, youth and adults who practice their faith at preconventional and conventional levels, the "public church requires a substantial number of adults who appropriate the tradition in the . . . [postconventional] stages of faith."[11] Fowler contends that faith communities should be intentionally aiming in their educational and congregational life toward growing Christians to a postconventional level of faith development. The phrase Fowler utilizes to capture the importance of the community to this growth in faith development is "church as an ecology of faith nurture."[12]

In this ecology of faith nurture, Fowler suggests that persons in the various faith stages are to be regularly interacting with one another,

---

[8]Gabriel Moran, "Where Now, What Next," in *Foundations of Religious Education*, ed. Padraic O'Hare (New York: Paulist, 1978), pp. 92-110.

[9]Gabriel Moran, *Interplay: A Theory of Religion and Education* (Winona, MN: Saint Mary's College Press, 1981), p. 109.

[10]James W. Fowler, *Weaving the New Creation: Stages of Faith and the Public Church* (New York: HarperCollins, 1991).

[11]Ibid., p. 191.

[12]Ibid., p. 189.

growing each other toward the more mature levels of faith as they participate in *kerygma* (story, preaching), *leitourgia* (worship and sacrament), *diakonia* (mission and service), *koinonia* (intimate community), and *paideia* (formation and instruction) together.[13] According to Fowler, these intergenerational interactions foster progressive faith development.[14]

Strong-group entity. Hellerman offers a detailed and colorful description of the first-century family culture as a strong group.[15] He contrasts this first-century "strong-group" mentality with the current western "weak-group" mentality. The point of Hellerman's book is that churches should be strong-group entities, made up of children, teens, singles, married couples, families and seniors for whom the welfare of their group—in this case, the whole faith community—takes priority over their own individual happiness and relational satisfaction. Hellerman believes that Jesus calls us into a new strong-group entity, the church, where our brothers and sisters of all ages are our new primary family.

Nelson's "community of believers," Westerhoff's "faith enculturation," Moran's "interplay across the generations," Fowler's "church as an ecology of faith nurture" and Hellerman's "strong-group entity" are all phrases that capture the idea that an intergenerational perspective within the community of faith, the church, is crucial to Christian formation for all ages.

During the last few decades, while Westerhoff, Fowler and others have been calling faith communities to a more whole-body-of-Christ outlook, other Christian scholars and ministry leaders have intentionally employed the explicit term *intergenerational* in order to express directly their conviction that spiritual formation and cross-generational settings are interconnected.

---

[13]Ibid.

[14]James Loder (see, e.g., "Reflections on Fowler's 'Stages of Faith,'" *Religious Education*, 77 [1982]: 133-39) has critiqued Fowler's understanding of faith, saying Fowler elevates the *natural process* of development in the faith journey, which inevitably diminishes the role of radical grace. However, these concepts are not mutually exclusive. As Osmer points out, a person's radical need for grace in light of sin does not thereby negate the crucial role of the faith community in the *process* of development toward faith maturity (Richard Osmer, "James W. Fowler and the Reformed Tradition: An Exercise in Theological Reflection in Religious Education," *Religious Education*, 85 [1990]: 51-68).

[15]Joseph Hellerman, *When the Church Was a Family: Recapturing Jesus' Vision for Authentic Christian Community* (Nashville: B & H Academic, 2009).

FROM INTERGENERATIONAL RELIGIOUS EDUCATION TO INTERGENERATIONAL FAITH FORMATION

The move from "intergenerational religious education" to "intergenerational faith formation" has taken place over the past three decades. The change of terms parallels the perceptual shift away from the term *education* and toward *formation* among influential Christian educators, theologians and ministry leaders.

Intergenerational religious education. Charles Foster, emeritus professor of religious education, wrote in 1984 that intergenerational religious education (IGRE) "gathers people from at least two and preferably three or more age groups or generations into a teaching-learning process in which all members give and receive from the experience."[16] Foster's definition emphasizes the teaching/learning aspect of IGRE, although Foster himself realized that this terminology was problematic. Many religious educators limited IGRE as they tended to plan "from the vantage point or angle of vision of the child in the group" rather than providing experiential opportunities for the generations to mutually engage with one another.[17]

James White, who was considered the main authority on IGRE for two decades, expanded Foster's definition into a richer, more complex one: "two or more different age groups of people in a religious community together learning/growing/living in faith through in-common experiences, parallel learning, contributive-occasions, and interactive sharing."[18] Though the "E" in IGRE stands for *education,* White really uses the word far more broadly than it is typically understood. The word *experiences* would connote White's meaning more accurately—that is, intergenerational religious *experiences*—not *education* in the more narrow classroom sense. When White quotes the editors of *Quarterly Intergenerational Guide* as defining the intergenerational experience as "one in which two or more generations come together intentionally for an occasion of worship, fel-

---

[16]Charles Foster, "Intergenerational Religious Education," in *Changing Patterns of Religious Education,* ed. Marvin J. Taylor (Nashville: Abingdon, 1984), p. 282.

[17]Ibid., pp. 287-88.

[18]James W. White, *Intergenerational Religious Education: Models, Theories, and Prescription for Interage Life and Learning in the Faith Community* (Birmingham, AL: Religious Education Press, 1988), p. 18.

lowship, study, decision-making, mission, or any combination of these functions," he retains this broader understanding of IGRE.[19]

Intergenerational Christian education. Allan Harkness's focus since 1996 has been specifically intergenerational Christian education (IGCE), not the more general religious education. Harkness describes IGCE also in terms of experiences, rather than the more narrow implication of education.[20] Harkness says that "intentional intergenerational strategies are those in which an integral part of the process of faith communities encourages interpersonal interactions across generational boundaries, and in which a sense of mutuality and equality is encouraged between participants."[21]

The general idea of IGCE is that children, teenagers, young adults (single and married), parents and grandparents gather in settings where all members give and receive from each other. All ages can participate actively in prayer and worship and, in some settings, share spiritual insights, read Scripture and minister to one other.

Harkness's main claim is that IGCE stands in contrast to the typical way "church is done" in the contemporary context. For example, in many formal worship experiences, children, young adults and women are rarely heard from. Activities in faith communities are often age-group oriented, and consequently children seldom hear older children or lay adults express spiritual thoughts, and adults rarely hear the spiritual insights of children. Even Sunday school classes, whether they follow the traditional educational model (teacher-centered, content-oriented) or have adopted more contemporary educational approaches such as discovery learning, active participation and cooperative learning, tend to be age-segregated. IGCE calls for more common learning experiences involving mixed age groups.

Intentional intergenerational ministry. The term *intentional intergenerational ministry* (IIM) was coined by James Gambone, author and con-

---

[19]Ibid., p. 19.

[20]Allan Harkness, "Intergenerational Christian Education: Reclaiming a Significant Educational Strategy in Christian Faith Communities" (doctoral dissertation, Murdoch University, Perth, Australia, 1996).

[21]Allan Harkness, "Intergenerational and Homogeneous-Age Education: Mutually Exclusive Strategies for Faith Communities?" *Religious Education* 95 (2000): 52.

sultant regarding intentional intergenerational dialogue.[22] Gambone's *Primer* provides a basic overview of IIM and outlines how a faith community could organize and implement an intergenerational dialogue event that would initiate an intergenerational mindset within a congregation.[23] Gambone's use of the term *ministry* broadens intergenerationality beyond education. Gambone believes that IGCE programs failed to make significant inroads into the church culture because intergenerationality tended to be seen as something "outside of the core mission of the congregation."[24] He teaches that the entire congregation needs to commit to *intentional* intergenerational ministry, and that IIM must be part of the core mission of a congregation rather than only a part of the educational/programmatic arm of the church: "It is important to understand that intentional intergenerational ministry is not simply another Christian education program or just another ministry."[25] He also points out that by nature churches are *multigenerational*, that is, they are made up of people from various generations. However, churches do not always capitalize on this natural aspect. Faith communities that are intentional about *intergenerational* ministry will look for ways to bring all generations that make up the body of Christ together in a variety of venues within the church ministry, such as worship, fellowship, discipleship and service.[26]

During a presentation to students of the Director of Christian Education Program at Concordia University in Irvine, California, Reverend Donald Smidt, a contributor to Gambone's *Primer*, shared his "Ten Principles of Intentional Intergenerational Ministry," which outlines the mindset congregational members must have in order to implement IIM effectively.[27] The first principle indicates that IIM "is a perspective and

---

[22]James V. Gambone, *Together for Tomorrow: Building Community Through Intergenerational Dialogue* (Crystal Bay, MN: Elder Eye Press, 1997); James V. Gambone, *All Are Welcome: A Primer for Intentional Intergenerational Ministry and Dialogue* (Crystal Bay, MN: Elder Eye Press, 1998).

[23]Gambone, *All Are Welcome*.

[24]Ibid., p. vi.

[25]Ibid.

[26]Ibid.

[27]Don Smidt, "Ten Principles of Intentional Intergenerational Ministry" (paper presented at Concordia University, Irvine, CA, October 2004).

attitude before it ever becomes plans, activities, or facilities."[28] Smidt's master plan provides an example of how one church developed the structure by which an intergenerational model could flourish. Smidt's congregation and his IIM philosophy were highlighted in the book *Passing on the Faith: A Radical New Model for Youth and Family Ministry* by Strommen and Hardel.[29]

Intergenerational faith formation. The recent book by Mariette Martineau, Joan Weber and Lief Kehrwald offers this phrase in its title: *Intergenerational Faith Formation: All Ages Learning Together.*[30] The book's primary purpose is to examine, explain and assess the theory and practice of a ten-step intergenerational faith formation approach to Catholic catechesis (the Generations of Faith Project[31]). The ultimate concern of the Generations of Faith Project is *lifelong* faith formation, and the phrase *intergenerational faith formation* emerged out of this project.

In general, intergenerational faith formation represents a shift away from "education" (or catechesis) as it has been traditionally perceived, and a concomitant shift toward a "formation" approach. According to Martineau, Weber and Kehrwald, the goals for intergenerational faith formation include: moving away from a "children-only" focus in learning; changing the "start/stop" perception of catechesis (e.g., baptism, confirmation); reducing age segregation; moving away from a textbook-oriented approach via implementing a more event-centered, experiential, service-oriented approach; and adopting a more integrative, collaborative model of faith formation.[32] The authors make a compelling case for intergenerational learning as "one of the ways people can best learn about and grow in faith"[33]; they say that intergenerational faith formation can be "magical, powerful, and dramatic."[34]

---

[28]Ibid.

[29]Merton P. Strommen and Richard A. Hardel, *Passing on the Faith: A Radical New Model for Youth and Family Ministry* (Winona, MN: St. Mary' s Press, 2000).

[30]Mariette Martineau, Joan Weber and Lief Kehrwald, *Intergenerational Faith Formation: All Ages Learning Together* (New London, CT: Twenty-Third Publications, 2008).

[31]*Generations of Faith Project* (Gig Harbor, WA: Center for Ministry Development, 1997).

[32]Martineau, Weber and Kehrwald, *Intergenerational Faith Formation*, pp. 3-4.

[33]Ibid., back cover.

[34]Ibid.

John Roberto, one of the senior writers for the Generations of Faith Project, now edits a new quarterly journal entitled *Lifelong Faith: The Theory and Practice of Lifelong Faith Formation*, produced by the Center for Ministry Development (as is the Generations of Faith Project). The first edition of the journal was published in 2007. Though typically each issue of the journal focuses on a specific area of faith formation (e.g., family faith formation, Summer 2007; or emerging adulthood faith formation, Summer 2010), a common thread woven throughout is the importance of intergenerational faith formation. One issue focused directly on the topic (Spring 2009), and intergenerationality was a recurring theme in the forward-looking issue "Faith Formation 2020: Envisioning the Future" (Summer 2009).

PROPOSING THE PHRASE
INTERGENERATIONAL CHRISTIAN FORMATION

A kaleidoscope of descriptive terms and phrases is available to help illuminate the concept that believers are formed spiritually as they interact together in complex, authentic, intergenerational Christian faith communities. One more phrase that captures this construct is *intergenerational Christian formation*—the title of this book. A search of the ATLA database[35] yields no articles containing the exact phrase "intergenerational Christian formation," nor does Amazon sell a book so titled, other than this one. Though this phrase is (apparently) not currently a popular term, we find it particularly apt.

A closely related phrase that could be used is *intergenerational spiritual formation*. Spiritual formation has been an increasingly hot topic for over a couple of decades, so perhaps intergenerational spiritual formation will be the term of the future. The ATLA database yielded no recent articles (2000–2011) that contained the exact phrase "intergenerational spiritual formation" either; however, entering the shortened phrase "spiritual formation" yielded 867 articles compared to 52 articles that contained the terms "Christian formation" or "Christian spiritual formation." But there is a disadvantage in using the phrase "spiritual formation": not all of the

---

[35]The ATLA database is the American Theological Library Association's massive data bank for sources on religion, theology and ministry.

articles that addressed spiritual formation were specifically Christian. Spiritual formation is a phrase that can be operationalized across a wide spectrum of spiritual beliefs and practices—that is, it is not unique to the Christian realm and can be perceived as much broader than Christian spiritual formation. In fact, Dallas Willard says that spiritual formation is "a process that happens to everyone. The most despicable as well as the most admired of persons have a spiritual formation. . . . Their spirits or hearts have been formed"[36] in some way.

Therefore our hope is that the phrase *intergenerational Christian formation* will be increasingly utilized over the next several years.[37] But whether one uses Nelson's "community of believers," Westerhoff's "faith enculturation," Moran's "interplay across the generations," Fowler's "church as an ecology of faith nurture," Hellerman's "strong-group entity," or intergenerational religious education/experiences (White), intergenerational Christian education/experiences (Harkness), intentional intergenerational ministry (Gambone), intergenerational faith formation (Martineau, Weber, and Kehrwald) or intergenerational Christian formation (Allen and Ross), the emphasis is on the importance of fostering intentionally cross-generational opportunities for the purpose of nurturing Christian learning, growth and formation.

The next section, part two, is the heart of this book. It addresses the question: *Why* might intergenerational faith experiences uniquely nurture Christian formation? Initially—and most importantly—we will explore biblical foundations for intergenerationality. Then we will unpack several theories that intersect with intergenerational principles, and introduce a macrotheory that explains *why* intergenerationality is so effective. Along the way, we aim to draw further theological connections that correlate with intergenerationality and Christian formation.

---

[36]Dallas Willard, *Renovation of the Heart: Putting on the Character of Christ* (Colorado Springs: NavPress, 2002), p. 19.

[37]Though we have not read this phrase in our research, we may not be able to claim that we are the first to employ it.

Part Two

■   ■   ■

BIBLICAL, THEOLOGICAL AND THEORETICAL SUPPORT

5

FEASTS, JEHOSHAPHAT AND HOUSE CHURCHES

Biblical Foundations

Blow the trumpet in Zion; consecrate a fast; call a solemn assembly;
*   gather the people.*
Consecrate the congregation; assemble the elders; gather the children, even
*   nursing infants.*

Joel 2:15-16 (ESV)

One generation commends your works to another;
*   they tell of your mighty acts.*

Psalm 145:4

SCRIPTURE PRESUMES THAT FAITH FORMATION occurs within intergenerational, familial and community settings.[1] This assumption is reflected in sociocultural and social learning theories described in later
chapters in this text, and it provides insight to those who seek to evan-
gelize, catechize, disciple and form persons into Christlikeness.

---

[1]Parts of this chapter were adapted from or previously published in Allen, "Bringing the Generations Together" (2005); Allen, "Bringing the Generations Together" (2009); and Allen, "No Better Place" (2010). See permissions, page 4.

THE OLD TESTAMENT AND GENERATIONAL COMMUNITY

Intergenerational writer and speaker Daphne Kirk describes both the familial and communal nature of Old Testament relationships, stating, "When God set His people Israel in order, he placed each individual within a family, each family within a tribe, and each tribe within the nation. No generation was excluded, no child left out, no older person put aside. Within each tribe were the components of family; they were community."[2]

Special occasions. When Israel gathered for important events—even critical moments—all the generations were present. For example, when Moses gave his farewell address, all were present: "All of you are standing today in the presence of the LORD your God—your leaders and chief men, your elders and officials, and all the other men of Israel, together with your children and your wives, and the foreigners living in your camps. . . . You are standing here in order to enter into a covenant with the LORD your God" (Deut 29:10-12).

Sometime later, after the first few battles in the land of Canaan, after the Israelites had defeated Jericho and (eventually) Ai, Joshua called the people together to renew the covenant and to read the law: "And afterward he read all the words of the law, the blessing and the curse, according to all that is written in the Book of the Law. There was not a word of all that Moses commanded that Joshua did not read before all the assembly of Israel, and the women, and the little ones, and the sojourners who lived among them" (Josh 8:34-35 ESV).

Another time that all of God's people gathered together, from youngest to oldest, was during Jehoshaphat's reign. Jehoshaphat was one of the kings of Judah who did "what was right in the sight of the LORD" (2 Chron 20:32 ESV). When a vast army of Moabites and Ammonites marched upon Judah, Jehoshaphat "resolved to inquire of the LORD, and he proclaimed a fast for all Judah" (2 Chron 20:3), and people came from all over Judah to seek the Lord's help. The writer of Chronicles describes the scene at the temple: "All the men of Judah, with their wives and children and little ones, stood there before the LORD" (2 Chron 20:13).

---

[2]Daphne Kirk, *Heirs Together: Establishing Intergenerational Church*, rev. ed. (Suffolk, UK: Kevin Mayhew, 2003), p. 17.

When all were gathered, Jehoshaphat prayed loudly:

- calling on God's name
- attributing to God power and might
- recalling that God drove out the inhabitants of the land of Canaan for his people
- acknowledging that he and all the people were gathered before the temple to cry out for deliverance from this enemy
- asking God to judge these enemies

Then Jehoshaphat closed his prayer with profound words: "We do not know what to do, but our eyes are on you" (2 Chron 20:12).

Then the Spirit of the Lord came upon a prophet named Jahaziel, and he spoke God's words: "Do not be afraid or discouraged because of this vast army. For the battle is not yours, but God's" (2 Chron 20:15).

What a day! Threatened by powerful enemies, the children, parents, aunts, uncles, cousins, grandparents, brothers, sisters, neighbors, friends—*everyone*—heard their king entreat Yahweh, and then heard the Lord respond through a prophet. The events of this memorable day were experienced *en masse*, then told and retold to the generations yet unborn, even to this present day.

Near the end of recorded biblical history before Christ, after the Jews had returned from captivity to Jerusalem, "Ezra the priest brought the Law before the assembly, both men and women and all who could understand what they heard. . . . And he read from it facing the square before the Water Gate from early morning until midday, in the presence of the men and the women and those who could understand. And the ears of all the people were attentive to the Book of the Law" (Neh 8:2-3 ESV). And sometime later, when the wall of Jerusalem was dedicated, there was singing, music, sacrifices and much rejoicing among the people, and "the women and children also rejoiced" (Neh 12:43).

The feasts. In the religion of Israel, all ages were not just included, they were drawn in, assimilated, absorbed into the whole community with a deep sense of belonging.[3] The intergenerational examples just described

---

[3]Allan G. Harkness, "Intergenerational Education for an Intergenerational Church?" *Religious*

are illustrative, but the directives for feasts and celebrations depict this point best. These commanded festivals were celebrated annually and included elaborate meals, dancing, instrumental music, singing and sacrifices.[4] All of Israel participated, from the youngest to the oldest.

Before he died, Moses gave the following instructions for one of these festivals, the Feast of Booths: "Assemble the people, men, women, and little ones, and the sojourner within your towns, that they may hear and learn to fear the LORD your God, and be careful to do all the words of this law, and that their children, who have not known it, may hear and learn to fear the LORD your God, as long as you live in the land that you are going over the Jordan to possess" (Deut 31:12-13 ESV).

The purpose of these festivals was to remind the Israelites of who they were, who God was and what God had done for them in ages past. As children and teens danced, sang, ate, listened to the stories and asked questions, they came to *know* who they were and who they were to be. This *knowing* carried the sense of the Hebrew word *yada'*, which connotes more than intellectual information, but rather knowing by experiencing.[5]

In these settings, God clearly expected the older generation to be available to the younger to answer questions and to offer explanations. For example, Exodus 12:26-27 says, "And when your children ask you, 'What does this ceremony mean to you?' then tell them, 'It is the Passover sacrifice to the LORD, who passed over the houses of the Israelites in Egypt and spared our homes when he struck down the Egyptians.'" The adults participated with their children, singing, dancing, eating, hearing the stories and responding to questions.

Generations passing on the faith. Many biblical texts further emphasize the idea that older generations are responsible for passing on God's truths to the younger generations. However, some passages offer examples of the younger generation leading or teaching the elders. Psalm 145:4 declares:

Education 93 (1998a): 436.

[4]These festivals included Passover (Ex 12; 23:15; 34:18, 25; Lev 23:5-8; Num 9:1-14; 28:16-25; Deut 16:1-8; Ezek 45:21-24); the Feast of Weeks (Ex 23:16; 34:22; Lev 23:15-21; Num 28:26-31; Deut 16:9-10); the Feast of Booths (Ex 23:16; 34:22; Lev 23:33-36; Num 29:12-39; Deut 16:13-18); and the Feast of Trumpets (Lev 23:23-25; Num 29:1-6).

[5]Terence E. Fretheim, "Yada," in *New International Dictionary of Old Testament Theology and Exegesis,* ed. Willem A. VanGemeren (Grand Rapids: Zondervan, 1997), 2:410.

"One generation commends your works to another; they tell of your mighty acts," indicating that each generation has a responsibility to share God's work in their lives with people of other generations so that all can worship and praise God together.

The young boy Samuel "was ministering to the LORD in the presence of Eli the priest" (1 Sam 2:11 ESV) and the Lord spoke to him and told him what would happen to Eli's sons (1 Sam 3). King Josiah was eight years old when he began to reign over Judah. Even as a young boy he "did what was right in the eyes of the LORD and followed completely the ways of his father David" (2 Kings 22:2), and under his reign the whole nation of Judah was more aligned with the ways of the Lord (2 Kings 22–23). Samuel and Eli's relationship is one example of a mutually beneficial cross-generational relationship in the Old Testament; other significant relationships among nonfamilial persons of different generations are Elijah and Elisha (see 1 Kings 19:19-21; 2 Kings 2:1-18), David and King Saul (in the early years; see 1 Sam 18:18-27), and Ruth and Naomi (see Ruth 1–4).

Deuteronomy 6:6-9 clearly signifies the importance of generational transmission for spiritual formation: "And these words that I command you today shall be on your heart. You shall teach them diligently to your children, and shall talk of them when you sit in your house, and when you walk by the way, and when you lie down, and when you rise. You shall bind them as a sign on your hand, and they shall be as frontlets between your eyes. You shall write them on the doorposts of your house and on your gates" (ESV).

Though these verses have often been assumed to be speaking exclusively to parents, these words convey the communal sense that faith in God is to be modeled and taught in the home as well as among the faith community, across the generations. Parents, grandparents and all extended family (that is, *all of Israel* since they were all descendants of Jacob and therefore related) are to participate in the telling of God's faithfulness to those coming along behind them. Another passage, Psalm 78:1-8, carries a similar implication:

> My people, hear my teaching;
> listen to the words of my mouth.

I will open my mouth with a parable;
    I will utter hidden things, things from of old—
things we have heard and known,
    things our ancestors have told us.
We will not hide them from their descendants;
    we will tell the next generation
    the praiseworthy deeds of the LORD,
    his power, and the wonders he has done.
He decreed statutes for Jacob
    and established the law in Israel,
    which he commanded our ancestors
    to teach their children,
so the next generation would know them,
    even the children yet to be born,
    and they in turn would tell their children.
Then they would put their trust in God
    and would not forget his deeds
    but would keep his commands.
They would not be like their ancestors—
    a stubborn and rebellious generation,
    whose hearts were not loyal to God,
    whose spirits were not faithful to him.

In order for those of the next generation to be able to place their trust in God, this psalmist says that they must hear repeatedly about this God in whom they are to trust. Whole generations are to pass to the next generations the truths of Yahweh, so that they will not forget who he is and what he has done for those he loves. In order for this progression to be possible, the generations must *be together, not just occasionally or sporadically, but often*—for important events, for rejoicing, for critical moments, for prayer, for solemn occasions, for feasts and celebrations, and for reading the Word, as well as for ordinary happenings.

THE NEW TESTAMENT AND INTERGENERATIONALITY

Emerging from their Jewish heritage, the first-century churches were multigenerational entities, with children present for worship, healings, prayer meetings, even perhaps when persecutions were perpetrated. "Inherent in these communities was a radical mutuality and interdependence which crossed age boundaries, a feature consistently stressed by the New Testament writers."[6]

House churches. In the early church as a whole, the generations met together in homes. Several whole families, including the extended family and household servants, came together as the church. All generations met together, breaking bread, praying together, ministering to one another in the context of the home (Acts 2:46-47; 4:32-35; 16:31-34). "Children observed the faith commitments of their parents [and other known adults] in real, concrete ways."[7]

Paul's letters, written to churches in Asia Minor, offered directives to believers across the life span. In these house church settings, when Paul's letters arrived, all ages listened as his directives were read to wives and husbands (Eph 5:22, 25, "Wives, submit yourselves to your own husbands" and "Husbands, love your wives"), to slaves and masters (Eph 6:5, 9, "Slaves, obey your earthly masters" and "Masters, treat your slaves in the same way. Do not threaten them"), and to children and parents (Col 3:20, 21, "Children, obey your parents" and "Fathers, do not embitter your children").

And in Paul's letters to Timothy and Titus, Paul assumed multigenerational settings in which all ages were interacting. Paul recognizes that "older men," "older women," "younger women" and "young men" need specific guidance and indicates that some of that teaching is to be cross-generational.

Besides the house church gatherings, all ages were present in other spiritual settings as well. Jesus communicated his intentions for children to be part of his kingdom when he rebuked the disciples for not allowing children to "bother" him (Mt 19:13-14); when he taught that his disciples must have the faith and humility of children and must welcome them into Christ's presence (Mt 18:1-6); and when he laid hands upon the children and blessed them (Mk 10:13-16). In Acts 16:15, Lydia was baptized "with the members of her household," and in Acts 16:33, the jailer was baptized with "all his household." Also in Acts is the story of the young Eutychus, who, while listening to Paul preach until midnight, fell out of a window

---

[6]Allan G. Harkness, "Intergenerational Christian Education: An Imperative for Effective Education in Local Churches (Part 1)," *Journal of Christian Education* 41, no. 2 (1998b): 11.

[7]M. Scott Miles, *Families Growing Together* (Wheaton, IL: Victor Books, 1990), p. 12.

(Acts 20:7-12). Luke also reports that children accompanied those bidding farewell to Paul as he boarded a ship at Tyre (Acts 21:5-6).

The intergenerational body of Christ. Lewis and Demarest, in offering several purposes for the church, say that a "church . . . should stimulate enriching fellowship within the membership (Acts 2:42). It should encourage mutual caring among all its members intergenerationally, irrespective of gender, marital status, and socioeconomic standing."[8] In other words, *all* are the body of Christ. "Speaking the truth in love, we are to grow up in every way into him who is the head, into Christ, from whom the whole body, joined and held together by every joint with which it is equipped, when each part is working properly, makes the body grow so that it builds itself up in love" (Eph 4:15-16 esv). Drawing from Romans 12:4-6, Glassford states that "fostering such a climate in Christ's church includes valuing, nurturing, and employing the gifts of every person," from young to old.[9]

This chapter, noting explicit intergenerational concepts in Scripture, clarifies that religious community as described in the Bible assumed the idea that children, young people, adults, and the elders and leaders were actually present together often. Of course, there were times when only portions of God's people met together (e.g., in Acts 15 when church leaders met in Jerusalem to discuss Gentile-Jewish issues), and indeed there are important reasons to meet separately (as chapters three and thirteen explain). But throughout Scripture there is a pervasive sense that all generations were typically present when faith communities gathered for worship, for celebration, for feasting, for praise, for encouragement, for reading of Scripture, in times of danger, and for support and service.

Community as practiced in contemporary churches often is segmented by age or stage of life. Separating the generations may sometimes be helpful for specific purposes, but to experience authentic Christian community and reap the unique blessings of intergenerationality, the generations must be together regularly and often—infants to octogenarians.

---

[8]Gordon Russell Lewis and Bruce A. Demarest, *Integrative Theology* (Grand Rapids: Zondervan, 1994), 3:275.

[9]Darwin Glassford, "Fostering an Intergenerational Culture," in *The Church of All Ages: Generations Worshiping Together*, ed. Howard Vanderwell (Herndon, VA: Alban Institute, 2008), p. 79.

6

Theoretical Foundations

In the United States, it is now possible for a person eighteen years of age, female as well as male, to graduate from high school, college, or university without ever having cared for, or even held, a baby; without ever having comforted or assisted another human being who really needed help. . . . No society can long sustain itself unless its members have learned the sensitivities, motivations, and skills involved in assisting and caring for other human beings.

Urie Bronfenbrenner, *The Ecology of Human Development*

The continuity of all cultures depends on the living presence of at least three generations.

Margaret Mead, *Culture and Commitment*

IN THE FOUR YEARS that the Allens worshiped with a vibrant, growing new church plant in Texas, they and their children (ages 7, 9 and 15 when they first became a part of this group of spiritual pilgrims) participated weekly in intergenerational small groups. All of the Allens, but especially their children, flourished in those hothouse environments, basking in the unconditional love of college students and young, middle and older adults, and contributing to cross-age discussions that addressed fears, moral dilemmas, successes, theological conundrums, loss and grief, hopes, parenting questions, and interpersonal tensions.

Recently their daughter Bethany (now 25) was visiting with the family when Holly was speaking about intergenerationality at a gathering of church leaders. One of the attendees asked Bethany about her memories in the small groups. This is what she said:

> It was so natural, sitting with everyone in our intergenerational small groups. I felt like I belonged, like we all belonged there; age wasn't a factor. We'd all sing songs, and pray, and do a fun ice-breaker, and I participated on every level. Sometimes, the group leader would ask me to choose a song, or would ask me a particular question, like maybe how I felt about a certain verse or story in the Bible, and everyone listened to my response. I felt important, like what I had to say mattered. I remember so many of the adults in my small groups, and they were my friends, not just my parents' friends. I remember listening to them talk about what was going on in their lives, or what new insights they'd had recently about God, and I felt a sense of intimacy.

When Holly speaks now on intergenerationality, she reads Bethany's description, and adds that those intergenerational small groups were powerful, life-forming experiences for her children—as well as for her husband, for her and for hundreds of others.

RATIONALE FOR EXPLORING THEORETICAL FOUNDATIONS

The last chapter laid out the idea that not only was intergenerationality the common and accepted practice of God's people throughout Scripture, but that God's directives (through Moses, Paul and others) indicated that the generations were intended to be mutually influential. This chapter examines intergenerationality from the perspectives of developmental theory, social learning theory and ecological systems theory. One might ask: if a strong biblical case can be made for intergenerationality, why might we cite secular theories to strengthen our case? The short answer is the recognition that all truth is God's truth. Other seemingly inexplicable directives given by God have ultimately been supported in the hard or social sciences as having validity outside the biblical directive; for example, the wisdom of separating from the camp those with unhealthy discharges or infectious diseases (Lev 13–15) has of course been confirmed by modern medical science. Finding connections between God's directives and current theory can help us understand why God has given those directives. These connections further affirm that the Creator knows his creation well and that his guidelines for living indeed bless. Therefore in this chapter we will explore several theoretical perspectives that offer corroboration of intergenerationality as an influential element in growth and development.

DEVELOPMENTAL THEORY

Erik Erikson's psychosocial developmental theory and Jean Piaget's cognitive developmental theory have been utilized most commonly to understand processes of individual developmental growth; however, these theories also offer significant insight regarding the influence and importance of social interaction, though this aspect of the theories has been somewhat neglected. Erikson's work particularly addresses the interaction of generations, which he calls *mutuality*.[1] He would say that the generations benefit from each other, that is, they grow each other up. Lawrence Kohlberg's insights on moral development and James Fowler's work regarding faith development strongly connect development in moral and faith realms to social interaction.

Jean Piaget. Piaget (1896–1980) is most widely known as a cognitive psychologist. His attempt to describe normal and healthy cognitive growth was not primarily concerned with the social aspects of development; he was more focused on the intellect. Nevertheless, he had much to say about interrelationships and the effect they have on cognitive development in persons.

Throughout his works, Piaget describes four stages of cognitive development: sensorimotor (birth to age 2), characterized by motor responses by the infant; preoperational (ages 2-7), characterized by intuitive thought rather than logic; concrete operational (ages 7-11), characterized by concrete understanding of reality; and formal operations (as early as age 11, but often later), the capability of abstract conceptualization.[2]

As Piaget describes these stages and the movement from one stage to the next, it is clear that several factors, not just age and genetic unfolding,

---

[1]Erik H. Erikson, *Childhood and Society,* 2nd ed. (New York: Norton, 1963).
[2]Jean Piaget and Bärbel Inhelder, *The Psychology of the Child,* trans. Helen Weaver (New York: Basic Books, 1969).

impact the change. Ginsburg and Opper, who spent decades studying Piaget's extensive writings, have summarized Piaget's thinking on factors that contribute to cognitive development.[3] They describe five factors: maturation, experience, social transmission, equilibration and contradictions. Besides the inclusion of social transmission, three other factors—experience, equilibration and contradictions—commonly take place in social settings. For example, Piaget describes disequilibration as what happens when the stage the person is experiencing no longer satisfactorily explains what is happening; the person begins to move to the next stage to achieve equilibrium. This process often happens in a social context through interrelationships or social experience, Piaget says. Persons do not necessarily move through the stages simply by growing older; the process requires social interaction. Piaget's early investigation of children's moral development especially highlights cooperation during pair interaction as a necessary condition for cognitive changes.[4]

Though this social aspect of Piaget's work is often overlooked due to the human tendency to simplify complex theory, Piaget nevertheless recognized the crucial role social interaction plays in cognitive development.

Erik Erikson. Though Erikson (1902–1994) is known as an ego psychologist and a Piagetian cognitivist, he is also classified as a social psychologist, that is, his works reflect a strong social and cultural orientation. Erikson's famous epigenetic principle offers the idea that persons develop through a predetermined unfolding of their personalities in eight stages. Each stage involves certain developmental tasks that are psychosocial in nature, and these tasks are learned through complex social interactions of family, school, church and other social environments.

Erikson's eight stages are described as psychosocial crises.[5] These crises are trust vs. mistrust, autonomy vs. shame and doubt, initiative vs. guilt, industry vs. inferiority, identity vs. role confusion, intimacy vs. isolation, generativity vs. stagnation, and ego integrity vs. despair. Erikson calls these psycho*social* crises because he believed they are negotiated not

---

[3]Herbert P. Ginsburg and Sylvia Opper, *Piaget's Theory of Intellectual Development*, 3rd ed. (Englewood Cliffs, NJ: Prentice Hall, 1988), pp. 213-29.
[4]Jean Piaget, *Moral Judgment of the Child*, trans. Marjorie Gabain, 3rd ed. (London: Routledge & Kegan Paul, 1932).
[5]Erikson, *Childhood and Society*.

only cognitively and psychologically but socially; that is, satisfactory navigation of any of these developmental tasks is highly dependent on social interchange.[6]

Erikson's work particularly addresses the interaction of generations, which he calls mutuality. Obviously children are influenced by their parents, but Erikson makes it clear that children influence their parents' development as well.[7]

Another point Erikson emphasizes is that any task (e.g., development of trust, autonomy or intimacy) once done, is never completely finished. The "sense of basic trust," for example, must be maintained by the infant as well as the septuagenarian. In other words, each of the tasks continues to be developed throughout a lifetime. Erikson's work serves to highlight the role of socialization in the growth and development of persons, especially socialization across the generations.

Lawrence Kohlberg. Kohlberg's work with moral reasoning is applicable in that Kohlberg recognizes the important role socialization plays in moral development.[8] Kohlberg says that for those with "preconventional morality" (typically children ages four to ten), moral values are oriented toward punishment (obedience to rules to avoid punishment) or satisfying one's own needs (obedience to rules to obtain rewards); those with "conventional morality," that is, some adolescents and most adults, value conforming to society's general standards, acting "right" either to avoid disapproval of others or to avoid guilt. Kohlberg describes the highest morality—"postconventional morality"—as the moral principled level that only some adults attain; he says that those who achieve this level of morality either conform to standards that are agreed upon by the whole society (out of concern for the good of all in the society) or adhere to self-chosen ethical principles defined by conscience.[9]

Kohlberg describes moral growth as a developmental process that re-

---

[6]Ibid.

[7]Ibid., p. 69.

[8]Lawrence Kohlberg, *Essays on Moral Development: Vol. II. The Psychology of Moral Development* (San Francisco: Harper & Row, 1984).

[9]Lawrence Kohlberg, *Collected Papers on Moral Development and Moral Education* (Cambridge, MA: Center for Moral Development and Education, Harvard Graduate School of Education, 1973), pp. 72-73.

quires interaction. He further explains the process, saying that changes and processes going on *inside* a person are meeting with objects, challenges and people *outside* the person. In these meetings, the person moves into more advanced stages of moral reasoning as the person interacts with others, especially those who challenge the current stage.[10] Interpersonal relationships are a key to developing a moral framework.[11]

James Fowler. In developmentalist fashion, Fowler has woven strands of Erikson, Piaget and Kohlberg (as well as Freud and, theologically, H. Richard Niebuhr) into a developmental theory of faith structures. However, in describing his progressive stages of faith, Fowler also emphasizes the crucial role community plays in faith development.[12] Community facilitates this growth by offering intellectual stimulation, affection, advanced stage modeling, challenge and interaction.[13]

For understanding the dynamics of faith-building, Fowler describes a triangular figure he calls the "dynamic triad of faith"[14]; the triangle includes the self, others, and a center of values and power. Fowler says that each self is always in relation to other people as well as to some center of values and power, which is shared with these others. Fowler says faith develops among these relationships. Again the importance of *social interaction* for growth is emphasized.[15]

---

[10]Lawrence Kohlberg and Rochelle Mayer, "Development as the Aim of Education," *Harvard Education Review* 41 (1972): 456.

[11]Carol Gilligan's view on moral development is more interactionist than is Kohlberg's. Gilligan criticizes Kohlberg's work as too male-oriented, noting particularly that his original research was conducted with males only. Gilligan replicated some of Kohlberg's study with female participants and found that females emphasize relationships with people more so than justice issues as Gilligan believes Kohlberg's work does. However, both Gilligan and Kohlberg would say that an essential ingredient in moral development is interacting with other people. Carol Gilligan, *In a Different Voice: Psychological Theory and Women's Development.* (Cambridge, MA: Harvard University Press, 1982).

[12]James W. Fowler, *Stages of Faith: The Psychology of Human Development and the Quest for Meaning* (San Francisco: Harper, 1981); James W. Fowler, *Weaving the New Creation: Stages of Faith and the Public Church* (New York: HarperCollins, 1991).

[13]Fowler, *Weaving the New Creation*, pp. 189-95.

[14]Fowler, *Stages of Faith*, pp. 7, 92.

[15]As mentioned earlier, James Loder (see, e.g., "Reflections on Fowler's 'Stages of Faith,'" *Religious Education*, 77 [1982]: 133-39) has critiqued Fowler's understanding of faith, saying Fowler elevates the *natural process* of development in the faith journey, which inevitably diminishes the role of radical grace. However, these concepts are not mutually exclusive. As Osmer points out, a person's radical need for grace in light of sin does not thereby negate the crucial role of the faith community in the *process* of development toward faith maturity (Richard Osmer, "James W. Fowler and the

SOCIAL LEARNING THEORY

Social learning theory also offers important ideas to consider when examining intergenerationality; in particular, Margaret Mead's work as well as the ongoing research of Albert Bandura. In the past three decades, social learning theory has been evolving, and sociocultural learning theory has emerged as a separate but related theoretical construct. A whole chapter (chapter seven) is reserved to address what *sociocultural* learning theory has to say regarding the construct of intergenerationality.

Though the previous section on developmental theory interfaces somewhat with the construct of social learning, this section focuses directly on theorists who are known explicitly for their contribution to social learning theory.

Margaret Mead. As a social scientist, Mead (1901–1978) is most widely known for her cultural anthropological work on island cultures of the South Pacific in the 1920s and 1930s. She studied particularly how culture is transmitted from generation to generation. Though her earlier work engendered heavy criticism in the mid-twentieth century, her later work was more positively received.

In her last book, Mead concluded her lifelong discourse on how cultures are transmitted.[16] In it she says most of the cultures of the world are moving out of the "postfigurative" way of passing on culture. Postfigurative cultures are those in which "change is slow and a child's expectations could be defined at birth."[17] In these cultures grandparents play an important role, and they pass on the mores and norms of their lives to their children and grandchildren, expecting the culture to stay essentially the same.

Some cultures have moved to what Mead calls the "cofigurative" style. Mead describes the cofigurative culture as one in which the "prevailing model for members of the society is the behavior of their contemporaries."[18] In this type of culture, the grandparents are absent or disregarded, and concentration is on the nuclear family.

Reformed Tradition: An Exercise in Theological Reflection in Religious Education," *Religious Education*, 85 [1990]: 51-68).

[16]Margaret Mead, *Culture and Commitment: The New Relationships Between the Generations in the 1970s*, rev. ed. (New York: Columbia University Press, 1978).

[17]Ibid., p. 13.

[18]Ibid., p. 39.

Mead labels a third type of culture as "prefigurative." In this type of culture, children are born into a very different world than the one their parents knew when they were young. These children face a vastly different future than their parents can envision. Mead states essentially that the generations born after World War II are prefigurative. She explains, "Today nowhere in the world are there elders who know what the children know, no matter how remote and simple the societies are in which the children live. In the past there were always some elders who knew more than any children in terms of their experience of having grown up within a cultural system. Today there are none."[19] Mead's words are as true today as when she wrote them decades ago.

Mead concedes, however, that "the continuity of all cultures depends on the living presence of at least three generations."[20] The key to harmony, growth and the future in this prefigurative society is communication, dialogue among the generations and willingness to learn from one another. Mead's work generally fits within social learning theory, and it clearly speaks uniquely and directly to intergenerational issues as well.

Albert Bandura. Bandura's continuing work in social learning theory has emphasized the strong role of observation and modeling in acquiring the basic protocols and customs of a culture as well as in acquiring a personal lifestyle and values.[21] A basic assumption in Bandura's work through the decades is that persons need not learn everything through direct experience; in other words, acquiring new ways of being, new knowledge and new values *only* by trial and error would be tedious and problematic. Fortunately, Bandura says, human beings can learn many things through observation and modeling. In his recent work, Bandura extends his social learning theory into the spiritual realm, centering on "the influential role

[19]Ibid., p. 75.

[20]Ibid., p. 14.

[21]Albert Bandura, *Social Foundations of Thought and Action: A Social Cognitive Theory* (Englewood Cliffs, NJ: Prentice Hall, 1986); Albert Bandura, "A Social Cognitive Theory of Personality," in *Handbook of Personality: Theory and Research,* ed. Lawrence A. Pervin and Oliver P. John, 2nd ed. (New York: Guilford, 1999); Albert Bandura, "Social Cognitive Theory: An Agentic Perspective," *Annual Review of Psychology* (Palo Alto, CA: Annual Reviews, Inc., 2001), 52:1-26. Retrieved from <search.ebscohost.com.ezproxy.jbu.edu/login.aspx?direct=true&db=afh&AN=444 5594&site=ehost-live>.

BOX 6.1

Janette

When Holly was eleven, Janette, a fortysomething woman in her church, became ill with cancer. Janette's son, Richard, was a teenager in the youth group. Though Holly wasn't old enough to be in the youth group, she knew Richard because, in years past, the children of the church played Red Rover and other spontaneous games after church, so Holly knew all the children—those older and those younger.

As Janette began the rounds of chemotherapy, her hair began to fall out and she came to church with a rainbow of brightly colored scarves and interesting hats; the church prayed for her on a regular basis. One summer, Janette's younger sister, Nancy, a nurse who lived in California, came to live with Janette. Nancy had taken a leave from her job—and from her husband and teenage children—to come to Holly's small town to care for her dying sister. Nancy stayed in their midst for about six months, while her sister was losing her hair, losing weight and losing her battle with cancer. Though Janette could no longer worship with the faith community, Nancy was often among them as they prayed for Janette.

Though Holly was just a little girl, she observed this scene, this love, this loss, and absorbed it into her being. And in 2002, when her older sister, Judy, was diagnosed with bone cancer, Holly left California, the ongoing work on her doctoral dissertation, her teenage children and her husband to fly to Florida to stay with Judy, to care for her, to accompany her on this journey. Holly did this because she loved her sister, but also because she remembered another pair of devoted sisters who had vividly graced her childhood memories in an intergenerational faith community.

of modeling in transmitting values, spiritual belief systems and spiritual lifestyle practices."[22]

Bandura connects several social modeling concepts to spiritual modeling. For instance, Bandura notes that abstract social principles alone are

---

[22]Albert Bandura, "On the Psychosocial Impact and Mechanisms of Spiritual Modeling," *International Journal for the Psychology of Religion* 13, no. 3 (2003): 171.

poorly applied; that is, people need concrete examples of these principles to understand them and practice them. Bandura connects this concept to spirituality by noting that doctrinal abstracts are likewise difficult to grasp concretely, but faith communities offer multiple models of people who live their lives in ways that embody their doctrinal beliefs.

Translating this principle in terms of the basic premise of this book, intergenerational Christian settings provide spiritual models up and down the age spectrum for believers to *observe* and emulate on their own formative spiritual journeys.

ECOLOGICAL SYSTEMS THEORY

Ecological systems theory, particularly the interconnections among the systems, also sheds light on the principles surrounding intergenerationality. Urie Bronfenbrenner was a Russian-born American psychologist who spent most of his career as professor of human development and psychology at Cornell University. He is perhaps best known as cofounder of the nation's Head Start program.

Bronfenbrenner created a holistic model of human development, asserting that human development is influenced by several environmental systems:

- *Microsystems* are the social settings in which an individual has the most direct interaction, such as family, school, neighborhood, church and peers.

- *Mesosystems* refers to interrelationships that occur between a person's microsystems; for example, when a parent attends a child's school event or a family attends a neighborhood church along with other neighborhood families. The healthiest environment for child development is one with many interconnections between the child's microsystems.

- *Exosystems* are external environmental settings that only indirectly affect development; for example, a husband's or child's experience at home may be influenced by the wife or mother's experiences at work. Bronfenbrenner wrote: "One of the most significant effects of age segregation in our society has been the isolation of children from the world of work. Whereas in the past children not only saw what their parents did for a living but even shared substantially in the task, many children nowadays have only a vague notion of the nature of the parent's job, and have had little or no opportunity to observe the parent, or for that matter any other adult, when he is fully engaged in his work."[23]

- The *macrosystem* is the overarching cultural context in which an individual lives. An example of a macrosystem is the American culture of individualism and self-sufficiency; it also includes the national economy, individual socioeconomic status, political culture, ethnicity and various subcultures. Regarding the macrosystem of age segregation, Bronfenbrenner asserts, "In the United States, it is now possible for a person eighteen years of age, female as well as male, to graduate from high school, college, or university without ever having cared for, or even held, a baby; without ever having comforted or assisted another human being who really needed help. . . . No society can long sustain itself unless its members have learned the sensitivities, motivations, and skills involved in assisting and caring for other human beings."[24]

Bronfenbrenner theorized that connections across the various systems enhance development, a key insight for the purposes of this book. Thus a child who knows his parents' coworkers, or a child who relates with her teacher both at school and church is more likely to develop to his or her full potential than children whose systems are more disconnected.

The interconnection of systems promotes intergenerational relationships; without this interconnection, social discord and the eventual demise of society can occur. The institutions of society have "created and perpetuate the age-segregated, and thereby often amoral or antisocial world in which children live and grow."[25] Age segregation has become a macrosystem, and as such, it is impossible for parents to combat such a culture alone; parents must position themselves to provide nonfamilial adult mentors for children and youth.

Bronfenbrenner laments the weakening role of churches in the social

---

[23]Urie Bronfenbrenner, *Two Worlds of Childhood: U.S. and U.S.S.R.* (New York: Simon and Schuster, 1970), preface.

[24]Urie Bronfenbrenner, *The Ecology of Human Development: Experiments by Nature and Design* (Boston: Harvard University Press, 1979), pp. 52-53.

[25]Bronfenbrenner, *Two Worlds of Childhood*, p. 152.

development of children, as churches are natural places for cross-system connections for children, youth and adults. He views churches and community involvement as a way for young people both to work together with people of other generations and to give back to their community; through these cross-generational opportunities for work and care, all of society benefits, and "hostility gives way when groups pull together to achieve goals which are real and compelling for all concerned."[26]

In sum, Bronfenbrenner's theory indicates that activities, roles and interpersonal relationships within one system affect the other systems, for good or ill. The good news is that intergenerational interactions within faith communities may be one significant step toward changing the ideology of age segregation and its resulting negative stereotyping of people of another generation.

DRAWING CONNECTIONS BETWEEN THEORY AND INTERGENERATIONALITY

What is going on when the generations interact? Far more than we know. The developmental theorists in this chapter indicate that social interaction is crucial for cognitive, moral, psychosocial and faith development. When persons of any generation are perennially present only with those who inhabit their own developmental level, it is more difficult to progress to the next stage of development. Opportunities for Piaget's disequilibration increase in cross-generational settings; Erikson's mutuality across the ages enhances all generations; movement toward higher levels of moral development is enabled in cross-generational settings; sharing life with and hearing stories from those in Fowler's later faith stages permits those in the earlier stages to glimpse a more substantive, complex faith that can call them deeper into Christ. Interage connections across all the generations foster development cognitively, morally, psychosocially and spiritually.

Mead's contention that the continuity of *all cultures* depends on the presence of at least three generations is applicable to faith cultures as well; for harmony and growth Mead recommends dialogue across the generations and willingness to learn from one another.[27] Bandura's emphasis

---

[26]Ibid., p. 147.
[27]Mead, *Culture and Commitment*. Interestingly, John Westerhoff says something similar: "True

over the years has focused on the power of observing those who are farther ahead on the human journey. But for cross-generational dialogue, learning or even observation to take place, the generations must *be* together—there must be regular opportunities for conversation, interaction and mutual activities. And Bronfenbrenner's contention that age segregation is now a macrosystem underscores the importance of faith communities becoming more intentionally intergenerational.

Building on the biblical model, the insights presented in this chapter from developmental psychology, social learning theory and ecological systems further substantiate the importance of cross-generational mutuality for healthy growth and development. However, none of these theoretical perspectives explains *why* intergenerationality is so powerful; another theory is needed to connect the dots. Chapter seven introduces the situative-sociocultural perspective on learning as a cohesive undergirding macrotheory to explain the centrality of the intergenerational nature of faith communities for spiritual growth and formation.

---

community necessitates the presence and interaction of three generations. . . . Without interaction between and among the generations, each making its own unique contribution, Christian community is difficult to maintain" (John H. Westerhoff III, *Will Our Children Have Faith?* rev. ed. [Toronto: Morehouse, 2000], pp. 52-53).

7

MIDWIVES, TAILORS AND COMMUNITIES OF PRACTICE

Learning Theory

Communities of practice are groups of people who share a concern or a passion for something they do and learn how to do it better as they interact regularly.
Etienne Wenger, "Communities of Practice: A Brief Introduction"

POTTY TRAINING THEIR FIRST SON, David, was an interminable process, says Holly. After locating a popular book on the subject, creating a chart for stickers and purchasing small treats as rewards, they began the arduous process. Months later they were still slogging through. When it came time to train their second son, Daniel, they reluctantly dug out the book, bleakly sought courage to tackle the task and generally dreaded the ordeal. One day as Holly walked into the laundry room/bathroom with a load of clothes, she came upon David demonstrating to a very intent younger brother the basic technique of aiming straight; David had pulled up a small stool for his little brother to stand on, and Daniel was well on his way to proficiency. Holly was delighted.

This potty-training phenomenon—that second and subsequent children tend to pick up basic knowledge, skills and understandings from older siblings—illustrates well one aspect of the learning theory that follows.[1]

---

[1]Parts of this chapter were adapted from or previously published in Allen, "Nurturing Children's Spirituality" (2003); Allen, "Nurturing Children's Spirituality" (2004); Allen, "Bringing the Generations Together" (2009); and Allen, "No Better Place" (2010). See permissions, page 4.

Intergenerational Christian experience has been a practice in search of a theory. Outside biblical and theological support, those who extol the benefits of intergenerationality[2] have sought theoretical support in the work of social scientists such as G. H. Mead, Margaret Mead and Erik Erikson (chapter six), and religious educationists such as John Westerhoff III, Donald Miller, Ellis Nelson and James Michael Lee (chapter nine). Principles from systems theory (e.g., that all parts of a system are important and interrelated) and insights from generational theory (chapter eleven) as well as developmental and ecological systems theory (chapter six) contribute to the theoretical discussion. Yet, no broad *learning* theory has been proposed that would explain why intergenerational settings might be especially conducive places for *learning, growing* and *being formed spiritually*.

This chapter will propose the situative-sociocultural perspective as introduced by Lev Vygotsky and developed and elaborated by contemporary educational psychologists and social scientists to explain the basic learning principles at work in an intergenerational Christian community. The situative-sociocultural perspective on knowing and learning places a stronger emphasis on the social interaction of the learning environment than do cognitivist and behaviorist theories (see box 7.1) and promotes the idea that *the social setting itself* is crucial to the learning process. Lev Vygotsky (see box 7.2) is the best-known theorist in this category.[3]

THE SOCIOCULTURAL LEARNING THEORY

During Vygotsky's era, psychologists were divided on the issue of human development and learning into two basic camps, either behaviorist or cognitivist (see box 7.1). Vygotsky felt that both cognitivists and behaviorists had misconceptualized human development and that a new theory needed to be constructed—one that would not be merely a cobbling together of these two

[2]James White, *Intergenerational Religious Education* (Birmingham, AL: Religious Education Press, 1988); Catherine Stonehouse, *Joining Children on the Spiritual Journey: Nurturing a Life of Faith* (Grand Rapids: Baker, 1998); Allan Harkness, "Intergenerational and Homogeneous-Age Education: Mutually Exclusive Strategies for Faith Communities?" *Religious Education* 95 (2000): 51-63; Patty Meyers, *Live, Learn, Pass It On!—The Practical Benefits of Generations Growing Together in Faith* (Nashville: Discipleship Resources, 2006).
[3]Jerome Bruner, also a well-known proponent of the sociocultural theory, gradually shifted from the cognitive to the sociocultural over his decades-long career. Jerome S. Bruner and Helen Haste, eds., *Making Sense: The Child's Construction of the World* (New York: Methuen, 1987).

inadequate theories. In his well-known analogy to water, Vygotsky said that explaining human growth and learning in behaviorist and cognitivist terminology would be as useful as explaining the properties of water by studying hydrogen and oxygen, "neither of which possesses the properties of the whole and each of which possesses properties not present in the whole."[4]

Vygotsky initially identified more closely with the behaviorist view but was also in contact with Piaget and those from the Gestalt camp. He eventually rejected both theories. Rieber and Carton explain it best: "Vygotsky argued that [psychological processes] have their source not in biological

---

BOX 7.1

During the first half of the twentieth century, educational psychologists tended to support either the behavioral or the cognitive learning perspectives.

In the behaviorist/empiricist *view, knowing is an organized collection of associations and skills. Behavioral learning theories have tended to view persons as neutral human animals whose behavior can be controlled through training and manipulation in the form of reinforcement (and lack thereof). Learning can be defined as a change in behavior or performance resulting from experience and practice.[a] B. F. Skinner is the name most associated with this viewpoint.*

Around mid-century some behavioral learning theorists began to shift the field away from behavior toward a cognitive *approach that focuses on what happens inside the mind rather than merely focusing on the outward changes in behavior. Learning came to be defined more as a restructuring of knowledge and a change in understanding. In general, the cognitive/rationalist perspective is concerned with how persons organize knowledge about their world. It focuses on understanding the individual mind—its abilities or achievements in perceptions, reasoning and problem solving.[b] Jean Piaget is the name most associated with this viewpoint.*

---

[a]James G. Greeno, Allan M. Collins and Lauren B. Resnick, "Cognition and Learning," in *Handbook of Educational Psychology*, ed. David C. Berliner and Robert C. Calfee (New York: Macmillan, 1996), pp. 15-46.
[b]Ibid.

---

[4]Lev S. Vygotsky, *Thought and Language*, trans. Alex Kozulin, rev. ed. (Cambridge, MA: MIT Press, 1986), p. 3.

BOX 7.2

Lev Semyonovich Vygotsky (1896–1934)

Lev Vygotsky was born in Orsha, Byelorussia, in November 1896 to middle-class Jewish parents. He graduated with a law degree from Moscow University in 1917 and studied history and philosophy at Shanyansky's Popular University just before the Bolshevik revolution. He began teaching at Moscow University's Psychological Institute in 1924 and wrote and taught in the area of psychology, human development and learning over the next ten years (1924-1934), in which he authored approximately 200 papers, most of which have only recently been published in English. He died of tuberculosis in 1934 at age 37.

After Vygotsky's death, his work was suppressed during Stalin's reign. His works began to be published in the 1950s in Russia, but only in 1978 with the publication of his works in English has Vygotsky's thought begun to widely impact educational thought and practice in the West. His insights regarding the importance of the social aspects of learning were especially instrumental in the discussions about mainstreaming and inclusion in public education in the 1990s.[a]

[a]Ibid.; Lev S. Vygotsky, *Mind in Society: The Development of Higher Psychological Process*, ed. Michael Cole, Vera John-Steiner, Sylvia Scribner and Ellen Souberman (Cambridge, MA: Harvard University Press, 1978).

structures or the learning of the isolated individual but in historically developed *socio-cultural experience.*"[5] Vygotsky came to believe that for persons to learn concepts, they must experience them and socially negotiate their meaning in authentic, complex learning environments.

Vygotsky describes three zones of developmental activity:

- The zone of actual development: Where the learner *actually* is developmentally;

- The zone of potential development: Where the learner *potentially* could or should be; and

[5]Robert W. Rieber and Aaron S. Carton, eds., *The Collected Works of L. S. Vygotsky* (New York: Plenum Press, 1987), 1:19, emphasis ours.

- The zone of proximal development: The amount of assistance required for a learner to move from the zone of actual development to the zone of potential development.[6]

The zone of proximal development (ZPD) is a subset of Vygotsky's sociocultural theory that intersects with intergenerational theory. The concept of ZPD is that when a person is ready to learn the next thing, the best way to learn it is to be with those who are just ahead on the learning journey. Wertsch and Rogoff have conceptualized the ZPD as: "that phase in development in which the [person] has only partially mastered a task but can participate in its execution with the assistance and supervision of an adult or more capable peer. Thus, the zone of proximal development is a dynamic region of sensitivity in learning the skills of culture, in which [persons] develop *through participation . . . with more experienced members of the culture.*"[7]

This concept is not a new one, though perhaps it has not been well articulated in educational terms. As mentioned earlier, mothers who have several children would recognize ZPD as the "potty-training phenomenon."

Thus a sociocultural learning perspective would submit that persons learn to be members of their community as they actively participate in that particular social community, learning *alongside* those who are further ahead in the journey. Intergenerational Christian settings are authentic, complex, *formative* environments, made up of individuals at various stages in their faith journeys, teaching some and learning from others as they participate in their community of believers.[8]

SITUATED LEARNING AND COMMUNITIES OF PRACTICE: MIDWIVES, TAILORS AND BUTCHERS

Another aspect of the situative-sociocultural theory is the concept of "situated learning," the kind of learning that happens in apprenticeships. In order for Holly's friend Allison to become a midwife, she spent a year ap-

---

[6]James R. Estep Jr., "Spiritual Formation as Social: Toward a Vygotskyan Developmental Perspective" (paper presented at North American Professors of Christian Education Annual Conference, San Diego, CA, October 1999), p. 15.

[7]James Wertsch and Barbara Rogoff, "Editors' Notes," in *Children's Learning in the "Zone of Proximal Development": New Directions for Child Development,* ed. Barbara Rogoff and James Wertsch (San Francisco: Jossey-Bass, 1984), p. 1, emphasis ours.

[8]Chapter nine will make further biblical and theological connections to the sociocultural theory.

prenticing with experienced midwives, attending dozens of home and hospital births. Though she was already a registered nurse with the required university degree, Allison has said that the year of apprenticeship amid the community of practicing midwives is what made her a midwife.

Jean Lave, a social anthropologist, and Etienne Wenger, a social learning theorist, coined the phrases *situative learning* and *communities of practice* (see box 7.3) as they examined studies of several apprenticeship settings, including midwives, tailors, meat cutters and recovering alcoholics.[9] In situated activity, learners must be given access to the practices that they are expected to learn and to genuine participation in the activities and concerns of the community of practice; thus, Allison's situated activities meant that she actually attended and participated in the birthing of babies. At first, learners are relatively peripheral in the activities of the community, but as they become more experienced and adept, their participation becomes more central and must be legitimate; that is, they must actually practice the activities themselves, not just observe or receive instruction about them. Eventually Allison coached a mother through childbirth with a master midwife watching quietly from the corner of the room.

As apprentices participate actively and relationally in communities of practice alongside more experienced members, the apprentices gain the knowledge, practice the skills and absorb the ethos of this particular community of practice. Ultimately, they come to *identify* with the community of practice—that is, they *become* midwives, tailors or butchers.[10]

Intergenerational faith settings provide situative learning opportunities that forge persons who identify with the Christian community of practice. Just as novice midwives and tailors learn to *be* midwives and tailors by participating authentically and relationally with "master" midwives and tailors, believers are formed spiritually while participating authentically and relationally with practicing Christians further along on the journey. Intergenerational events, activities and experiences provide continual opportunities *for all ages* to be learning with those just ahead of them.

---

[9]Jean Lave and Etienne Wenger, *Situated Learning: Legitimate Peripheral Participation* (New York: Cambridge University Press, 1991).

[10]Lave and Wenger, *Situated Learning*.

SITUATIVE-SOCIOCULTURAL THEORY
AND INTERGENERATIONALITY

This chapter has examined three aspects from the situative-sociocultural perspective that offer a rationale for intergenerationality as an effective approach:

1. the premise that persons learn best in authentic, complex environments;
2. the assertion that the best learning happens when persons participate with more experienced members of the culture (Vygotsky's zone of proximal development); and
3. Lave and Wenger's thesis that persons identify with their community of practice as they are allowed to participate legitimately in the activities to be learned.

BOX 7.3

Communities of Practice

Etienne Wenger has written extensively in the past two decades explicating the concept and principles of "communities of practice." He explains that learning has been seen in the past primarily as an individual enterprise, as a process that has a beginning and an end, as a separate entity from daily living, and as the result of teaching.[a] Wenger suggests, rather, that learning is social, that is, that it comes about primarily as we participate with others in daily living in communities of practice.

Wenger has developed and applied these principles to a variety of settings—business, health communities, education and government[b]—though not to Christian settings. However, many of the principles he describes can help envision intergenerational gatherings as communities of practice where all grow and learn together. For example, Wenger describes a community of practice as a joint venture; he says it involves mutual engagement among its participants.[c] He says that communities of practice are attuned to real practices; they are not merely think tanks. Another phrase that resonates with the Christian community is that a community of practice provides a home for identity.[d] When one's primary community of practice becomes one's home for identity, a profound sense of belonging results.

Wenger's communities of practice are "formed by people who engage in a process of collective learning in a shared domain of human endeavor"[e]; for example, a tribe learning to survive, a group of engineers working on a difficult problem or a network of surgeons exploring new surgery techniques. These communities of practice "share a concern or a passion for something they do and learn how to do it better as they interact regularly."[f]

The gathered body of Christ is another example of a "community of practice" that shares a passion and learns how to do it better as its participants interact regularly. "Mutual engagement," "a tribe learning to survive," "real practices" and "home[s] for identity" are concepts that especially characterize intergenerational Christian communities.

---

[a]Etienne Wenger, "Communities of Practice: Learning as a Social System," *The Systems Newsletter* 9, no. 5 (1998): 1-5.

[b]Business and education: Etienne Wenger, Richard A. McDermott and William Snyder, *Cultivating Communities of Practice: A Guide to Managing Knowledge* (Cambridge, MA: Harvard Business School Press, 2002); health communities: Etienne Wenger, "Communities of Practice," *Healthcare Forum Journal* 39, no. 4 (1996): 20-27; Etienne Wenger, *The Public Involvement Community of Practice at Health Canada: A Case Study* (Ottawa: Health Canada, Corporate Consultation Secretariat, 2003); government: William Snyder and Etienne Wenger, *Communities of Practice in Government: The Case for Sponsorship* (report to the CIO Council of the U.S. Federal Government, 2003).

[c]Wenger, "Communities of Practice: Learning as a Social System."

[d]Etienne Wenger, *Communities of Practice: Learning, Meaning, and Identity* (New York: Cambridge University Press, 1998).

[e]Etienne Wenger, "Communities of Practice: A Brief Introduction." Retrieved from <www.ewenger.com/theory/>.

[f]Ibid.

These situative-sociocultural principles are clearly interrelated, and more importantly for the purposes of this text, can be seen to transfer readily to the concept of children, new believers and older pilgrims learning, growing and becoming in intergenerational community. Intergenerational faith communities, as seen in Bob's story (see box 7.4), fit what situative-socioculturalists describe:

• The gathered church is the authentic, complex community being addressed here. June's faith community and the camp personnel were these communities for Bob.

- In intergenerational settings, children, teens, young adults and even older adults participate with "more experienced members of the culture." June, the camp personnel, and the other elderly members of the church were the more experienced members of the culture.

- As children and new believers (and others) participate in relational community doing "Christian" things with those further down the road, they comes to identify with the believing community—as Bob did.

This chapter has proposed the situative-sociocultural learning perspective as a cohesive, illuminating rationale for the idea that churches as relational intergenerational communities are uniquely and inherently suited to fostering growth, learning and Christian formation. The next chapter further develops the connections between the situative-sociocultural theory and the ever-present concept of community in Scripture.

BOX 7.4

Story of Bob

One summer day, long-haired fourteen-year-old Bob, draped in chains and wearing his trench coat, arrived at Trinity Lutheran Church's daycare to pick up his baby sister. Trinity offered the best preschool in town, which is the only reason Bob's mother, a vocal atheist, sent his sister there. As Bob walked up the steps, June, a slight, white-haired church member who was helping at the preschool that day, watched him. "Would you like to make some money?" she asked. "Our church camp is having a work day; I can drive you there and pay you for your work." Bob needed money to hang out with his friends, so the next week June picked Bob up from his house. As they drove to camp, June talked a little but she wasn't really the chatty type, which made Bob a little uncomfortable. They spent the day painting cabins. When Bob went to June's cabin to get more paint, he was embarrassed to discover that June had painted all four of that cabin's walls in the same amount of time it took Bob to paint one wall. Where does this old lady get her strength? he wondered. Despite his work ethic, June invited him back to the camp to rake leaves the following week. As

Bob completed one pile, he saw June's four. Again he mused, Where does that strength come from? At lunch the camp director asked June how her chemotherapy was going. Bob had no idea she had cancer; she certainly didn't look or act sick. As they drove home, June offered to pay for Bob to spend a week as a camper. She explained to him that there would be lots of young people his age.

Immediately upon entering the camp, Bob took in the scene of squeaky-clean, short-haired kids being hugged by parents and grandparents, and he realized that he was trapped in enemy territory. He knew he didn't fit in; Bob's world didn't look like this. He realized that he would have to lie low to survive the week. His aloofness served him well until midweek when he looked out the cabin window and heard the camp director telling his mother that she couldn't walk barefoot here, she couldn't smoke here and she definitely couldn't take Bob out of camp early. Bob's mom flicked her cigarette as she explained, "He's gotta go one way or another. If I don't take him to complete his community service time, a police car will." Bob left quickly with his mom.

Bob returned afterward, expecting the camp counselors to have packed his bags. But no, three of them sat down with him. They talked about life, Jesus and forgiveness. At first Bob was mad, but he was also intrigued; for the first time he experienced people who cared about him and heard of a God who cared too. Bob's friends got pregnant; his friends got in trouble and went to juvenile hall; one friend committed suicide there. But Bob started listening more to the Bible studies; he started asking questions. By the end of the week, the camp director asked Bob to stay on and work through the remainder of the summer. So he worked and read the Bible for the first time, and June came up for work days and seemed happy to see him.

By the end of the summer, Bob wanted to believe. He asked June if he could go to her church. June was there with him every week, talking to him about Jesus and helping the other elderly members adjust to Bob's presence. June was there for Bob's baptism, June gave him his first cross, June shared her faith with love and consistency.

June was dying of an inoperable brain tumor. Before she left town to go live her final days with family, Bob had an opportunity to thank her. June didn't speak a lot, she didn't preach, but she did speak of her faith; she told him that her favorite hymn was "Lift High the Cross," and she spoke with quiet courage—courage that Bob now understood came from Christ. June had become closer than family to Bob, but Bob thinks she must have spoken to people at church before she left because they quickly became family also. They didn't always know how to deal with him, but they encouraged him and they seemed to like having him around. The elderly women purchased hair bands for him and told him how handsome he looked with his hair tied back (Bob believes they unconsciously would have preferred he cut his hair). This faith family made up of mainly elderly members paid for his college degree and paid for him to attend seminary. But that's not all. Bob had taught them that they could reach out to young people despite the generational differences. Thus from then on, the church members were constantly on the lookout for other young people who needed a stable family and a loving Lord. Besides Bob, Trinity has put two other boys through seminary and one girl through college to become a Lutheran teacher. [a]

---

[a]Personal conversation between Christine Ross and Rev. Robert (Bob) Sundquist, Pastor at Christ the King Lutheran Church, Coeur d' Alene, ID, January 29, 2012. Rev. Sundquist is the Bob in this story.

8

THE TRINITY, *KOINONIA* AND THE BODY

Theological Foundations

I do not ask for these only, but also for those who will believe in me through their word, that they may all be one, just as you, Father, are in me, and I in you, that they also may be in us, so that the world may believe that you have sent me.

John 17:20-21 (ESV)

IN HER CHILDHOOD AND YOUTH Holly erroneously embraced the understanding that *believing* the right things and *doing* the right things constituted Christianity in its entirety; somehow she missed the *being* part of Christian formation. In her twenties she had the opportunity to participate occasionally in a Bible class with women who were two generations older than she was, stoic believers every one. The various women in the class had survived the Depression, buried children, lost husbands in World War II; some had endured difficult marriages with men who were alcoholics, unfaithful or physically abusive. Every week the teacher of this class, Patricia, would listen patiently to the spiritual and physical needs of the elderly women, and then she would pray long, passionate prayers for God's mighty hand to bless, heal and empower these faithful believers. Over a period of years Holly saw God at work in these women, binding up their broken hearts (Is 61:1), releasing them from shame, redeeming the years the locusts had stolen (Joel 2:25), pouring over them the oil of gladness (Is 61:3), replacing the spirit of despair with the fruit of the Spirit (Is 61:3; Gal 5:22-23).

Observing this transformation caused Holly to question whether Christianity was more than believing the right things and doing the right things. These had always seemed adequate to her before; they seemed incomplete now. Around this time Holly saw a strange insurance advertisement on television that opened the eyes of her heart to a new truth. The advertisement dwelt for several long seconds on an unusual rendering of Leonardo da Vinci's *Mona Lisa*. As the camera panned closer to the famous face, Holly could see that it was actually a paint-by-number version of that great painting. It was, of course, quite distressing. The point of the advertisement was the value of authenticity or genuineness. In a moment of piercing insight, Holly pictured herself as a paint-by-number Christian, rather than one who had allowed the Master to transform her into an authentic work of art. It was not an attractive picture.

Witnessing Patricia's compassionate interaction with this community of hurting women, hearing her authentic, relational prayers, and beholding the spiritual formation among the elderly women of the class opened the eyes of Holly's heart to truths that God had been pouring over her for years, but to which she had been blind. The *Mona Lisa* advertisement would doubtless have passed unnoticed had she not witnessed Christ being formed in Patricia and the other women. Holly wanted what they had.

Why is Christianity presented as such a communal enterprise in Scripture? Why does one's sociocultural environment, that is, one's community, play such a vital role in Christian formation? While chapter five focused on explicit intergenerational concepts in Scripture, this chapter will draw theological connections between the crucial role of *faith communities* and the basic tenets of the situative-sociocultural theory. As the previous chapter explained, the sociocultural theory places a stronger emphasis on *the social interaction* of the learning environment than do other learning theories; it promotes the idea that the social setting itself is crucial to the learning process. Specifically, this chapter unpacks the theological significance of faith communities as authentic, complex, spiritually formative environments where believers learn Christian concepts, experience them and negotiate their meaning as they are being formed spiritually.

GOD IN TRINITARIAN RELATIONSHIP

Community is evident in the first words of the Bible: "In the beginning God created the heavens and the earth. Now the earth was formless and empty, darkness was over the surface of the deep, and the Spirit of God was hovering over the waters" (Gen 1:1-2). "Then God said, 'Let us make mankind in our image, in our likeness'" (Gen 1:26). One aspect of the image of God is that God exists in community, that is, in trinitarian relationship. Therefore, since we are made in his image, we are to reflect this communal nature. We are to be "social beings—an extension of God's image on earth."[1]

The idea of the social Trinity is that God is a communion of three Persons who exist in mutual relations with one another—one God yet three Persons. Each is distinct from the others, but each is who he is in relation to the others. The Father is a father in relationship to the Son, and the Son is a son in relationship to the Father. They both have relationship with the Spirit, who proceeds from the Father and descends on the Son, pouring out the power of God's love on him.[2] They delight in giving glory to each other. The Father, Son and Holy Spirit interweave "their distinctive patterns of personhood within an essential unit," and display a "characteristic attitude of love and interpersonal communion as servants of one another, always glorifying and deferring to one another."[3] The relationship that exists among the Trinity is to be reflected among the body of Christ in similar attitudes of love, connectedness, honor and deference.

Thus the basic theological support for the importance of community can be built around the concept of God's corporate, *relational* nature, and that God created his people in his image, that is, for *koinonia* or "familyness"[4]; they are meant to live in relationship "with a deep sense of togetherness and belonging."[5]

---

[1]Eddie Prest, *From One Generation to Another* (Capetown, South Africa: Training for Leadership, 1993), pp. 7-8.

[2]Stanley J. Grenz, *Theology for the Community of God* (Nashville: Broadman & Holman, 1994), p. 86; Clark Pinnock, *Flame of Love: A Theology of the Holy Spirit* (Downers Grove, IL: InterVarsity Press, 1996), p. 31.

[3]Royce G. Gruenler, "John 17:20-26," *Interpretation* 43, vol. 2 (1989): 178.

[4]Prest, *From One Generation to Another,* p. 11.

[5]Ibid., p. 7.

JESUS' EXAMPLE AND TEACHING

"And he went up on the mountain and called to him those whom he desired, and they came to him. And he appointed twelve (whom he also named apostles) *so that they might be with him* and *he might send them out to preach and have authority to cast out demons*" (Mk 3:13-15 ESV, emphasis ours). Over a period of three years, Jesus chose his apostles, walked with them, talked with them, ate with them, taught them, and modeled prayer, healing and servanthood for them. He dwelt in community with them. God could have chosen a more "academic" approach to train and form these disciples; he could have simply written down the truths he wished them to know, the attitudes he wished them to embody, the behaviors he wished them to display. Instead he became flesh and lived among these men, providing opportunity for them to learn, to develop, to become—together, and in the presence of Jesus in whom all these qualities already existed. Jesus' approach with his disciples demonstrates well the essence of situative-sociocultural perspective.

And while Jesus was on earth, he taught about community—though he spoke very little about the church per se. His teaching in the Beatitudes (Mt 5:3-11) assumes a relational social community; his teachings about the law, hatred and anger are all principles for living in community.

Jesus gives several word pictures that assume a relational community. In John 15:1-17 Jesus speaks of himself as the vine and his followers as the branches. His most important point here is that the branches (his followers) must abide in the vine (in him). But the concept of relationality among the branches can be gleaned from the passage. Believers are branches united in one vine, representing "the vital, organic unity of believers in Christ."[6] Community depends on a continuing spiritual relationship to Christ the vine.

The branch is composed of all the boughs including the smallest tendrils that shoot out from the parent stalk. All are in relationship to each other because they are related to the vine. If one branch grows strong and healthy yet produces no fruit, it may shade or injure producing plants, and

---

[6]Gordon R. Lewis and Bruce A. Demarest, *Integrative Theology* (Grand Rapids: Zondervan, 1994), 3:270.

it must be pruned. All branches must bear fruit, which they are able to do by abiding in the vine. Bearing fruit is a "symbol of possessing divine life and involves communicating that life to others."[7] Sharing that life is done basically through love for one another. Jesus explains that as the Father loves Jesus, so Jesus loves the disciples, and they are to love one another. This chain of love is a continuing theme in John and represents the identifying characteristic of the relational community.

Another strong image that Jesus uses to illustrate the relational aspect of community harks back to the trinitarian bond among the Godhead. In Jesus' powerful prayer for unity in John 17:20-24, fellowship is characterized by perfect oneness grounded in the close relationship between Father and Son:

> I do not ask for these only, but also for those who will believe in me through their word, that they may all be one, just as you, Father, are in me, and I in you, that they also may be in us, so that the world may believe that you have sent me. The glory that you have given me I have given to them, that they may be one even as we are one, I in them and you in me, that they may become perfectly one, so that the world may know that you sent me and loved them even as you loved me. Father, I desire that they also, whom you have given me, may be with me where I am, to see my glory that you have given me because you loved me before the foundation of the world. (ESV)

In the same prayer Jesus declares, "I made known to them your name, and I will continue to make it known, that the love with which you have loved me may be in them, and I in them" (Jn 17:26 ESV). He is here referring to the third part of the relational Trinity, the Spirit, whom Jesus promises to send to his believers after his departure for heaven (Jn 16:7; Acts 1:8).

In this prayer, Jesus specifically calls disciples to community as modeled in the unity of his own relationship with his Father. Thus in this prayer over Jesus' disciples, the doctrine of the Trinity—the quintessential motivation for community—is made clearer. The Trinity reveals God's heart for relational community.

---

[7]Raymond E. Brown, *The Gospel According to John*, Anchor Bible Commentary (Garden City, NY: Doubleday, 1966), 29a:680.

As he dwelt and taught among his followers, Jesus represented relational community as the way his people were to live, not primarily as individuals worshiping and serving God alone, but as a body of believers serving and loving each other and learning how to serve and love from one another.

COMMUNITY AS FAMILY, BODY AND *KOINONIA*

Adult church members may wonder what use infants are to congregational worship life (and thus place them out of sight and out of mind in a nursery), and young members may become frustrated with the seeming inflexibility of older people and desire to worship away from these members of their body; however, just as it would hurt the physical body to detach limbs, it also damages the spiritual body when we disengage with one another. Those parts of our church body who seem easier to get along without may actually be the most important part of our spiritual growth.

The church is presented in Acts as a distinct community of faith by empowerment of the Holy Spirit. Believers met together in each other's homes, eating together, praying together, learning together. It was the place Christians grew each other up into Christ.

Paul's writings concerning community build on the concepts first practiced in Acts. Paul uses two basic images of the church as relational community—the family and the body. Paul expects believers to relate to one another and grow together as loving family, practicing "patience, humility, tolerance, kindness, resilience, generosity, confidence, perseverance, and optimism."[8] In 1 Corinthians 12:12-30, Paul describes the inherent interrelatedness of the human body to illustrate the relationality of the church. He describes the church as a diverse unity by saying, "Just as a body, though one, has many parts, but all its many parts form one body, so it is with Christ" (1 Cor 12:12). He urges the honoring and valuing of each church member by saying: "The eye cannot say to the hand, 'I don't need you!' And the head cannot say to the feet, 'I don't need you!' On the contrary, those parts of the body that seem to be weaker are indispensable, and the parts that we think are less honorable we treat with special honor.

---

[8]Robert Banks, *Paul's Idea of Community: The Early House Churches*, rev. ed. (Peabody, MA: Hendrickson, 1994), p. 53.

And the parts that are unpresentable are treated with special modesty" (1 Cor 12:21-23).

What does church as family or church as body look like? Paul answers this partly with his "one another" passages. Be kind to one another; honor one another; live in harmony with one another; instruct one another; wait for one another; serve one another; carry each other's burdens; encourage one another and build each other up; live in peace with each other; bear with one another in love; submit to one another.[9] As children and new believers as well as seasoned saints participate in a community where others are kind to one another, love one another, bear one another's burdens and encourage one another, and they themselves are treated kindly with love and encouragement, they *learn* these concepts, *experience* them and *socially negotiate* their meaning; they are being formed spiritually into the image of Christ.

John's first epistle uses a word that exemplifies the concept of participatory community. That word is *koinonia*, often translated "fellowship" or "community."[10] It signifies participation with one another. It is used to "refer to both Christians' participation in the life of God and to the communal life it creates."[11] And *koinonos*, the person form of the word, is used to describe a "participant" or "fellow."[12] *Koinonia* and *koinonos* are words that align with the situative-sociocultural perspective, that is, the idea that growing-becoming—being formed—is intrinsically embedded in the social community.

SITUATIVE-SOCIOCULTURAL THEORY AND COMMUNITY

Anthony[13] grew up as a committed believer, but during his teen years, he was introduced to pornography. In his twenties he regularly viewed sexually explicit material but assumed that when he married, his desire

---

[9]Rom 12 and 15; 1 Cor 11; Gal 5 and 6; 1 Thess 5; Eph 4 and 5.

[10]Joseph A. Komonchak, Mary Collins and Dermot A. Lane, eds., *The New Dictionary of Theology* (Wilmington, DE: Michael Glazier, 1987), p. 557; Friedrich Hauck, "Koinonia," in *Theological Dictionary of the New Testament*, ed. Gerhard Kittel and Gerhard Friedrich (Grand Rapids: Eerdmans, 1965), 3:797.

[11]Komonchak, Collins and Lane, *New Dictionary of Theology*, p. 557.

[12]Hauck, "Koinonia," p. 802.

[13]"Anthony" is a pseudonym; certain details as well as his name have been changed to protect his anonymity.

for it would wane. In his thirties, though actively involved with a growing church and happily married, he still sought solace and comfort in sexual images on a regular basis. As pornography became more easily available via the Internet, Anthony's daily habit became more time consuming. In his forties, Anthony moved into chat rooms, and sexual images and scenarios began to overwhelm his thoughts, impacting his work and his marriage.

Eventually Anthony crossed the "flesh line," meeting one of his Internet connections at a coffee shop. She became Anthony's first extramarital affair. By this time he had been living a double existence for a couple of decades and was good at covering for himself. But he was wracked with guilt and decided not to pursue other relational affairs. Instead, he began to seek out prostitutes. This continued until he was caught in a sting operation.

Anthony lost his position as a city planner in his small community due to his arrest and conviction. His wife, his children and his faith community were stunned. Anthony was humiliated, ashamed and suicidal. Over the next few months his counselor urged him to join a sexual addiction recovery group that met at a large church in a nearby city. Anthony refused, maintaining that he was not a sex addict. His marriage continued to deteriorate as his long history of sexual encounters came to light, and Anthony recognized that he needed more help than his counselor could give. He went to his first recovery meeting, feeling belligerent and embarrassed. The men at that meeting admitted they were sex addicts, acknowledged their inability to control their sexual addictions and voiced their dependence on God.

Anthony went back the next week. Each week, he heard men tell of dozens of affairs and how it had cost them their marriages. He comforted himself by saying, "I'm not like that." Other men told of scores of anonymous encounters with other men in bathrooms and health clubs; again Anthony thought, "I'm not like that." But every week, he heard stories of men who were no longer enslaved to whatever form of sexual addiction had captured them. And he thought, "I *want* to be like that—I want to live a life free from sexual captivity."

Each week, Anthony joined the other men as they read together statements of reality acknowledging the true nature of their addictions and their radical reliance on God for healing and sobriety.

Anthony began attending several meetings a week. He was encouraged on his new path by men who had traveled the same difficult journey in years past. Some men had been in recovery for over a decade, but were still walking the walk one day at a time. Part of their reason for continuing to be a part of the recovery group was to accompany and support those who were just entering the recovering community. One man became Anthony's sponsor; he and Anthony were in touch almost every day, working at recovery and holding each other accountable for living clean.

It has been six years since Anthony was arrested. He still attends recovery meetings, and he sponsors several young (and older) Christian men who have come to their first meeting frightened, belligerent and ashamed, unwilling to acknowledge their need for God's healing power, yet unable to live abundant lives.

Anthony's story graphically illustrates the principles of the situative-sociocultural theory as it relates to Christian formation in community. Speaking from the situative-sociocultural perspective, we could say that:

- persons (in this case, Anthony)
- learn to be members of their community of practice (in this case, Christians recovering from sexual addiction)
- as they actively participate (attend meetings, read together basic statements of reality, listen to each other's stories, speak the truth in love/hear the truth spoken in love)
- in that particular social community (recovery group)
- learning alongside those who are farther ahead in the journey (the men who had been in recovery for years).

Though at first Anthony said, "I am not like these men," he eventually came to identify himself as a grateful, recovering sex addict, just as did the other men in the group. Though each man struggled with his own form of sexual compulsion, they were all being formed in community into the image of Christ. Anthony could not have made this journey alone; his recovery from captivity into abundant life *required* community. He needed others who were ahead of him on the journey to accompany, encourage and model for him this new life.

Though not all Christians are struggling with sexual addiction, we are all learning to live abundant lives while sometimes (or regularly) coping with failure, loss, woundedness, broken relationships, temptation, emptiness and/or fear. As we live in community, journeying with others, we long for Christ to be so formed in us that our mourning will be turned into dancing, that our lives will be characterized by hope, that faithfulness and godliness so shine from us that others will say, "I want *that*."

Intergenerational Christian settings are authentic, complex learning environments, made up of individuals at various stages in their faith journeys, teaching some and learning from others as they participate in their community of believers. And though the Spirit is at work in every believer fostering the growth of love, joy, peace, patience, kindness, goodness, faithfulness, gentleness and self-control (Gal 5:22-23), we must also acknowledge that this spiritual fruit grows *in community*. Intergenerational faith communities are God-designed places for Christian formation.

The next section of the book, part three, offers sociological and empirical support for the idea that intergenerational Christian communities provide exceptional opportunities for learning, growing and being formed spiritually.

Part Three

■   ■   ■

SUPPORT FROM THE SOCIAL SCIENCES

9

BECOMING CHRISTIAN IN COMMUNITY

"Religious Socialization"

*New members of any society are always inducted into the group by
elder members who form them in different ways to become active
participants of various sorts. This is done through role modeling, teaching,
taking-things-for-granted, sanctioning, training, practicing, and other
means of inculcating and internalizing basic categories, assumptions,
symbols, habits, values, desires, norms, and practices. This is simply how
most [people] learn religion and everything else.*

Christian Smith, *Souls in Transition*

IN SOCIOLOGICAL RESEARCH, the construct that most keenly interfaces
with intergenerationality is a concept often referred to as "religious socialization." Christian Smith stands in a long line of sociological researchers
who have studied this construct, which is the central focus of this chapter.[1]
Religious socialization is the process by which persons learn and internalize attitudes, values and behaviors within the framework of a religious
system of beliefs and practices.[2]

---

[1]Parts of this chapter were adapted from Holly's dissertation, "A Qualitative Study" (2002).
[2]Young-Shin Kang, "The Role of Religious Socialization in Asian Families for Children's Self-
Perceived Early Academic Success and Social Competence" (Doctoral dissertation, Northeastern
University, Boston, MA, 2010. Counseling Psychology Dissertations. Paper 12). <http://iris.lib.
neu.edu/couns_psych_diss/12/>; Diane R. Brown and Lawrence E. Gary, "Religious Socialization
and Educational Attainment Among African Americans: An Empirical Assessment," *Journal of
Negro Education* 60 (1991): 411-26. <www.jstor.org/stable/pdfplus/2295493.pdf?acceptTC=true>.

BOX 9.1

Kristen's Story

In Soul Searching, Christian Smith tells the story of sixteen-year-old Kristen, whose dad died by suicide when she was six years old. Kristen is one of 267 teens Smith and his colleagues interviewed for the National Study of Youth and Religion (NSYR).[a] Initially, because Smith had heard other stories from teens emerging from tragic childhood events, he expected to hear "another case of troubled family, traumatic loss, at-risk childhood, and bad teen outcomes."[b]

However, Kristen's story surprised him. She described the time after her dad's death as a religious turning point for her family. She said her mom "really trusted in God and went to the Word," and taught Kristen and her four brothers and sisters that "God is a father to the fatherless."[c] Over the next ten years, Kristen's family became deeply involved in a church where she currently participates in several ministries and is part of the youth group. Kristen reads her Bible and prays daily; she is able to articulate her Christian beliefs eloquently and passionately to Smith. Her family is close, and her parents (her mom is now remarried) know her friends as well as the parents of her friends from school and church. Kristen says that she knows her teachers at her Christian school and the adults at the church well. Kristen intentionally integrates her beliefs and commitment to God into her lifestyle: she respects her parents, works hard in school, doesn't drink or do drugs, volunteers at a soup kitchen and participates in mission trips.

---

[a]Christian Smith with Melinda Denton, Soul Searching: The Religious and Spiritual Lives of American Teenagers (Oxford: Oxford University Press, 2005). Smith's interview with Kristen was part of the National Study of Youth and Religion (NSYR), a research project that was conducted between 2001 and 2005. In 2002-2003, researchers with NSYR conducted a phone survey with 3,290 nationally representative thirteen- to seventeen-year-old teens; then seventeen trained project researchers (including Smith) conducted 267 in-depth face-to-face interviews with a subsample of those phone survey respondents in 45 states. These respondents were chosen to represent a range of demographic and religious characteristics such as age, race, gender, socioeconomic status, rural-suburban-urban residence, region of the country, and religion (Jewish, evangelical Christian, mainline Christian, Catholic, LDS).
[b]Ibid., p. 18.
[c]Ibid.

Kristen's story (see box 9.1) illustrates some of the key features of religious socialization; for example, deep involvement with a faith community, regular spiritual practices with others in the community, strong community relationships (with family, peers and nonparental adults), congruent lifestyle with beliefs and values of the community. The key premise of this book is that a cross-generational group of believing people uniquely fosters healthy spiritual growth and development among its constituents. Sociological research on religious socialization examines key aspects of this same premise.

SOCIOLOGICAL RESEARCH AND RELIGIOUS SOCIALIZATION

In the past several decades important sociologists of religion have included Gerhard Lenski, Stan Gaede, Kevin Welch and Marie Cornwall; more recently Christian Smith is continuing to conduct sociological religious research. Also in the twenty-first century, the Commission on Children at Risk has issued a report offering sociological insight that highlights the importance of what it calls "authoritative communities." This chapter will also explore the concept of authoritative communities as it relates to intergenerational faith contexts.

One of the basic questions sociologists of religion seek to answer is: "Why do some people exhibit more spiritual commitment than others?" These sociologists of religion have repeatedly, consistently found that faith communities play crucial roles. An intergenerational outlook taps into this complex question, especially as it reveals the role of faith communities in Christian formation. Sociological religious research connects most directly with intergenerationality when it examines religious *socialization* as a factor in spiritual and religious attitudes, understandings and behavior. Beginning with Gerhard Lenski's sociological surveys in the 1950s and 1960s, sociologists of religion began to study this construct in earnest.

Subcommunity. Gerhard Lenski's 1961 book reported the seminal work that launched decades of subsequent research on the interrelationships between sociological factors and religious factors. In his field research in Detroit, Lenski measured strength of religious commitment to a socio-religious group in two ways: (1) commitment to the religious group as *asso-*

ciation, and (2) commitment to the group as *community.*[3]

A major finding of Lenski's study deals with the distinction between associational and communal involvement. Lenski points out that formal association with a socioreligious group is not equivalent to being a part of the subcommunity of that socioreligious group. A network of informal primary-type relations usually is established among members of every religious association, and Lenski calls this network the religious subcommunity. The existence of the subcommunity "greatly facilitates the [training] of the young in the norms and standards" of the religious group.[4] In fact, Lenski points out that it is in these subcommunities—these crossgenerational primary relationships—that the participants learn and absorb the key understandings and beliefs of the group.

Lenski's work establishes that the subcommunity is an important instrument for extending the influence of religious groups in the life of the community. Intergenerational Christian formation seeks to make these primary groups, or subcommunities, more intentional.

Communal relationships. Stan Gaede's work builds on Lenski's research, though he attempts specifically to establish sociological *causes* of religious belief. The data for Gaede's study was gathered from five Mennonite denominations in North America. Communal involvement was determined in two ways—*secondary* interaction and *primary* interaction. *Secondary* interaction was assessed by determining the participant's involvement with nonreligious, secondary, voluntary associations. *Primary* interaction was assessed based on the percentage of close friends who belonged to the participant's local church. Belief-orthodoxy was measured

---

[3]Gerhard Lenski, *The Religious Factor: A Sociological Study of Religion's Impact on Politics, Economics, and Family Life* (Garden City, NY: Doubleday, 1961); Lenski's research is based on interviews with 656 Detroit residents conducted in 1958. Lenski utilized an experienced survey research organization, the Detroit Area Study, a facility of the Department of Sociology at the University of Michigan, to select the random sample, conduct the interviews, and complete the statistical work. The research itself is considered well-conducted in the literature that has been built around Lenski's work. The participants were Protestant, Catholic and Jewish (and a few "other" or "no religious preference"), both genders, all adult ages, several ethnicities, and all socioeconomic levels.

This research yielded an enormous number of significant findings. The central finding was that religion in various ways is constantly influencing individuals and society. The major limitation of Lenski's original research is the geographical sample (all from Detroit). But his work has spawned further research interrelating sociological factors and religious factors (in many other locations), which has supported, expanded and refined his major findings.

[4]Ibid., p. 301.

on two scales, both designed to determine the degree of the participant's commitment to basic Christian beliefs.[5]

Gaede found that communal involvement is a significant predictor of belief-orthodoxy. His study, like others, confirms particularly the importance of *communal relationships* in the development and maintenance of religious beliefs and practice.

Association with other believers. Building on Gaede's work, Kevin Welch's study examines several theories that propose to explain religious commitment, one of which is an interaction/social participation theory.[6] Welch's research participants were from ten denominations in California. Welch's study supported the *interactionist* perspective, which reflects a similar finding of the earlier studies: that "religious commitment is developed through the transmission of religious norms in a group context through association with other believers."[7]

Integration into a religious community. Maria Cornwall's study examines the social processes that influence religious belief and behavior within a specific religious group (in this case Latter-day Saints). She looks at five categories of factors—group involvement, belief-orthodoxy, religious commitment, religious socialization and sociodemographic charac-

---

[5]Stan Gaede, "A Causal Model of Belief-Orthodoxy: Proposal and Empirical Test," *Sociological Analysis* 37 (1976): 205-17; Gaede found that communal involvement is a significant predictor of belief-orthodoxy. Both aspects of communal involvement were indicative of belief. That is, "those individuals who establish primary group relationships with non-religious group members and those who become involved in non-religious, secondary associations are less inclined to accept orthodox Christian beliefs than those who do not" (p. 214).

One obvious limitation of this study is that the data was collected from the Mennonite population only, thus limiting the generalizability of the results. However, this study stands in a long line of research examining some of the same variables among different religious populations. This study, like many others, reconfirms particularly the importance of *communal relationships* in the development and maintenance of religious beliefs and practice.

[6]Kevin Welch, "An Interpersonal Influence Model of Traditional Religious Commitment," *Sociological Quarterly* 22 (1981): 81-92; Welch utilized data from a 1963 Northern California church member sample. Data from 1,571 respondents in ten denominations was analyzed. The study examines four theories that propose to explain religious commitment: (1) deprivation/compensation arguments, (2) sociodemographic approaches, (3) the localistic reference orientations argument, and (4) interaction/social participation theories. His study tests three of the theories and builds directly on Gaede's (1976) work.

Welch's large sample, broad and representative denominational base, and detailed statistical analysis lend strength to this study. And though the participants were all from California, not a national sample, the study generally supports other studies from other populations.

[7]Ibid., p. 81.

teristics. Religious behavior for this study was measured by frequency of personal prayer, church attendance and home religious observance.[8]

The results of Cornwall's survey indicate that all five factors have a significant impact on religious behavior. Cornwall references several other studies (including those of the previously mentioned Lenski, Gaede and Welch) that offer evidence to support her basic finding that "religious belief and commitment are highly dependent upon the extent to which an individual is *integrated into a religious community.*"[9]

Sacred umbrellas and subcultural identity. In 1996 Christian Smith conducted a national survey to evaluate the faith commitment of adults in five American religious communities: evangelical, fundamentalist, mainline, liberal and Catholic. The survey elicited responses concerning religious commitment, beliefs, attitudes and behaviors as well as opinions about issues of education, gender, morality and responsibility in society.[10]

In his explanation of the findings of the study, Smith coined a new

---

[8]Maria Cornwall, "The Determinants of Religious Behavior: A Theoretical Model and Empirical Test," *Social Forces* 68 (1989): 572-92. To gather data, Cornwall distributed a thirty-two-page questionnaire to randomly selected families from twenty-seven different Mormon wards (congregations) from all parts of the United States. Religious behavior for this study was measured in terms of frequency of personal prayer, church attendance and home religious observance.

From her research Cornwall created a model of the predictors of religious behavior. In her model, religious socialization has a direct positive influence on personal community relationships, and personal community relationships influence religious belief and commitment, and belief and commitment influence conformity to the norms of the religious group (p. 578).

Though Cornwall's data was collected entirely within the Latter Day Saints and thus limits the generalizability to other religious groups, Cornwall references several other studies (including those of previously mentioned Lenski, Gaede and Welch) that offer growing evidence to support her basic finding that "religious belief and commitment are highly dependent upon the extent to which an individual is integrated into a religious community" (p. 588).

[9]Ibid., p. 588, emphasis added.

[10]Christian Smith, *American Evangelicalism: Embattled and Thriving* (Chicago: University of Chicago Press, 1998). In 1996 a cross-sectional, nationally representative telephone survey called the "Religious Identity and Influence Survey" was conducted by FGI, a national survey research firm in Chapel Hill, North Carolina. The moving force behind this survey was Christian Smith. The randomly generated sample was designed to represent all telephones in the continental United States; the research design required ten attempts to reach each phone number, and at least three callbacks to convert initial refusals. The survey produced 2,591 completed surveys, and the response rate was 69 percent. Reviews of the survey and research design were very positive. Smith designed the survey to evaluate the faith commitment of adults in five American religious communities: evangelical, fundamentalist, mainline, liberal and Catholic (participants self-identified their religious community).

phrase: *sacred umbrella* (an adaptation of Peter Berger's *sacred canopy*[11]). Smith said that some religious groups in America have built strong and vibrant faith communities through erecting "sacred umbrellas" under which their members gather and define themselves as they dwell in an indifferent culture.[12] He calls his explanation the "subcultural identity theory."[13] Though Smith calls his theory a new paradigm, it is reminiscent of Lenski's "subcommunity" language: "The subcommunity is a vehicle by means of which large numbers of persons are effectively [taught] the norms of the group."[14] Smith's purpose was broader than identifying factors of religious commitment; however, his analysis supports the idea that religious socialization in a subcommunity is an essential aspect of strong and sustainable religious commitment, a conclusion reached also by Lenski, Gaede, Welch and Cornwall.

Authoritative communities. Another supportive piece from the sociological world is the report from the Commission for Children at Risk, called "Hardwired to Connect," released in September of 2003.[15] This commission convened a group of thirty-three pediatricians, neuroscientists, social scientists and psychologists to address what it called "the crisis in the 'ecology' of childhood," that is, the continually upwardly spiraling number of children and youth suffering from mental illness, emotional distress and behavioral problems. This group of scholars and practitioners, interrelating biology, brain research, developmental principles, attachment theory, gene research, moralization processes and spirituality with child well-being, offers a two-fold conclusion: (1) that human beings are "hardwired" to connect, and (2) that the crisis of American childhood is due in large part to a lack of *connectedness*. These conclusions led the commission

---

[11]Peter Berger (*The Sacred Canopy* [New York: Anchor, 1967]) developed the idea that religion in the past was like a large encompassing sacred canopy under which whole religious societies felt covered and protected from outside chaotic forces. Berger further argued that in the highly pluralistic twentieth-century world, these sacred canopies collapsed. Smith contends that Berger's vast, pervasive sacred canopies are actually not needed to sustain religious vitality, and that sacred umbrellas, that is, smaller, more portable versions of Berger's sacred canopies, are adequate, even necessary, to maintain a robust religious subculture today.

[12]Ibid., p. 106.

[13]Ibid., p. 89.

[14]Lenski, *The Religious Factor*, p. 296.

[15]The Commission for Children at Risk is an initiative jointly sponsored by Dartmouth Medical School along with the YMCA of the USA, and the Institute for American Values.

to its definitive recommendation: "We believe that building and strengthening *authoritative communities* is likely to be our society's best strategy for ameliorating the current crisis of childhood and improving the lives of U.S. children and adolescents."[16]

The report describes authoritative communities as groups that foster the types of connectedness that children (and others) need for healthy emotional, psychological and spiritual well-being. The Hardwired to Connect report delineates ten basic characteristics of an authoritative community (emphasis ours):

1. *It is a social institution that includes children and youth.*
2. It treats children as ends in themselves.
3. *It is warm and nurturing.*
4. It establishes clear limits and expectations.
5. *The core of its work is performed largely by nonspecialists.*
6. *It is multigenerational.*
7. *It has a long-term focus.*
8. *It reflects and transmits a shared understanding of what it means to be a good person.*
9. *It encourages spiritual and religious development.*
10. *It is philosophically oriented to the equal dignity of all persons and to the principle of love of neighbor.*[17]

The italicized characteristics sound very much like intergenerational faith communities, that is, *churches.* This report says children need authoritative communities in their lives to restore the missing connectedness of previous generations. Churches, more than any other social institution in America, bear in their DNA the key characteristics of authoritative communities as described in this report: intergenerational faith communities are warm, nurturing, *multigenerational* social institutions that teach children and youth and that promote religious and spiritual development for all the generations.

Christian formation and religious socialization. Some of the most recent

---

[16]Kathleen Kovner Kline, *Authoritative Communities: The Scientific Case for Nurturing the Whole Child* (New York: Springer Verlag, 2008), p. 26, emphasis ours.
[17]Ibid., p. 26.

sociological research regarding religious socialization is reported in Christian Smith's book *Souls in Transition: The Religious and Spiritual Lives of Emerging Adults.*[18] This research builds directly on the NSYR study with teenagers cited at the beginning of this chapter. In 2007 and 2008, the National Study of Youth and Religion conducted a follow-up survey with over 2,000 participants who could be located from the earlier study; the participants were now eighteen to twenty-three years of age. Interviews were conducted with 230 of the participants. In *Souls in Transition* Smith chronicles the transitions these young people face in emerging adulthood, seeking "to discover what happens, in the midst of those transitions, to their religious faith, practices, beliefs, associations, and commitments."[19]

In general, the findings reveal that these eighteen- to twenty-three-year-olds are coping with the typical developmental issues earlier generations of young adults have faced, such as multiple transitions, autonomy and financial struggles. Smith notes, however, that these common developmental issues are compounded by "moral relativism, individualistic subjectivism, pervasive drugs, extensive partying, amorphous relationships [and] sexual license."[20] And due to "their own (self-described) stupid and self-destructive choices," many of the young adults reported difficulty, struggles and trouble.[21]

However, Smith also reports that the most religious of the emerging adults in the study are consistently doing better (than the least religious study participants) on measures of life outcomes such as "relationship with parents, giving and volunteering, participation in organized activities, substance abuse, risky behaviors, moral compassion, physical health, bodily self-image, mental and emotional well-being, locus of control, life satisfaction, life purpose, feeling gratitude, educational achievement, resistance to consumerism, pornography use, or potentially problematic sexual activity."[22]

---

[18]Christian Smith with Patricia Snell, *Souls in Transition: The Religious and Spiritual Lives of Emerging Adults* (Oxford: Oxford University Press, 2009). Smith mines the same data for his most recent book, *Lost in Transition: The Dark Side of Emerging Adulthood* with Kari Christoffersen, Hilary Davidson and Patricia Snell Herzog (Oxford: Oxford University Press, 2011).

[19]Smith, *Souls in Transition*, p. 4.

[20]Ibid., p. 85.

[21]Ibid.

[22]Ibid., p. 297.

Smith explains these positive outcomes in terms of the sociological principle of religious socialization. He says that "new members of any society are always inducted into the group by elder members who form them in different ways to become active participants of various sorts. This is done through role modeling, teaching, taking-things-for-granted, sanctioning, training, practicing, and other means of inculcating and internalizing basic categories, assumptions, symbols, habits, values, desires, norms, and practices. This is simply how most [people] learn religion and everything else."[23]

Smith says that religious socialization in America takes places in two spheres: *individual family households* and *multigenerational religious congregations*. He concludes, "If nothing else, what the findings of this book clearly show is that for better or worse, these are the two crucial contexts of . . . religious formation in the United States. If formation does not happen here, it will—with rare exceptions—not happen anywhere."[24]

SUMMARY OF SOCIOLOGICAL RESEARCH AND INTERGENERATIONAL ISSUES

The basic point of the sociological studies in this chapter is that Christian commitment is formed and strengthened as persons *develop relationships* and *actively participate* in faith communities that teach, model and live out the communities' beliefs. Smith takes that point somewhat further by saying that these communities must be cross-generational. David Kinnaman agrees. In the conclusion to his 2011 book that examines why emerging adults are leaving Christian churches, Kinnaman describes three things he has learned from five years of research.[25] The first thing he has learned is that *intergenerational relationships in faith communities are crucial*.[26] Kinnaman's conclusion aligns closely with Smith's insight as well as the premise of this book: that intergenerational Christian communities

---

[23]Ibid., pp. 285-86.
[24]Ibid., p. 286.
[25]David Kinnaman with Aly Hawkins, *You Lost Me: Why Young Christians Are Leaving the Church . . . and Rethinking Faith* (Grand Rapids: Baker Books, 2011), pp. 203-5. Kinnaman is referring to eighteen studies conducted by the Barna Group primarily over the past five years; Kinnaman draws from all of these studies in *You Lost Me*.
[26]Ibid., p. 203.

uniquely and profoundly nurture Christian faith and development. A story from Smith's research illustrates the key construct at work here.

One of the recurring themes in Smith's book *Souls in Transition* is that some of the emerging adults who participated in the study are finding communities of faith to aid them as they recover from poor life choices made in their teens and early twenties. Smith tells the story of Andrea, a twenty-one-year-old whose nonreligious childhood was followed with teen years characterized by promiscuity, drug and alcohol abuse, poor relationships with family members and trouble with the law. At the time of the interview Andrea is attempting to pull out of her damaged past and has found a faith community where she regularly attends Sunday worship as well as weekly classes to learn about Christianity. She also actively participates in a life group—a small fellowship group in which people "of *various ages* discuss recent sermons, read the Bible, share what is going on in their lives, and pray together" (emphasis ours).[27] Though Andrea hasn't yet committed, she says that she is learning and that she wants to know more. She says, "I like the people at my church and their beliefs. I'm learning something, and it gives me a sense of belonging somewhere . . . where I feel secure, at church. So I feel an interest in going because I know I'll need people, and church is kind of a real close group of people."[28]

Smith says that "religious beliefs, relationships, and practices often offer [Andrea and others] helpful resources for getting their lives back in order."[29] In intergenerational faith communities, Smith indicates, these recovering twentysomethings find people who care about them, belief systems that help them set boundaries regarding what is healthy and unhealthy and right and wrong, and new relationships with men and women across the generations who can function as role models and can provide accountability.

Andrea is beginning the process of religious socialization that the sociologists in this chapter have described. She is beginning to enter, experience and participate in Lenski's subcommunity, Gaede's communal relationships, Welch's association with other believers, Cornwall's integration into

---

[27]Smith, *Souls in Transition*, p. 171.
[28]Ibid., p. 173.
[29]Ibid., p. 85.

a religious community, and the Children at Risk Commission's authoritative community, placing herself under one of Smith's sacred umbrellas.

The process of becoming Christlike in one's attitudes, values, beliefs and behaviors—that is, Christian formation—does not happen alone. To paraphrase Smith, for those like Andrea whose parents did not provide religious guidance, spiritual/religious formation—if it happens at all—will happen in authentic, complex, intergenerational faith communities such as the one Andrea has found.

10

Contributions from Gerontology

Is not wisdom found among the aged? Does not long life bring understanding?
Job 12:12

Age segregation has separated the old from the young and violated the continuity and wholeness of the life cycle.
Margaret Kuhn, foreword to *Intergenerational Programs*

THE HERITAGE DAY HEALTH CENTERS (HDHC) in Ohio offers two daycares, one for preschool children with special needs and one for older adults.[1] Because of HDHC's commitment to intergenerational programming, several times each day the two groups come together for mutually enjoyable cross-age activities. HDHC makes the key point that the elderly and preschoolers have many things in common, and perhaps see life in similar ways:

> Said the little boy, "Sometimes I drop my spoon."
> Said the old man, "I do that, too."
>
> The little boy whispered: "I wet my pants."
> "I do that, too," laughed the little old man.

---

[1] Parts of this chapter were adapted from Holly's dissertation, "A Qualitative Study" (2002).

Said the little boy, "I often cry."
The old man nodded. "So do I."

"But worst of all," said the boy, "it seems grownups don't pay attention to me."
And he felt the warmth of a wrinkled hand. "I know what you mean,"
said the little old man.[2]

In 1963 the University of Florida's P. K. Yonge Laboratory School began the Adopt a Grandparent Program—the first known intergenerational program in the country. In this program students from the school's elementary classes regularly visited a neighboring convalescent home and "adopted" an older adult there. Students would not only visit their adopted grandparent, but also write cards and create gifts for them. In 1965 the federal government became involved in intergenerational programming when it provided funding for the Foster Grandparent Program,[3] which continues today. Information about it can be found on the Senior Corps Website.[4] Current intergenerational programs typically embrace one of the following three types: older adults serving children or youth; children or youth serving older adults; or children/youth and older adults working together to serve others.[5]

GERONTOLOGICAL CONCERN AND INTERGENERATIONAL ISSUES

Gerontologists—those who study aging populations—are keenly interested in intergenerational issues. The burgeoning elderly population in North America is increasingly being perceived as a burden that younger generations and the government will be required to bear. Gerontologists are seeking ways for the growing population of seniors to be seen as a re-

---

[2]This vignette is played audibly on the website for The Heritage Day Health Centers <www.heritagedayhealth.org/about.html>.

[3]Sally Newman, "History and Evolution of Intergenerational Programs," in *Intergenerational Programs: Past, Present and Future*, ed. Sally Newman et al. (Washington, DC: Taylor and Francis, 1997), pp. 55-70.

[4]<www.seniorcorps.gov/about/programs/fg.asp>.

[5]Christopher Ward, "The Context of Intergenerational Programs," in *Intergenerational Programs: Past, Present and Future*, ed. Sally Newman et al. (Washington, DC: Taylor and Francis, 1997), pp. 21-36; Sally Newman and Timothy Smith, "Developmental Theories as the Basis for Intergenerational Programs," in *Intergenerational Programs: Past, Present and Future*, ed. Sally Newman et al. (Washington, DC: Taylor and Francis, 1997); Barbara Smith and Annette Yeager, "Intergenerational Communities: Where Learning and Interaction Go Hand in Hand," in *Intergenerational Programming: Understanding What We Have Created*, ed. Valerie Kuehne (New York: Haworth Press, 1999), pp. 25-45.

source, an asset, rather than as an oppressive burden on society.

Numerous institutional and governmental organizations are producing information aimed at providing avenues for utilizing the important human resource of aging Boomers. These organizations gather and disseminate data about aging, lobby for gerontological concerns, and seek opportunities to draw the generations together. One such group is the Gray Panthers, founded by Margaret Kuhn, who says: "Aging is a universal human experience shared by all living creatures. All are born of seed, mature, bear progeny, wither and die. The experience should unite us, but in the western developed world, old age is considered a pathological state and people have become segregated by age, as well as social class, income and ethnicity. Age segregation has separated the old from the young and violated the continuity and wholeness of the life cycle."[6]

Another organization, the powerful American Association of Retired Persons (AARP), is a national group with offices in Washington, D.C. The AARP provides travel and entertainment discounts for members, lobbies in Congress, and produces a prodigious amount of literature. One concern the AARP is addressing is how to integrate the separated generations.[7]

Generations Together,[8] a program of the University of Pittsburgh's Center for Social and Urban Research, was founded in 1981 by Sally Newman, who was a pioneer in intergenerational programs and, though now retired, is still known nationally and internationally as an author, educator, spokesperson and researcher. Newman coedited the first textbook on intergenerational issues, *Intergenerational Programs: Imperatives, Strategies, Impacts, Trends,* and is senior author of *Intergenerational Programs: Past, Present and Future.*[9] The latter book describes dozens of state, national or international intergenerational events, programs and initiatives that illustrate the growing field, including intergenerational child care centers, retired seniors volunteer programs, conferences on aging and

---

[6]Margaret Kuhn, "Foreword," p. xi.

[7]Karen A. Struntz and Shari Reville, eds., *Growing Together: An Intergenerational Sourcebook* (Palm Springs, CA: The Elvirita Lewis Foundation, 1985); AARP, *Intergenerational Projects Ideas Book* (Washington, DC: American Association of Retired Persons, 1993).

[8]See the Generations Together website at <www.gt.pitt.edu>.

[9]Sally Newman and Steven W. Brummel, eds., *Intergenerational Programs: Imperatives, Strategies, Impacts, Trends* (New York: Haworth Press, 1989); Sally Newman, *Intergenerational Programs: Past, Present and Future* (Washington, DC: Taylor & Francis, 1997).

intergenerational program guide manuals. Intergenerational programming most often refers to activities between young children or youth and older adults. Newman and Thomas Smith, former Intergenerational Early Childhood Program Director at Generations Together, define intergenerational programming as "a social phenomenon that brings together the nation's oldest and youngest generations."[10]

Besides Newman's Generations Together program at the University of Pittsburg, several other national and international centers now exist that promote intergenerationality, including the Intergenerational Center at Temple University, the Centre for Intergenerational Practice in the UK, and the International Consortium for Intergenerational Programmes, also in the UK. Enough interest in intergenerational issues exists at the national and international levels to support the *Journal of Intergenerational Relationships*, which is published four times a year by the University of Pittsburg and Generations Together.

GERONTOLOGICAL ISSUES AND FINDINGS

Two major issues gerontologists are studying include (1) the effects of age segregation on individuals, and (2) the impact of intergenerational programs on individuals, families and society. Twenty years ago Newman noted that the number of age-segregated communities was increasing while interactions among younger and older members of families was decreasing.[11] Newman comments that the outcome of this social phenomenon for the elderly has been "a decline in self-esteem and self-worth, and an increase in feelings of loneliness," and for the children and youth, there has been "an observed loss of the traditional elder/child nurturing."[12]

Over the last four decades scores of intergenerational programs involving seniors and children have gradually been implemented, and many have been evaluated to determine their impact on the participants. Rosencranz and McNevin found that children viewed older persons more posi-

---

[10]Sally Newman and Thomas Smith, "Developmental Theories as the Basis for Intergenerational Programs," in *Intergenerational Programs: Past, Present and Future*, ed. Sally Newman et al. (Washington, DC: Taylor and Francis, 1997), p. 3.

[11]Newman and Brummel, *Intergenerational Programs*.

[12]Ibid., p. 1.

tively after contact with the elderly.[13] An assessment of a foster grandparenting program indicated that the seniors in the program "were better adjusted both personally and socially and were more satisfied with their lives than a comparable group of older persons who did not participate in the project."[14] Seefelt, Jantz, Galper and Serock reported that children aged four to eight evaluated older persons more positively than before participation in a curriculum that included contact with older persons.[15]

Kocarnik and Ponzetti reported that children viewed older persons more positively after visiting the elderly in nursing homes.[16] Proller reported a study with fifth and sixth graders involved in visiting residents of nursing homes. Proller says that "the elderlies' negative attitudes were reversed, depression levels were decreased, and their self-esteem was increased," and children "developed significantly improved attitudes toward the elderly."[17] Tice, who has been working with gerontological issues since the late 1960s, has found repeatedly that seniors report increased feelings of life satisfaction when they work in the Teaching-Learning Communities, which involve seniors in an arts and humanities exchange with children ages five through twelve in the public schools.[18] Tice also reports positive outcomes for the children in basic academic performance and in the art curriculum.[19] Reporting on foster grandparenting programs, Saltz describes multiple benefits named by the participating "grandparents," among which were deep emotional satisfaction, increased self-esteem, renewed feelings of health and vigor, a gratifying sense of important and meaningful activity, and direction in their lives. The programs also had a

---

[13]Howard A. Rosencranz and Tony E. McNevin, "A Factor Analysis of Attitudes Toward the Aged," *The Gerontologist* 9, no. 1 (1969): 55-59.

[14]Robert M. Gray and Josephine M. Kasterler, "An Evaluation of the Effectiveness of a Foster Grandparent Project," *Sociology and Social Research* 54 (1970): 188.

[15]Carol Seefelt et al., "Children's Attitudes Toward the Elderly: Educational Implications," *Educational Gerontology* 2 (1977): 301-10.

[16]Rosanne R. Kocarnik and James J. Ponzetti, "The Influence of Intergenerational Contact on Child Care Participants," *Child Care Quarterly* 15 (1986): 244-50.

[17]Norman L. Proller, "The Effects of an Adoptive Grandparent Program on Youth and Elderly Participants," in *Intergenerational Programs: Imperatives, Strategies, Impacts, Trends,* ed. Sally Newman and S. W. Brummel (New York: Haworth Press, 1989), p. 202.

[18]Carol Tice, "Teaching-Learning Communities: An Investment in Learning and Wellness," in *Growing Together: An Intergenerational Sourcebook,* ed. Karen Struntz and Shari ReVille (Palm Springs, CA: The Elvirita Lewis Foundation, 1985), pp. 61-64.

[19]Ibid., p. 61.

positive effect on the children's intellectual and social development.[20]

In the 1990s gerontologists began to recognize that many healthy older persons have the time, the desire and the ability to encourage, nurture, teach and simply accompany persons from younger generations on their journey through life. Thus a concentrated effort was made in gerontological circles to bring together the aging but active population with the younger and needy population in school settings, an idea that gained popularity in educational circles also.[21]

A number of benefits for both older and younger participants have been well documented. Recent studies have shown that the older persons involved in intentional, well-designed intergenerational programs with children or young people show a reduction in depressive symptoms, watch less television, increase their mobility, exhibit enhanced memory and other cognitive skills, and enjoy satisfaction of feeling productive.[22] MacCallum et al. recently conducted a meta-analysis of 120 intergenerational programs in Australia. This meta-analysis identified over twenty important benefits for the aging population, including increased ability to cope with physical and mental illness, reintegration into community life, friendships with younger people, increased self-esteem and motivation, decreased isolation, and respect and recognition of their contribution to the community.[23]

The children and young people who participated in these intergenerational programs with the older population also exhibited growth and change in positive ways. Knapp and Stubblefield describe a program in which adolescents and adults attended a course (together) on aging, which

[20]Rosalyn Saltz, "We Help Each Other: The U.S. Foster Grandparent Program," in *Growing Together: An Intergenerational Sourcebook*, ed. Karen Struntz and Shari ReVille (Palm Springs, CA: The Elvirita Lewis Foundation, 1985), pp. 24-28.

[21]Kevin Brabazon and Robert Disch, eds., *Intergenerational Approaches in Aging: Implications for Education, Policy, and Practice* (New York: Haworth Press, 1997).

[22]Linda P. Fried et al., "The Experience Corps: A Social Model for Health Promotion, Generativity, and Decreasing Structural Lag for Older Adults" (symposium presented at the 53rd Annual Meeting of the Gerontological Society of America, November 17-21, 2000, Washington, DC); Sally Newman, Emin Karip and Robert B. Faux, "Everyday Memory Function of Older Adults: The Impact of Intergenerational School Volunteer Programs," *Educational Gerontology* 21 (1995): 569-80; Sally Newman and Barbara Larimer, *Senior Citizen School Volunteer Program: Report on Cumulative Data. 1988-1995* (Pittsburgh, PA: Generations Together, 1995).

[23]Judith MacCallum et al., *Community Building Through Intergenerational Exchange Programs* (Australia: National Youth Affairs Research Scheme, 2006).

also included a cooperative service component.[24] Following the course, the participating students knew more about aging and had more positive perceptions of older persons than did others who had not been involved in an intergenerational activity.[25] Benefits for children or youth in other studies show increased empathy toward older persons, enhanced prosocial conduct such as sharing, increased self-esteem, more resiliency, and increased school attendance and better behavior at school.[26] The MacCallum et al. meta-analysis of 120 intergenerational programs noted earlier also yielded a long list of benefits for children and youth including less loneliness, less involvement in violence and drug use, more optimism, increased respect for the achievements of adults, and greater awareness of heterogeneity of older persons.[27]

In general, these studies show that both younger and older participants of intergenerational programs mutually benefit. Children and youth who spend time with older persons view them more positively and experience growth in understanding of the aging process. Depending on the program, the children also exhibited academic and/or social growth. The older adults in the studies reported increased life satisfaction and self-esteem, heightened feelings of health and vigor, and a stronger sense of meaningful activity. "Healthy, mutually beneficial interaction occurs between young and old participants in intergenerational programs," according to Brummel, and these "myriad benefits of intergenerational interactions can strengthen the fabric of our societal structure."[28]

GERONTOLOGICAL FINDINGS AND INTERGENERATIONAL FAITH COMMUNITIES

Most children do not ordinarily desire to spend time with elderly people

[24]James Knapp and Patricia Stubblefield, "Changing Students' Perceptions of Aging: The Impact of an Intergenerational Service Learning Course," *Educational Gerontology* [serial online] 26 (October 2000):611-21.

[25]Ibid., p. 70.

[26]Marcia Marx et al., "Community-Service Activities Versus Traditional Activities in an Intergenerational Visiting Program," *Educational Gerontology* 31 (2004): 263-71; Andrea S. Taylor et al., "The Mentoring Factor: Evaluation of the Across Ages' Intergenerational Approach to Drug Abuse Prevention," in *Intergenerational Programs: Understanding What We Have Created*, ed. V. S. Kuehne (Binghamton, NY: Haworth Press, 1998), pp. 77-99.

[27]MacCallum et al., *Community Building*.

[28]Newman and Brummel, *Intergenerational Programs*, p. xiii.

in their faith communities. These same children may thoroughly enjoy spending time with their own grandparents, but research shows that children—and others—tend to exhibit ageism; that is, they have negative views of older people in general. Children tend to view the elderly as sickly and frail or simply as boring.[29]

Sadly, ageism exists in faith communities as well as in society in general. And sometimes, older people have negative views of children and youth as well. Spending time together can teach both groups to honor the other.

Children and youth, even those active in faith communities, tend to spend most of their time (other than school time) with their nuclear families or doing fun things with others their own age. Intentional opportunities to spend time with older faith pilgrims can provide young believers with ways to see outside themselves, ways to begin to practice the "one another" passages of life in Christ: honor one another (Rom 12:10); wait for one another (1 Cor 11:33); serve one another (Gal 5:13); carry each other's burdens (Gal 6:2). Most older persons have experienced several losses, and the presence and attention of the young can bring cheer, hope and childlike faith to those suffering from loneliness, pain and loss.

Happily, older adults have much to offer the younger generations. "Like all people, they want to be needed and loved and often seek out opportunities to be in service to others."[30] However, due to the isolated nature of our society, older adults may have few opportunities for loving and serving others, especially if they live far away from their families. Therefore when the young and the old spend time together, the old may also practice the "one another" passages of life in Christ: honor one another (Rom 12:10); instruct one another (Rom 15:14); encourage one another and build each other up (1 Thess 5:11). Older adults who are not harried by immediate responsibilities have time to listen, to play games, to encourage and to be "spiritual directors" of the young.

---

[29]Bill Bytheway, "Ageism and Age Categorization," *Journal of Social Issues* 61 (June 2005): 361-74; Jon F. Nussbaum et al., "Ageism and Ageist Language Across the Life Span: Intimate Relationships and Non-intimate Interactions," *Journal of Social Issues* [serial online] 61 (June 2005): 287-305; Dagmar Grefe, "Combating Ageism with Narrative and Intergroup Contact: Possibilities of Intergenerational Connections," *Pastoral Psychology* 60 (February 2011).
[30]Richard Gentzler, *Designing an Older Adult Ministry* (Nashville: Discipleship Resources, 1999), p. 25.

Margaret Guenther in *Holy Listening: The Art of Spiritual Direction*[31] compares spiritual direction to midwifery. Her favorite midwife image is the wise, resourceful, experienced "Appalachian granny woman" who assists at the birth of babies in remote and difficult-to-reach mountain areas.[32] The role of the midwife is to be present, to encourage, to listen, to wait with—in order to assist in bringing babies to term; the role of the spiritual director is to be present, to encourage, to listen, to wait with—in order to assist in bringing souls to term. Perhaps the older saints in our faith communities—whose primary roles are not training, feeding, transporting, clothing or financially supporting the young—are uniquely suited for bringing the souls of the young to term; they have the time and the wisdom to wait and listen.

Data from four decades of research suggests that intergenerational interaction has a positive effect on both the older and younger populations involved. The studies reported in this chapter show that children's attitudes toward the elderly improve when they spend time with them, and that the older people experience less negativity, more satisfaction with life and an increase in self-worth. Due to the win-win results reported in these studies, educators and leaders of governmental agencies and other gerontological organizations are seeking to create more intergenerational programs that can positively impact both young and old. Faith communities offer natural opportunities for young and old to bless one another. Creating intentional opportunities for young and old to meet together, to share stories, to create something together or merely to talk can be mutually beneficial and can bless the whole body of Christ.

---

[31]Margaret Guenther, *Holy Listening: The Art of Spiritual Direction* (Cambridge, MA: Cowley Publications, 1992).
[32]Ibid., p. 86.

11

MILLENNIALS, XERS, BOOMERS AND SILENTS

Generational Theory

How great are his signs, how mighty his wonders! His kingdom is an eternal kingdom; his dominion endures from generation to generation.
Daniel 4:3

For as in one body we have many members, and the members do not all have the same function, so we, though many, are one body in Christ, and individually members one of another.
Romans 12:4-5

The church is a partnership of generations fulfilling God's purposes in their time.
David Kinnaman, *You Lost Me*

DURING AN ADULT EDUCATION COURSE, Christine invited adults from three generations to share with students their joys, struggles, faith journeys and understanding of their generation. After the Boomer generation class period, students commented that they now understood their parents and teachers better. Several weeks later one young man shared how his new understanding had changed him, "I have more compassion for my mom now that I realize she is struggling with the empty nest syndrome. I've been able to speak more patiently with her."

Christine's greatest surprise came during the class in which those from the Silent generation shared. At the end of class students left their seats to hug these adults and tell them how much they appreciated each one taking time to attend. Guests and students remained standing and talking together informally for quite some time. Students articulated their newly found appreciation of the Silent generation and their realization that their grandparents were of this generation. Having positive relationships with grandparents, these young adults now felt more comfortable about making positive connections with other Silents. Students also realized that older adults may have extraordinarily interesting life stories, and students' interest in these stories increased. Later, one of the millennial students shared how he put his recent awareness to practice: "I purposely engaged [in conversation with] a Silent generation woman at church who has been vocal about not wanting too many changes to the traditional worship service. I learned that her husband died ten years ago, she is caring for her thirty-six-year-old daughter who has cerebral palsy, and her older son just moved back home after a divorce. Yet she also talked about how the Lord gives her strength and she is blessed to have the means to serve her family. I thought I might be able to encourage her, but she encouraged me! Now I understand why she doesn't want changes to the traditional liturgy; church is one of the few stable environments in her life!"

GENERATIONAL THEORY

Christine first learned about William Strauss and Neil Howe's influential book on generational theory[1] through the pastors she interviewed for her dissertation research. One pastor was already working toward a philosophy of intergenerational faith formation when he read Strauss and Howe's book on generations; the book then became the impetus for teaching his congregation about the needs of various generations. Another pastor read Strauss and Howe's book but did not immediately connect the material to his congregation. Over time he recognized that generational

---

[1]William Strauss and Neil Howe, *Generations: The History of America's Future, 1584 to 2069* (New York: Quill, William Morrow, 1991).

differences were causing certain difficulties within the church, especially regarding worship style, and he began teaching generational theory as a way to nurture unity among congregants. Since Strauss and Howe's seminal work was published in 1991, several books have been published that explain generational theory as it pertains to the church setting, to aid congregational ministry.[2]

Generational theory is different from gerontology, the topic of the previous chapter, and developmental theories. Gerontology focuses specifically on the development and needs of older adults. Developmental differences correlate to differences in people of various ages. Generational theory spans all ages and suggests that there are differences in age-related groups of people due to a cyclical pattern driven by changing values and attitudes of each new generation. That most fifty-year-olds will think more maturely and have different social needs and health issues than most twenty-year-olds is mainly related to years of life. Generational theory indicates that a fifty-year-old Boomer will view life very differently from the way an older Silent saw life at that same age. Not only did society change between the time the Silent was fifty and the time the Boomer turned fifty, but the characteristics common to each generation mean they will view even similar circumstances differently.

Scripture uses the word *generation* in three ways. The most common Old Testament usage designates a period of time. When the Psalmist writes "from generation to generation we will recount your praise" (Ps 79:13 ESV), he could have written, "forever or for all ages we will recount your praise." Another usage is seen in the genealogical lists of descendants found in both the Old and New Testaments (Gen 5; Mt 1). The final usage relates most directly to generational theory and is defined by McIntosh as "a group of people who are connected by their place in time with common boundaries and a common character."[3] Judges 2:10 highlights this usage: "After that whole generation had been gathered to their an-

---

[2]Jackson Carroll and Wade Roof, *Bridging Divided Worlds: Generational Cultures in Congregations* (San Francisco: Jossey-Bass, 2002); Gary L. McIntosh, *One Church, Four Generations: Understanding and Reaching All Generations in Your Church* (Grand Rapids: Baker Books, 2002); Peter Menconi, *The Intergenerational Church: Understanding Congregations from WWII to www.com* (Littleton, CO: Mt. Sage Publishing, 2010).

[3]McIntosh, *One Church, Four Generations*, p. 11.

cestors, another generation grew up who knew neither the LORD nor what he had done for Israel." Peter Menconi describes how the words *generation* and *generality* derive from the root word meaning "to bring forth." Thus generational theory will *bring forth* certain generalities that may not fit every member of a generation but will represent the majority of generational members.[4] Strauss and Howe define a generation as a "cohort-group whose length approximates the span of a phase of life [roughly 22 years] and whose boundaries are fixed by peer personality."[5]

We live in a time when as many as six generations are living simultaneously. The eldest of the generations, the G.I. generation, is passing on. Its members are eighty-five years old and older, yet their legacy continues to affect the following generations. On the other end of the spectrum, the youngest generation is still in the birth process, and few characteristics of this generation have been solidly formed.

CHARACTERISTICS OF THE GENERATIONS

The eldest generation—most commonly called the G.I. generation, but also known as the Greatest, Civic, Heroic[6] or Builder generation[7]—is made up of Americans born between 1901 and 1924.[8] In Strauss and Howe's repeating generational rubric, this generation is a *civic* generation[9]

---

[4]Menconi, *Intergenerational Church*, p. 14.
[5]Strauss and Howe, *Generations*, p. 60.
[6]Menconi, *Intergenerational Church*, p. 17.
[7]McIntosh, *One Church, Four Generations*, p. 28. Note: McIntosh uses the term *Builders* as an overarching title for three generations: G.I., Silent and what he calls the war babies born between 1940 and 1945.
[8]Unless otherwise noted, dates are from Strauss and Howe, *Generations*.
[9]As Strauss and Howe researched characteristics of past generations, they discovered four repeating patterns of generational characteristics, which they identify as "generational cycles," as well as revealed a correspondence between these cycles and recurring types of historical events. With this information they were able to envision possible future trends in American society. They label the four repeating generational types and explain each as follows:

> A dominant, outer-fixated CIVIC GENERATION grows up as increasingly protected youth after a spiritual awakening; comes of age overcoming a secular crisis; unites into a heroic and achieving cadre of rising adults; sustains that image while building institutions as powerful midlifers; and emerges as busy elders attacked by the next spiritual awakening.

> A recessive ADAPTIVE GENERATION grows up as overprotected and suffocated youths during a secular crisis; matures into risk-averse, conformist rising adults; produces indecisive midlife arbitrator-leaders during a spiritual awakening; and maintains influence (but less respect) as sensitive elders.

characterized by their upbeat, team-playing nature. World War II provided a national crisis that enabled this generation to rise up, work together and lead the country into a better standard of living. As mentioned, this generation is in the process of passing away, and many people today lament the crumbling of values and institutions that the people of the G.I. generation created.

The next generation, known as the Silent, Artist or Peacemaker generation, is composed of persons born between the years of 1925 and 1942. Strauss and Howe describe this type of generation as an *adaptive* generation. Living in the shadow of the outgoing, leadership-oriented G.I. generation, this postwar generation adapted and became trusted helpmeets to G.I. leaders and skilled managers of G.I.-created institutions. The Silent generation produced no United States presidents, but did produce trusted assistants to G.I. presidents. Silents honed their mediation skills and became good listeners, open and fair minded, and able to bring together people who have differing perspectives of a situation. A downfall to being fair-minded listeners is that Silents can also be indecisive, emotional and sometimes conflicted about their own beliefs. Men and women of this generation typically were passive parents preferring to provide their children with information for decision making rather than proffer their own opinions. It is not uncommon for children of Silent parents to comment that they didn't know what political party their parents were until they themselves were adults with their own views. Coming of age during a time when views of women in the workplace were changing, abortions were legal in some states and birth control pills were just becoming available, women of this generation were more likely than previous generations to work outside the home, abort children and divorce. However, as noted in the opening class scenario, many older Silents are

---

A dominant, inner-fixated IDEALIST GENERATION grows up as increasingly indulged youths after a secular crisis; comes of age inspiring a spiritual awakening; fragments into narcissistic rising adults; cultivates principle as moralistic midlifers; and emerges as visionary elders guiding the next secular crises.

A recessive REACTIVE GENERATION grows up as underprotected and criticized youth during a spiritual awakening; matures into risk-taking, alienated rising adults; mellows into pragmatic midlife leaders during a secular crisis; and maintains respect (but less influence) as reclusive elders.

now very involved with and respected by their Millennial grandchildren and adaptive great-grandchildren.

The next generation—the Boomers (born 1943-1960), also known as the Baby Boom, Hippie, Yuppie, TV, Flower Children and the Me Generation—is described by Strauss and Howe as being composed of values-obsessed *idealists*, a characteristic that typically fits the next repeating generation in Strauss and Howe's rubric. Boomers were raised to believe in themselves by a generation of G.I. leaders. The sky wasn't even a limit—astronauts first walked on the moon during Boomers' youth. However, Boomers weren't motivated so much by an outward national crisis as were their parents; rather, they were inspired by inward principles and utopian visions. The institutional adult world ran like a machine, a situation that seemed cold and heartless to Boomers with their passionate, internalized standards of right and wrong. Lacking a major crisis to bond them, Boomers' spiritual quest has led them down a variety of paths, but the search for a personalized truth guides many of them. This generation moved out of mainline churches and into New Age spirituality and evangelicalism, the latter movement birthing an active era of church formation and values-laden education stressing good works, service and family.

As the Boomers age, some find their Millennial children returning home. Thus they find themselves ushering in a rebirth of the extended family, and they are positioned to play a positive role in bridging generational tension and building intergenerational relationships. With the oldest Boomers just moving into retirement, this generation will continue to influence society for several more decades.

According to Strauss and Howe's cyclical rubric, the idealists are followed by a *reactive* generation, and indeed the pragmatism of the thirty- and fortysomethings Gen X generation (1961–1981) is a *reaction* to the seemingly unattainable ideals of the preceding generation. As children, this reactive generation was also called Busters, Latch-key, Boomerangs, Lost, At Risk and more. Currently they are most often known as Gen X. Growing up under Silent parents and under anything-but-silent Boomers, reactive Gen Xers have somehow found their own way in life with little parental direction or socially mandated mission. As youth in the 1980s, Gen Xers witnessed via media several worldview-shaping events: political and military scandals that uncovered hypocritical and dishonest behavior by leaders; the effects of a newly revealed disease known as AIDS; the discovery of the hole in the ozone; the Challenger shuttle explosion; and the Exxon Valdez oil spill. Many of them were also personally affected by the increased rate of divorce. Thus Xers are characterized by skepticism of leaders and realism about life; many are now over-protective parents. As they move toward midlife, their pragmatic character combined with their independent spirits and resourcefulness (learned by raising themselves) may enable them to step forward as leaders.

These four generations, approximately twenty years each, correlate to Strauss and Howe's four repeating generational types (civic, adaptive, idealist and reactive); thus the generation following Gen X should move full circle to become another civic generation. This generation, now in their teens and twenties, is best known as the Millennial generation. Other titles bestowed upon them have been Generation Y, the Bridger generation and Mosaics.[10] The Millennials include persons born between 1982 and 2003 and, according to Strauss and Howe, they are indeed characterized by the classic attributes of a civic generation. Like previous civic-generation children, Millennials have been protected, directly guided and expected to excel in everything they do. Millennials display their societal leadership abilities through community service activities as well as worldwide volunteer opportunities. Strauss and Howe describe Millennial civics as having "activity-oriented peer relationships, peer-enforced codes of conduct, and a strong sense of generational community." Strauss and Howe predict that "they [will] band together at a historic moment and—guided by the principled wisdom of elder Idealists and the realistic leadership of midlife Reactives—successfully shoulder a secular crisis."[11]

Tim Elmore, author of *Generation iY*,[12] segments the Millennial or iY generation into older (born 1984 through 1990) and younger (born after 1990) iYers, stating that "more than any previous group, this younger popu-

[10]George Barna, *Real Teens: A Contemporary Snapshot of Youth Culture* (Ventura, CA: Regal Books, 2001).

[11]Strauss and Howe, *Generations*, p. 361.

[12]Tim Elmore, *Generation iY: Our Last Chance to Save Their Future* (Atlanta: Poet Gardener Publishing, 2010).

BOX 11.1

Nuances of Generational Characteristics

It is possible that a person might identify with aspects of more than one generation or might place themselves in a generation other than their birth year indicates. The authors most cited in the generational descriptions above offer differing dates for the various generations by a two-to-four-year span. The term cusper *is often used to define people who are born during the years near a transition between generational cycles.[a] For example, according to Strauss and Howe the generational cycle transitions from Boomer to Gen Xer at 1960; however, someone born in 1959 may relate to some qualities of both generations, or a person born in 1962 may exhibit Boomer characteristics more than Gen X characteristics. In this latter case, perhaps the natural personality is more akin to the Boomer idealism, or this cusper was raised by Silent parents and was nurtured to become more skeptical and pragmatic. Christine is a cusper, and she resonates with the latter explanation. Her peers who were raised by young Boomer parents or raised in an urban environment seem to bear the Boomer characteristics more than she does, having been raised by Silent generation parents. However, as her parents have been married for over fifty years and she grew up in the same rural farm home that her father grew up in, she does not fully relate to all of the characteristics of Gen X either. Nurture, environment, family ethnicity, socioeconomic level and educational background all work together to make individuals unique.*

[a]Menconi, *Intergenerational Church*, p. 14.

lation has been defined by technology."[13] Elmore views the older Millennials as being more civic oriented and more self-sacrificing than their younger counterparts. He also remarks on the paradox of the Millennials being simultaneously self-absorbed yet generous. Elmore believes that the Millennials will need to spend time with older and younger generations and will need proper mentoring by adults in order to "develop their empathy

[13]Ibid., p. 13.

muscles."[14] He also cites Vygotsky, stating that the best learning for Millennials will occur in social contexts [15] (for more on Vygotsky see chapter seven).

The sixth living generation, children born after 2004, is as yet unnamed, although Strauss and Howe's generational theory indicates that they will bear the characteristics of an adaptive generation.

Concepts and terms from generational theory are ubiquitous; the use of the word *Boomer* to describe the first postwar generation has been perhaps the most commonly used descriptor. But the key question for this book is, How can insights from generational theory contribute to the rationale for intergenerational Christian formation?

GENERATIONAL THEORY AND CONGREGATIONAL MINISTRY

While explaining why church leaders should be interested in building intergenerational relationships, Menconi states, "How [the] generations relate to each other over the next years and decades will determine the course of America and American churches. Over the next several decades, intergenerational churches have great potential to impact individual lives and transform society. The degree to which churches are successful in achieving effective intergenerational ministry will determine the effectiveness of their overall ministries."[16]

No matter how a church leader determines to minister to and with the various generations within the congregation, understanding the characteristics of each generation will be helpful. Menconi as well as Gambone, McIntosh and Dittmer [17] have used Strauss and Howe's theory to consider how generational characteristics are typically showing themselves in the four generations that compose the largest percentage of congregants today. The following lists are summaries of these various authors' insights about the Silents, Boomers, Gen Xers and Millennials who currently populate churches in North America.

---

[14]Ibid., p. 69.
[15]Ibid., p. 185.
[16]Ibid., p. 21.
[17]Ibid., pp. 48-142; James V. Gambone, *All Are Welcome: A Primer for Intentional Intergenerational Ministry and Dialogue* (Crystal Bay, MN: Elder Eye Press, 1998), pp. 11-15; McIntosh, *One Church, Four Generations;* Terry Dittmer, "Ministry Among the Generations: Challenges and Opportunities," *Issues in Christian Education* 41, no. 2 (Fall 2007): 10-13.

Silent Generation—*Adaptive*

- Consensus builders who are generally liked by all generations and can mediate between generations
- Private; reserved about sharing their faith, will need encouragement to do so
- Loyal to church
- Endure authority (i.e., pastoral leadership)
- Most often in smaller congregations
- Share themselves and their wealth
- Prefer didactic teaching and a variety of topics
- More interested in having a spiritual impact on their grandchildren than changing the world through service or mission opportunities
- Seek to stabilize the future for upcoming generations
- Accustomed to programmatic models of ministry

A church dominated by this generation will typically mirror the civics' preference for traditional worship. However, Silents are more likely to be flexible about worship style *if* they understand how a new style will help the younger generations.

Boomer Generation—*Idealist*

- Have high standards for themselves and others; ministry must be done well
- Inner-focus driven and willing to fight for what they believe in
- Values-driven and moralistic, making it easy for them to focus more on the law in Scripture than the gospel
- Want the best for their children and are highly active in children's lives
- May focus more on enabling children to be good people than on having a life-changing relationship with Jesus
- Not likely to be concerned about church membership or maintaining civic-created institutions
- Prefer planning service projects rather than actively participating in them

- Tend to clash with Gen Xers and may control Millennials

- Prefer teaching that provides practical, useful information and interaction

A majority Boomer church will most likely have a contemporary worship format. Boomers are the initiators of "worship wars," as they like praise music, guitars and drums, and they tend to believe that contemporary music will keep the younger generations in church.

Gen X Generation—Reactive

- "Just do it" mentality

- Like to serve

- Jump in if they believe a mission project will make a difference

- Desire a church that offers adventurous, exciting outreach and service

- Skeptical and suspicious of Boomers and of civic-created institutions

- Tend to be overprotective, "helicopter" parents

- Comfortable without absolute truth and prefer teaching that allows for questions and questioning

- The least represented generation in churches—church as an organization is unimportant

- Desire caring relationships; friends become family

- Prefer early, mystical, church practices and/or authentic and technologically advanced worship

- Initiators of the emerging church movement

A Gen X–led church would tend to blend modern technology with artistic design and ancient worship practices to provide a multisensory and participatory experience.

Millennial Generation—Civic

- Doers; philosophize less than their Boomer parents

- Community/team oriented, like to work together and bring people together (however, need help getting out of their own cliques)

- Service oriented with both a local and global perspective; want to change the world and believe they can do so better than their elders

- Impatient, need help making long-term commitments
- Look to Silents for care, Boomers for philosophical guidance and Gen Xers for models of action
- Interested in a church that clearly teaches doctrine *and* practices it
- Likely to be loyal to their church, but also comfortable with people who don't believe as they do
- Enjoy a blend of traditional, contemporary and mystical worship, but may become most comfortable with the traditional church of their grandparents

The Millennials' positive relationship with their elders and openness to diversity enables majority Millennial churches to embrace a wide variety of worship practices and styles in such a way that all ages and cultures might worship and build community together.

■   ■   ■

A comparison of the characteristics of the generations indicates both likely places of potential connection between the generations (such as all previous generations having relationships with the Millennial generation) as well as likely places of division (such as each generation's preferred type of learning). Generational characteristics can help church leaders understand what might best motivate a generation. For example, Silents might be motivated to give financially through their sense of responsibility for and duty to their church or to younger generations; Boomers may be motivated if they understand giving as a way to improve their own spiritual or financial health; Gen Xers and Millennials may be more likely to give to friends with whom they have personal relationships or to projects they believe will make the world a better place. Hymns such as "Blessed Be the Tie that Binds" may converge with the Silent penchant toward peacemaking; the praise song "He Has Made Me Glad" hits a chord with the Boomers' interest in the upbeat, clap-along music of their youth; Gen X music is often more Christocentric and melancholy like "Opener" (see below); Millennials' music may be a combination of all the above as they

BOX 11.2

"Opener"

I went to my church on Sunday, just to hear good news.

And I confess it's been years more or less since I've warmed these pews.

I am looking for something stronger than my own life these days,

But the church of my childhood seems like the YMCA.

Every Sunday is just like the last, as if the church has no history and the people have no past.

We just sing the songs we like to sing and we preach about the news

and we think up some new things just to fill up the pews.

I want palms on Palm Sunday, I want Pentecost still to be red,

I want to drink of the wine and eat of the bread.

But they strive for attendance while I starve for transcendence,

But I count among this body both the living and the dead.

Whether it's guitars and amps and video screens and cordless mics,

Or incense and robes and copes and candle light.

Let's stop all the fighting over words and ways

And tell about Jesus like in the good old days.[a]

---

[a]Lyrics from "Opener" by Lost and Found. Copyright 1995. Lyrics reprinted by permission. <www.speedwood.com>.

are accustomed to variety and choice and perhaps the music of their grandparents, parents and contemporaries.

FROM GENERATION TO GENERATION

Church leaders use generational characteristics in a variety of ways. Some choose to ignore generational theory; others keep the generations apart as much as possible in order to minister to each in a manner that promotes the least generational conflict; others use it to specifically target Boomers or Gen X generations in order to grow their churches through a homogeneous model; and some use it to foster unity across the generations. Scripture reminds us that God's "dominion endures from generation to generation" (Dan 4:3) and in Christ the diverse members of his church—Jew and Greek, male and female, Silent, Boomer, Gen Xer and Millennial—are one body (1 Cor 12:12-13). In the first-century church, various characteristics distinguished the Jew, Greek, slave or free persons; likewise today generational characteristics may distinguish members of Christ's body from one another, yet all generations are equally in need of Christ.

The church is the place where generational differences are to be transcended rather than reinforced. Gary McIntosh, professor of Christian Ministry and Leadership, recommends a blended model to unite the generations in worship and beyond. He describes the blended church as one that combines two or more philosophies of ministry, which typically results in (1) the use of more than one style of music in a worship service; (2) traditional and new ministries functioning simultaneously; and (3) a transitional atmosphere.[18]

Proponents of using generational theory in church settings encourage ministry leaders to meet the generational challenge head-on and to work to promote generational understanding and positive intergenerational relationships. Doing so exemplifies the biblical imagery of the body of Christ, enhances family relationships, benefits all ages and encourages mature Christian formation. Generational theory itself suggests that this time period in American history, with elder Silent peacemakers and community-building Millennials surrounding two generations (Boomers and Gen Xers) that desire the best for Millennials, is the right time for intentionally intergenerational churches to thrive and to offer a powerful witness of Christ's message and mission to the surrounding society.

---

[18]McIntosh, *One Church, Four Generations*, pp. 210-33.

12

Empirical Research

The record . . . for testing and validating [intergenerational] programs . . . is very limited. . . . I have yet to come across a report which tried to ascertain anything more about results other than whether what was offered was liked or not.

James White, *Intergenerational Religious Education*

AS JAMES WHITE NOTES ABOVE, empirical research that attempts to evaluate the impact of intergenerationality in faith-based settings is limited. Though White wrote this in 1988, research assessing intergenerational practices in Christian settings is still relatively scarce; it *is*, however, becoming more rigorous. A few studies over the last few decades have sought to measure this difficult-to-assess phenomenon. This chapter will describe nine studies that have sought to evaluate how intentionally intergenerational religious and spiritual experiences affect children, adolescents and adults.[1]

"LEARNING FROM CHILDREN"

In the early 1980s, Paul Welter conducted dozens of "Learning from Children" workshops in church settings across the United States. Welter asked the adult participants in these workshops to "write a story . . . about

---

[1]Parts of this chapter were adapted from Allen, "Nurturing Children's Spirituality" (2003) and Allen, "Nurturing Children's Spirituality" (2004). See permissions, page 4.

what they had learned from children."[2] Though Welter gives no information on how many attended the workshops, six hundred adults responded to his request over a period of two years. Welter records their responses, grouping the contributions into general categories, which form the structure for his book.

The six hundred contributors reported they had gained new spiritual ideas from children, particularly regarding faith, hope and love. These adults also said they had drawn fresh insights regarding how to heal, how to continue to grow ("growth as a way of life"), how to become honest again, how to regain trust, how to challenge their fears, how to forgive and how to mourn.

Welter notes that adults often learn to bury their sadness and grief, hiding it from others. In his research Welter gathered dozens of stories in which adults shared how children had helped them acknowledge their sorrow. The following was written by a college student who was reeling from a breakup with her boyfriend: "One of my little cousins (four years old) was with me one day, and wanted to know what was wrong. So I told her what was wrong and she said, 'Why don't you just cry?' I don't know if she had heard it from somebody or came up with it by herself, but it sure helped me." Welter notes in other stories that children's willingness to seek comfort sometimes gives adults permission also to seek comfort when they are experiencing loss and grief.

Welter's research methods in general do not adhere to rigorous academic research standards; however, the participants' poignant accounts do offer support for the idea that adults benefit in important ways when they spend time with children. Welter's conclusion is that churches must make more opportunities for adults to be experientially engaged with children in a wide spectrum of activities.

INTERGENERATIONAL RELIGIOUS EDUCATION

As mentioned earlier, James White's 1988 text, *Intergenerational Religious Education,* has been the most cited book on intergenerationality for the last couple of decades.[3] White's interest in intergenerational religious education

---

[2] Paul Welter, *Learning from Children* (Wheaton, IL: Tyndale House, 1984), p. 13.
[3] James White, *Intergenerational Religious Education* (Birmingham, AL: Religious Education Press, 1988).

grew originally out of his work with age-inclusive programming at a large mainline Christian denomination in the 1970s. White designed and implemented nine summer programs of cross-age worship, learning experiences and other activities. Embedded in the age-inclusive cognitive aspects (e.g., important Old Testament persons, the fruit of the Spirit, language descriptors of Jesus) and worship opportunities were numerous intergenerational activities such as dancing the Havah Nagila (Hebrew folk song), a preschool-to-senior-citizen marching band, children and teens presenting carnations to all men on Father's Day, a garden-planting project, and pairs of older and younger participants (ages four to eighty-one) jointly composing a message of joy and placing it in a helium balloon, then releasing the balloon.

White evaluated the impact of these intergenerational summer programs in a variety of ways, and he shares in his text two types of hard data he collected on the intergenerational programs he directed. One type of data is simply attendance data. White includes a table showing an increase in attendance during each summer's program.[4] Another type of data is content outcome data (e.g., knowledge of Old Testament characters such as Ruth, Elisha, Daniel, etc.). White conducted a pre- and postprogram inventory of content for several of the summer intergenerational religious education programs. All post-tests showed improvement.[5] None of the tests utilized advanced statistical methods; nevertheless, they did demonstrate actual improvement in content knowledge.

White also offers soft data regarding affective, lifestyle and intergenerational outcomes; he reports that the participants stated that they enjoyed the intergenerational experiences using words such as *fantastic, excellent, terrific, creative* and *superb*[6]; these kinds of responses led to a positive global sense of feeling better about the church. Anecdotal data supported the goal of affecting lifestyles of participants. For example, one family held a council after the Zaccheus-in-a-tree day, which had emphasized loving people who are not very likable. This family decided to visit an older neighbor whom the family had previously avoided. In his ten-year evaluation of the whole intergenerational project, White said there was a strong sense among those

---

[4]Ibid., p. 223.
[5]Ibid., pp. 226-30.
[6]Ibid., p. 221.

who attended that "the church had indeed become more of a community with wholeness," and that they were "one across the ages."[7]

"GOD-TALK"

Kathleen O'Connell Chesto wrote her dissertation in response to the results of a National Catholic Education Association survey, which revealed that the existing religious education system was not producing committed Christians whose faith influenced the way they live their lives.[8] The study indicated that an important factor in passing on faith to children is the amount of "God-talk" in the home, and this factor is related to the involvement of parents in the religious instruction of the children.

Thus, the focus of Chesto's dissertation was to develop an alternative set of materials for religious education, based not on the typical school model, but rather on an intergenerational Christian community model. Chesto developed a full year's Family-Centered Intergenerational Religious Education (FIRE) curriculum,[9] which was utilized by eleven intergenerational family groups within a Roman Catholic parish in a Connecticut suburb.

At the conclusion of the first year, Chesto evaluated the FIRE program. Of the seventy-two families involved, sixty-seven returned the evaluation surveys. She also evaluated the FIRE program the next year as it was implemented in other churches in the area. Questions on Chesto's evaluative survey included the following: Why did you become involved in this program? Did you read Scripture before becoming involved in this program? Have those reading habits changed? Do you talk about God more as a family since joining FIRE? Has the program challenged you to become involved in ministry? In social justice issues? What do you see as the specific strengths of this program? What are its weaknesses?[10]

---

[7]Ibid., p. 239.

[8]Kathleen O'Connell Chesto, "FIRE (Family-Centered Intergenerational Religious Education): An Alternative Model of Religious Education" (D.Min. dissertation, Hartford Seminary, 1987, *Dissertation Abstracts International*, 48, 2034).

[9]Chesto's materials, though labeled "intergenerational," focus very tightly on nuclear family issues. Since her dissertation, Chesto has published a four-year curriculum based on her work for use in parishes. The titles reveal this strong nuclear-family focus; for example, *Family Prayer for Family Times: Traditions, Celebrations & Rituals* (1995) and *Raising Kids Who Care: About Themselves, About Their World, About Each Other* (1996).

[10]Kathleen O'Connell Chesto, *Family-Centered Intergenerational Religious Education: Director's Guide* (Kansas City, MO: Sheed & Ward, 1988), pp. 65-76.

The responses of the participants offer key insights into the program. In general the participants were very supportive and positive. Most importantly (for this book) was the success the program had in fostering "God-talk." Chesto reports that the program "enabled 100% of the households participating [in the evaluation] to discuss God and religion more frequently within the family setting."[11] Her later evaluation elicited the same results, prompting Chesto to write: "FIRE's greatest success appears to be in enabling 'God-talk' within families."[12]

The participants offered numerous strengths of the program. Though Chesto does not quantify the responses in any way, she reports several comments; for example, "It helps families to pray together, to share with other people, to be more open, to grow," and "the children become more comfortable expressing their feelings about God as they see their parents doing so."[13]

Interestingly, one weakness mentioned was the strong nuclear family focus, rendering the materials less usable across a broader intergenerational spectrum. Chesto says that as a result of this criticism she rewrote some of the Take Home experiences to be more inclusive. Though Chesto's evaluative methods were not highly analytical, the participants reported very positive responses in general as well as some specific spiritual benefits of the intergenerational materials.

INTERGENERATIONAL CELEBRATORY EVENTS

Peter Marr attempted to answer three questions in his dissertation:

1. Does intergenerational learning provide real education in the true sense of the word?
2. Can an approach to learning which is experiential and age-inclusive be relevant for adults, teens, and children at the same time?
3. What other effects would intergenerational education have for children, teens, and adults who are not used to such an approach?[14]

---

[11]Chesto, FIRE, abstract.
[12]Chesto, Director's Guide, p. 71.
[13]Ibid., p. 75.
[14]Peter R. Marr, "Development of an Intergenerational Curriculum for Christian Education Ministry in the Church" (doctoral dissertation, Eastern Baptist Theological Seminary, 1990, Dissertation Abstracts International, 51, 1182).

Marr's work describes and evaluates four experiential, intergenerational religious events at a mainline Protestant church. The programs centered around the Christian holidays—Thanksgiving (reenactment), Christmas (a marketplace event), Maundy Thursday (Seder and a "living" Lord's Supper) and Easter (*Walk with Us to Emmaus* drama). Marr evaluated the impact of the intergenerational events primarily through opinion surveys completed by all participants.

A survey of nine items was distributed after each intergenerational event. The first item was: "This program has been helpful to me in learning about Thanksgiving [or other event]." Other yes/no items were: "I enjoyed being in an event which included people of all ages"; "This event would have been better if children and teens had met separately"; and "The church should plan to have other events like this one, which include people of all ages."[15] In addition, the open-ended portions of the survey yielded comments that were interesting and helpful.

In general, good things happened in the intergenerational religious events Marr implemented, as the survey results indicate: adults and young people functioned together in roles of leadership; the education committee felt that all ages related well to one another; a high level of rapport and cooperation was reported among those who worked on the events. Marr's discussion offers very positive support for the general benefits of intergenerationality.

NURTURING FAITH IN COMMUNITY

In the 1990s the Search Institute, an organization founded in 1958 to initiate sociological and educational research in order to enable children and youth to become caring and responsible adults,[16] published several studies addressing Christian education and faith development occurring in North American mainline congregations, some of which draw connections between Christian formation and intergenerationality.

One study that surveyed a random sample of 150 congregations used "nurturing faith in community" as one of eight indicators of a mature faith. The research reported that 46 percent of Christian adults and 16

---

[15]Ibid., p. 153.
[16]Retrieved from <www.search-institute.org/about/mission-vision-values>.

percent of youth in this study have a mature understanding of what it means that their faith is nurtured in community.[17] The study reveals that:

- 20 percent of the congregations adequately promote intergenerational relationships
- 39 percent of youth say their churches do a good or excellent job of helping them get to know adults in the church
- "having a greater sense of community or family at church" is one of the top ten interests of both active and inactive adults.[18]

In analyzing the data from this study, Eugene Roehlkepartain reported several positive outcomes related to intergenerational interaction:

- Contact with older adults is more likely to give young people mentors with mature faith. This maturity can have a positive influence on teenagers' growth in faith.
- It builds for young people a sense of community in the congregation. As youth get to know people of all ages, they feel more comfortable in the church and more like a member of the family of God.
- Cross-generational contact can build positive and mutual respect between the generations.
- Intergenerational education is a way to build shared experiences for youth and parents, which can open doors for formal and informal conversations at home.

In the same research study, several approaches to Christian education were presented to the congregations' pastors, teachers and educational coordinators. These church leaders first placed the educational approaches in order by those most commonly utilized. The top four, in order, were: religious instruction, spiritual development, interpretation and faith community. However, the order changed when the participants were asked to order the choices by what they would *prefer* to emphasize: spiritual development, faith community, interpretation and religious instruction.[19] In-

---

[17]Eugene Roehlkepartain, *The Teaching Church: Moving Christian Education to Center Stage* (Nashville: Abingdon, 1993), pp. 36-37.
[18]Ibid., p. 183.
[19]Ibid., p. 92.

tergenerational Christian formation aligns most directly with the top two desired emphases of these church leaders, a possible indicator from the 1990s that these church leaders were interested in less segregated Christian education approaches.

INTERGENERATIONALITY AND CHILDREN'S SPIRITUALITY

In the field research for her dissertation, Holly interviewed forty children from two different types of church settings: 1) intergenerational churches—where children are intentionally included regularly in inter-generational activities, and 2) nonintergenerational churches—where children are almost always segregated from adults.[20]

The children were asked a series of questions during a personal interview, including such questions as: Who do you know who knows God? What is it about that person that makes you think they know God? What does it mean to know God? Do you know God? Holly also asked several feeling questions such as: When you think about God how do you feel? Can you tell me about a time when you felt surprised or amazed about God? Happy about (or with) God? Sad about God? Have you ever felt angry at God?

Toward the end of the interview Holly asked the children: Do you talk to God? What sorts of things do you talk to God about? Do you ever listen to God? In what ways does God talk to us? Have you ever thought God talked to you?

More than any other set of comments on a particular practice or subject, the children's comments concerning prayer shed light on the depth and

---

[20]Holly C. Allen, "A Qualitative Study Exploring the Similarities and Differences of the Spirituality of Children in Intergenerational and Non-Intergenerational Christian Contexts" (doctoral dissertation, Talbot School of Theology, Biola University, La Mirada, CA, 2002).

Altogether, forty nine-, ten- and eleven-year-old children were interviewed from six churches in Tennessee and California in 2001–2002. All of the children attended church regularly with their parents. The children represented a cross-section of evangelical churches—two Vineyard churches (one large, one small), a Baptist church, a Bible church, a renewal Presbyterian church and a progressive Church of Christ. In three churches, the children worshiped with the whole congregation, attended Sunday school and participated in an intergenerational small group. In the other three churches, the children attended Sunday school and participated in children's church on Sundays while their parents and other adults worshiped. The purpose of the dissertation was to explore connections between intergenerational Christian experiences and spiritual development in children.

quality of their spiritual lives. Also, this area yielded the largest differences between the two groups. Children in both settings (intergenerational and nonintergenerational) spoke of prayer frequently, said they knew God and described knowing God similarly. Children in both samples offered a wealth of evidence attesting to their perception of God as warm and caring. However, those from intergenerational settings more frequently referred to their relationship with God (a key construct in the working definition of spirituality in the research[21]).

Boaz,[22] an eleven-year-old participant in Holly's field research, meets regularly in an intergenerational small group and worships on Sunday mornings with his family at the church they attend. Boaz's prayer file[23] is 533 words; he mentioned talking with God in response to ten different questions before the prompted questions on prayer near the end of the interview. Martha, another eleven-year-old participant, attends Sunday school regularly and goes to children's church while her parents worship; Martha has not had the opportunity to participate in intergenerational activities in the church she attends. Martha's prayer file is 140 words; she mentioned praying in response to only one question before the prompted questions regarding prayer. See box 21.1 for the complete prayer files of both Boaz and Martha.

Some of the children from the nonintergenerational churches had fairly extensive prayer files; some did not. Though that was also true of the children in intergenerational settings, the intergenerational children referred to prayer significantly more often[24] (see figure 2) and exhibited relationality in more of their discussions of prayer than did the children from nonintergenerational settings. Analyses of the responses in other areas yielded differences also. For example, in defining the concept of

---

[21]The definition of children's spirituality in the Allen dissertation was "awareness of relationship with God" ("A Qualitative Study," p. 13).

[22]The participants chose pseudonyms from a list of biblical names.

[23]A "prayer file" consists of every comment the participant made concerning prayer, either in response to a question about their prayer life or an "unprompted" remark made in response to some of the other questions.

[24]Holly C. Allen, "Nurturing Children's Spirituality in Intergenerational Settings," *Lutheran Educational Journal* 139 (Winter 2003): 118. Significant difference between the two groups of children: The number of times a participant mentioned prayer (before the questions about prayer were asked) was tallied and statistical comparison was performed. The t-test was significant, $t(38)=2.37$, $p=0.02$.

BOX 12.1

Prayer file of Boaz, 11, of Smyrna:

- *Can you describe a time when you felt really happy about God? "Well, I've been praying for my great grandmother and she's been staying alive and that's pretty cool."*

- *Can you describe a time when you felt sad about God? "Well, sometimes I have prayed for somebody to get well and they don't."*

- *Can you describe a time when you felt angry at God? "Yes. Well, sometimes when I'm done praying for something and I don't get it, like something that I really wanted to happen."*

- *Can you describe a time when you felt an overwhelming love for God? "Well, a few nights ago I was just laying in my bed and I was just like, 'God you are so awesome.'"*

- *What does it mean to know God? "Like my friend Brandon, I can tell he knows God because I've been to church with him before and he just gets really into it." Gets into what? "The worship and prayer."*

- *How do you think someone gets to know God? "Praying, reading the Bible, listening to Him."*

- *What are some things that you do that help you know that you know God? "Well, I just pretty much every night I just talk to him a lot. If there's anything I want to say to him I just say it."*

- *What sort of things do you talk to God about? "I talk to him about Harry Potter and stuff like that, if he thinks I should stop reading it. So far I think he hasn't really told me anything about it, just kind of drawn me away from it just a little bit. . . . There's still only four but I have only read three of them. My dad's reading the first one to see if it's okay."*

- *What else do you pray about? "Well, if I like this girl or something I will pray that I don't go into anything bad or anything like that." What else do you talk to God about? "I pretty much pray about my family, if anybody is sick that they will get better." What else? "Sometimes I pray that I will get to know him better."*

- *Were you ever afraid or alone, and you think God helped you? Would you tell me about that? "Yes. At night when I was going to bed when I was younger I would see the tree shadow and I would be scared. I would like see shadows on the wall and like be really afraid and ask him to protect me. There was one time where I think a month ago when it was really good weather and the lights went out and I was really scared and I asked him for protection."*

- *Has your family ever needed special help and you think God helped? Would you tell me about that? "Well my other grandmother, my mom's mom had cancer and we prayed for her and she got better and now she's having cancer again but we don't think she's going to get better this time." How will you deal with it this time if she doesn't get better? "Well, I'll just ask God to comfort us. I think she's 74."*

Prayer file of Martha, 11, of Philippi:

- *Do you think you know God? "Yes." (strong answer) Tell me about that. "I know that I know God because my family grew up in a Christian home. Go to church. I asked him into my life. When I feel bad or something I sit in my room and talk to him."*

- *What sort of things do you talk to God about? "When my grandpa died—about that. When my grandma died; when my friend had a problem. They had to move out of their house, their apartment, they didn't have anywhere to go. They lived with some people awhile, but they didn't know where to go. But now she's with her aunt." How did you know her? "She used to come here."*

- *What else do you pray about? "About the homeless; help me be safe; help when I'm sick."*

knowing God, a larger number of intergenerational children gave relational descriptions of that concept than did nonintergenerational children.

In general, though children from both settings gave profound and eloquent testimony regarding their relationships with God, the intergenerational children in this study were more aware of their relationship with

	Intergenerational			Nonintergenerational	
Participant	**# times prayer mentioned**		**Participant**	**# times prayer mentioned**	
#14 Elijah	4		#7 Barnabas	2	
#32 Esther	3		#30 Bartholomew	5	
#27 Eve	5		#13 Cornelius	4	
#16 Caleb	5		#26 Dorcas	4	
#25 Joseph	2		#1 Joanna	6	
#34 Leah	5		#21 Junia	0	
#2 Levi	4		#35 Mark	3	
#29 Nathaniel	3		#17 Paul	3	
#11 Noah	1		#38 Priscilla	5	
#20 Rebeccah	6		#8 James	3	
#6 Sara	6		#22 Luke	1	
#15 Abigail	6		#4 Lydia	3	
#37 Adam	2		#40 Martha	1	
#3 Benjamin	6		#31 Mary	1	
#28 Boaz	6		#39 Philip	2	
#33 Hannah	7		#18 Stephen	4	
#10 Micah	2		#36 Tabitha	5	
#19 Miriam	3		#9 Thomas	4	
#24 Seth	3		#12 Julia	2	
#5 Zipporah	7		#23 Phoebe	2	

Figure 2.

God, that is, a larger number of them spoke more frequently and more reciprocally of that relationship.

STORYTELLING AND INTERGENERATIONALITY

A small study of intergenerational storytelling was conducted by John Williams, a minister in Maryland, for his Doctor of Ministry thesis. Williams' purpose in conducting his study was to provide opportunities for the teens and the seniors of his congregation to get to know one another, and in so doing, to reduce tension, create new bonds and foster cooperative intergenerational ministries.[25] The seniors and teens met together regularly over a

---

[25]John T. Williams, "If You Build It, They Will Come: Using Storytelling as an Intergenerational

year, with a senior telling a personal story and a teen responding at each meeting, followed by a teen telling a personal story and a senior responding with questions; then the teens joined the seniors in a ministry activity, or the seniors joined the teens in a chosen ministry opportunity.[26] Williams reported that the intergenerational storytelling and ministry activities yielded positive responses from all participants, older and younger; he said that the "bond which was formed in the first session lasted to the last."[27] One older participant said, "We learned that youth and adults are not too far apart. We can share and learn from each other."[28] A teen reported, "I thought it was very interesting to hear about an older person's life, and try to think about what I can learn from it."[29] Williams also reported that both older and younger participants indicated a desire to continue the relationship.[30]

BENEFITS OF INTERGENERATIONALITY FOR CONGREGATIONS

Most intergenerational research pursues evidence for the benefits of intergenerational interaction within specific types of programs, curricula and ministry models. Christine took another route for her dissertation research.[31] In order to understand key processes in implementing intergenerational ministry into churches, Christine observed intergenerational worship and activities and interviewed fifteen persons at four congregations committed to an intergenerational philosophy of ministry. Interview questions focused on describing the term *intergenerational*, describing how the interviewees and the congregation became interested in an intergenerational philosophy of ministry, what steps were taken to implement intergenerationality, and benefits, obstacles and dreams for the future. Each congregation's story of discovering and implementing intergenerational ministry is summarized throughout this text (see box 12.2 for one congregation's story).

Bridge" (D.Min. thesis, Wesley Theological Seminary, Washington, DC, 2006).
[26]<http://johntwilliams.org/Recap_Of_Events_In_Pictures.html>.
[27]<http://johntwilliams.org/Research_of_IM.html>.
[28]<http://johntwilliams.org/Endorsements.html>.
[29]Ibid.
[30]<http://johntwilliams.org/Research_of_IM.html>.
[31]Ross, "A Qualitative Study Exploring Churches."

BOX 12.2

Research Congregation: Midwestern Church

This small, traditional, century-old Midwestern church was led into inter-generational ministry in the mid-1980s when its new pastor and his wife realized that they wanted to adapt the family ministry model of a previous congregation. Having a small congregation of mainly elderly members, the number of young families was too small to start a traditional family ministry program, and the pastor wanted a form of ministry that would reach and bring together all ages of the family of God. Knowing the need to make changes slowly, the pastor began by implementing children's songs and hand motions with Psalm readings surrounding the children's messages. He also encouraged children to join adults as greeters and ushers, and he encouraged families to join the older women of the church in serving meals at funerals and supporting the needs of local homeless shelters.

Seven years later, the volunteer Sunday superintendent attended a con-ference where she heard about intergenerational Christian education ac-tivities involving all ages together in Sunday school, Vacation Bible School and evening fellowship activities. She realized that what she learned aligned with the pastor's vision; thus she, the pastor and the pastor's wife began working together to unify the generations within the congregation. They named this intergenerational philosophy "United Intergenerational Min-istry," believing this phrase would enable people to understand that inter-generational means everyone together—not just providing programs for people of each age group, but more importantly, providing opportunities for the various age groups to serve, learn, play and minister together. The mission statement of United Intergenerational Ministry was to "re-unite and strengthen the generations." This ministry has become almost full-time work for the pastor's wife, who writes the curriculum used for the church's intergenerational Sunday school, VBS, retreats, special events (Reformation, Advent, Lent evening activities) and worship.[a]

[a]Ibid.

Each of the four churches had leaders who mentioned the following three reasons they see intergenerationality as being a viable philosophy of ministry: the generations have much to offer one another; it is biblical; and it provides *family* for every person in the faith community. Other benefits described by at least two congregational leaders were: generations were no longer afraid of one another; adult minds were opened to new ideas; youth had a more positive perception of older adults; there were fewer discipline problems within activities; parents became more involved in congregational life; children and youth mature in faith as they see how to be faithful throughout life; a sense of unity suffused the churches rather than an "us/them" mentality; and intergenerationality provided faith support for all ages.

It is a considerable undertaking to alter the mindset of people who live in an age-segregated culture and are often most comfortable having age-separated church activities; however, this research indicates that such a task is possible and provides reasons why such an undertaking is worthwhile.

INTERGENERATIONAL FAITH FORMATION

The most comprehensive evaluation of intergenerationality to date was conducted from 2005 to 2007 by Mariette Martineau, Joan Weber and Leif Kehrwald, who gathered data from over five hundred Catholic parishes across North America, utilizing both qualitative and quantitative research methods.[32] All of these parishes had been using *Generations of Faith*, an intentionally intergenerational faith formation curriculum.[33]

Generations of Faith is an event-centered approach (as was Marr's material); the intergenerational events are organized around the church calendar, the sacraments, justice themes, prayer and spirituality, the Apostles' Creed, or morality. For example, one event is the Advent reconciliation service, with the learning focus on the sacrament of reconciliation; another event is the International Marriage Day, with the learning focus on the sacrament of marriage.

---

[32]Mariette Martineau, Joan Weber and Lief Kehrwald, *Intergenerational Faith Formation: All Ages Learning Together* (New London, CT: Twenty-Third Publications, 2008).

[33]John Roberto with Mariette Martineau, *Generations of Faith Resource Manual: Lifelong Faith Formation for the Whole Parish Community* (New London, CT: Twenty-Third Publications, 2005).

Martineau, Weber and Kehrwald's evaluation methods attempted to address the following general questions:

- Did participants enjoy the experience?
- Did participants change attitudes, improve knowledge or increase skill?
- Are participants transferring what they are learning into their real lives?
- How did the intergenerational experiences impact individual spiritual commitment and congregational engagement?[34]

Key findings that emerged from the data include: (1) Parishioners of all ages are developing a deeper understanding of the foundational themes of their faith—church year, sacraments, morality, prayer, justice—and learning how to live their faith in the parish, at home and in the world; and (2) Parishioners are building relationships with people across all ages, and this process is benefiting the whole parish community.[35]

Leaders from the parishes report that the benefits of this intergenerational, event-centered, lifelong faith formation approach include "providing a setting for each generation to share and learn from other generations (their faith, stories, wisdom, experience, and knowledge)"; "providing

---

[34]Martineau, Weber and Kehrwald, *Intergenerational Faith Formation*, pp. 88-89. The qualitative research for this study collected data from eighty-three parishes in nine dioceses. Each parish in the study had been using the *Generations of Faith (GOF)* intergenerational curriculum for at least one year. In each of the nine dioceses, two focus group interviews were conducted as well as one or two in-depth personal interviews. The questions for the focus groups included:

• When you chose to participate in the GOF project, what were your hopes for faith formation in your community?
• Describe faith formation in your community now:
What has changed?
What has remained consistent?
What do you think still needs to change?
• How did the GOF project help your community in developing your faith formation?

The key findings from the qualitative analysis were reframed into a quantitative survey for the purpose of canvassing a larger number of participants to "express their level of agreement or disagreement with the findings" (p. 146). Participants from 430 parishes responded to the survey, marking their level of agreement on a Likert scale from 1 to 5 on such items as "our parish is reaching new audiences, such as new adults and whole families, through intergenerational learning"; "families benefit from intergenerational learning though opportunities to pray, learn and be together"; "families are growing in the ways that they share faith"; "intergenerational learning strengthens the parish community through relationship building and participation in parish life" (appendix 2).

[35]Martineau, Weber, and Kehrwald, *Intergenerational Faith Formation*, pp. 4-5.

adult role models for children and youth"; and "promoting understanding of shared values and a common faith, as well as respect for individuals in all stages and ages of life."[36]

In the following scenarios, Martineau, Weber and Kehrwald illustrate how intergenerational faith formation offers opportunities for the whole community to learn and benefit from each other's experiences of God: "Hearing a woman with breast cancer describe the power of prayer provides a profound awareness of God's loving care in our lives. Listening to a teen describe what solidarity with the poor and vulnerable means to him, after experiencing the faith of the poor in a soup kitchen, can be transformative for all age groups. And watching the eighty-year-old who attends daily liturgy share what Eucharist means in her life can lead to a more meaningful experience of liturgy for those who hear her story."[37]

SUMMARY OF INTERGENERATIONALITY RESEARCH

Evaluative research on intergenerationality is still quite limited, though the last decade in particular has produced several dissertation studies as well as the strong Intergenerational Faith Formation initiative (Martineau et al.). The studies described in this chapter suggest that intergenerational experiences in faith-based settings nurture spiritual growth and development in several ways.

General findings. All of the studies indicate that people enjoy age-inclusive settings—they like interrelating with each other; that is, most participants offer positive global remarks. Though enjoying intergenerational activities is not necessarily a spiritual benefit, it must be acknowledged that if participants do not enjoy the activities, they will be less likely to receive the spiritual benefits that can ensue.

For children. Children who participated regularly in intergenerational small groups mentioned prayer more frequently and more relationally than did children who were not involved in intergenerational settings (Allen). Families with children reported that they talked about God and read the Bible more after participating in Chesto's FIRE program. Intentional cross-generational activities created access to role models for

---

[36]Ibid., p. 5.
[37]Ibid., p. 12.

children and youth (Intergenerational Faith Formation initiative) and opportunities for young people to find mentors with mature faith (Search Institute). And lastly, children who participated in intergenerational Christian educational experiences actually learned content (White; Marr; Martineau et al.).

For adults. Since some who object to intergenerational learning opportunities do so on the basis that the material would be too elementary for adults to gain new content, it is significant that adults (as well as children) who participated in intergenerational Christian educational experiences actually learned content (Marr; Martineau et al.). In Welter's study, adults reported that they had gleaned spiritual insights from children in the areas of trust, forgiveness, honesty, love and fear.

For congregations. White reported that attendance increased across summer-long intergenerational programs. The leaders of intentionally intergenerational congregations reported a stronger sense of unity (Ross), and both Ross and Williams noted that leaders perceived the generations were no longer afraid of one another; intergenerational events seem "to draw the people of a church closer together." [38] This global sense of unity and wholeness is reflective of Jesus' desire for his followers: "I do not ask for these only, but also for those who will believe in me through their word, that they may all be one, just as you, Father, are in me, and I in you, that they also may be in us, so that the world may believe that you have sent me" (Jn 17:20-21 esv).

Other research exists that supports in profound yet indirect ways the benefits of cross-generational experiences for old and young. Sociological research, reported in chapter nine—especially Christian Smith's work[39]—champions the importance of intergenerational community as a crucial spiritual influence. The gerontological research described in chapter ten, though not focused on faith communities per se, offers substantial and extensive evidence for the benefits of intergenerationality from which faith communities can nevertheless draw.

---

[38]Marr, *Development of an Intergenerational Curriculum*, p. 201.

[39]Christian Smith with Melinda Denton, *Soul Searching: The Religious and Spiritual Lives of American Teenagers* (Oxford: Oxford University Press, 2005); Christian Smith with Patricia Snell, *Souls in Transition: The Religious and Spiritual Lives of Emerging Adults* (Oxford: Oxford University Press, 2009).

There is still a need for further rigorous quantitative and qualitative research that explores intergenerational principles, practices and benefits in faith communities.[40] In the meantime, the studies examined in this chapter offer substantial support for the benefits of intergenerationality for spiritual formation.

---

[40]Several obstacles tend to discourage research in this arena. For example, definitional issues plague this type of research. If one is seeking to empirically study the spiritual impact of intergeneration-ality, one must construct an operational definition of spirituality/spiritual development/spiritual formation, and then locate or create an instrument that could validly and reliably measure that elusive quality. Longitudinal, comparative research—that is, data collected over a period of years comparing, for example, Christian spiritual formation in churches that do not offer intentional intergenerational experiences with churches that do—would be especially helpful. However, find-ing "matching" or similar churches across other variables is difficult, as is locating willing congre-gations, and obtaining funding for such research. Furthermore, influences on spiritual develop-ment are exceedingly complex; isolating intergenerationality as a key factor would be problematic. The obstacles that impede the pursuit of rigorous research regarding the impact of intergenera-tionality are indeed formidable. Nevertheless, further research is needed, and the topic should provide the next generation of doctoral students an exciting challenge.

Part Four

■ ■ ■

INTERGENERATIONAL CHRISTIAN FORMATION PRACTICES

13

CREATING A CULTURE
OF INTERGENERATIONALITY

"Intergenerational" is not something churches do—it is something they become.

Research participant, in Brenda Snailum, "Implementing Intergenerational Youth
Ministry Within Existing Evangelical Church Congregations"

*You may lose people who can't make the adjustment. But for everyone who
leaves you get three more. Why? Because most people understand the innate
wisdom of the generations relating to each other.*

Christine Ross, "A Qualitative Study Exploring Churches
Committed to Intergenerational Ministry"

MATTHEW, A YOUTH MINISTER with a church in the Northwest, attended a conference for youth ministers a couple of years ago where the idea of intergenerational faith community was promoted and described in glowing terms. Matthew came back full of new ideas about how to implement these new teachings. He shared some of the key insights from the conference at the next all-staff ministry meeting; the lead pastor, associate minister and the praise team leader, as well as several other staff members, were very encouraging and urged him to lead the youth toward a more integrated approach. First he brainstormed with his youth group about ways to serve the elderly, and they planned a dinner in which the youth would serve the oldest members. They invited the upper elementary children into one of their evening devotionals, and they asked their parents to share an evening of youth-led praise and worship.

Though each event went well, the teens began to complain that the youth group seemed to exist for other people—not for *them*. Some parents began to express the guilt they felt when they couldn't come to the youth event. The children's minister was frustrated with the absence of some of her key helpers on the evening they went to the youth meeting. The senior pastor and others on the ministry staff continued to encourage Matthew is his attempts at cross-age ministry. However, after a couple more events, Matthew felt generally discouraged and decided that intergenerationality was a great concept that worked in some places but not in the Northwest.[1]

Thus far, this book has offered biblical, theological, sociological, empirical, developmental and anecdotal support for the idea that age-integrated faith communities are places of spiritual blessing to all concerned, and the next several chapters will describe dozens of activities, events and ideas for integrating the generations. However, Zahn warns that though *introducing* people to intergenerational ministry through specific events is relatively easy, "building a permanent culture of intergenerational cooperation . . . is not."[2] Matthew found this insight to be profoundly true.

BARRIERS TO SUCCESSFULLY IMPLEMENTING INTERGENERATIONAL MINISTRY

Brenda Snailum recently asked four intergenerational experts for their suggestions for churches desiring to become more age-integrated faith communities.[3] Snailum's team of experts agreed that "transitioning from a predominantly age-stratified ministry mindset to an intergenerational culture requires a paradigmatic shift in philosophy and core values, and efforts to create intergenerational community need to be an integral part of the whole church's vision, mission, and purpose."[4] That is, intergenerationality is not a new *model* of ministry, but rather a new *mindset*. Con-

---

[1]"Matthew" is a pseudonym; certain details as well as his name have been changed to protect his anonymity.
[2]Drew Zahn, "Connecting the Generations: How Churches Are Building and Sustaining Age-Integrated, Multi-Generational Ministry," *Leadership* 23 (Spring 2002): 40.
[3]Brenda Snailum, "Implementing Intergenerational Youth Ministry Within Existing Evangelical Church Congregations: What Have We Learned?" *Christian Education Journal* (series 3) 9, no. 1 (Spring 2012): 165-81.
[4]Ibid., p. 168.

versely, Snailum's intergenerational specialists warned that the chief challenge to successfully transitioning to a more age-integrated outlook is that intergenerationality may be seen simply as a new method, rather than a mindset or core value. Some of the ministry leaders in Christine's 2006 research with four intentionally intergenerational congregations noted this same challenge.[5] In fact, the participants in Christine's study and the intergenerational ministry experts in Brenda Snailum's study agreed on several common barriers, challenges or hindrances to creating an intergenerational faith community:

- failure to transition to an intergenerational *paradigm*
- lack of understanding of the basis and need for intergenerationality
- self-centeredness (a focus of some age cohorts on their own needs and desires)
- lack of available resources to assist ministry leaders
- lack of perseverance (leaders must maintain the patience needed to fully transition the congregation to a new ministry mindset)[6]

The participants in both studies warned that movement toward intergenerationality is not easy; as the youth minister, Matthew, in this chapter's opening vignette experienced, change is hard and there will be complaints. Intergenerational experiences do not always meet the immediate felt needs of everyone present: the children *may not wish* to participate in an idea-oriented discussion; seniors *may not wish* to have young children disrupting a special event; the youth group *may not wish* their parents to be among them; the parents *may not wish* to be with their teens; and those whose offspring have recently flown the nest *may not wish* to reenter the world of children and chaos. The ministry leaders themselves can become discouraged reframing and tweaking already-existing community events and activities to embrace intergenerationality. Leading people out of their comfort zones may create initial uneasiness; moving into new forms of

---

[5]Christine M. Ross, "A Qualitative Study Exploring Churches Committed to Intergenerational Ministry" (doctoral dissertation, Saint Louis University, St. Louis, MO, 2006).

[6]Snailum, "Implementing Intergenerational Youth Ministry"; Ross, "A Qualitative Study Exploring Churches"; Christine M. Ross, "Four Congregations That Practice Intergenerationality," *Christian Education Journal* (series 3) 9, no. 1 (Spring 2012): 135-47.

ministry requires more energy and commitment than remaining on the well-known path.

So, what do those who have successfully led intergenerational ministries recommend? The rest of this chapter offers conceptual as well as concrete tried-and-true suggestions for ministry leaders who desire to cultivate a more intergenerational perspective.

IMPLEMENTING INTERGENERATIONALITY: LEADERSHIP LEVEL

Deep change within any entity—organization, family, government, university or church—requires a holistic reorientation; that is, mind, spirit and body must be involved. This head-heart-hands approach means that to move forward, persons must be persuaded in their minds that this new place is right or best, they must be convicted in their hearts that this is good, and they must have opportunity to experience the new place authentically.

Faith communities do not become intergenerational in their outlook and practice simply by adding an occasional intergenerational activity. A paradigm shift is required, and paradigm shifts must be guided by leaders who understand the issues and communicate well. All of Snailum's panelists agreed that "successfully transitioning to an intergenerational paradigm lives (or dies) with the leadership."[7]

As the research participants in Christine's research confirmed, typically only one or two ministry leaders are initially energized and excited about fostering an intergenerational culture.[8] The initial leader(s) becomes the catalyst for establishing intergenerationality as a congregational core value. However, for the faith community as a whole to move forward with this vision, the entire ministry team, particularly the senior pastor, will need to support the initial leader's vision and ultimately embrace it. As illustrated in Matthew's story, one champion cannot carry this vision alone.

The leader who has become excited about intergenerational faith formation must slowly, gently and persuasively share his or her own journey of discovering intergenerationality with other ministry leaders. At this point,

---

[7]Snailum, "Implementing Intergenerational Youth Ministry," p. 169.
[8]Ross, "A Qualitative Study Exploring Churches."

the initial leader's goal is to convince a few other ministry leaders to explore together the biblical foundations and spiritual benefits of intergenerationality for their community of faith. The leader may use the head-heart-hand approach outlined below to draw colleagues into the vision; then together this group may employ the same process to draw other ministry leaders into this paradigm, and eventually the whole community of faith.

Informational/cognitive (head). Healthy intergenerational relationships and activities will occur only if a ministry leader, and his or her teammates, are *convinced* that intergenerationality is a viable strategy for the spiritual growth and faith formation of all members of Christ's body and a positive and inviting witness to the unchurched. As leaders begin to discern a need for more cross-generational opportunities, they will need to acquire a deeper, more informed understanding of intergenerationality. The following recommendations will aid in acquiring that necessary knowledge.

Over a period of a few months, in a variety of settings, the leadership team should:

- Explore the biblical examples of Jewish community life and early house churches and the relational dynamics of such settings, as well as other biblical and doctrinal foundations for enhancing intergenerational relationships (see especially chapters five and eight of this text).

- Discuss the factors that have led faith communities to adopt age-segregated approaches to worship, service, learning, fellowship and outreach (e.g., developmental concerns, the influence of individualism, the expectation of societal norms; see chapter two in this text). As the rationale for dividing the generations is considered, the unique strengths of both age segregation and intergenerationality begin to emerge.

- Share the theoretical support for learning and growing authentically in communities of practice (see chapters six and seven in this text).

Read and discuss together books that have benefited ministry leaders involved in intergenerationality.[9]

---

[9]The reading resources most often mentioned by ministry leaders in Ross's research were William Strauss and Neil Howe, *Generations: The History of America's Future, 1584 to 2069* (New York: Quill, William Morrow, 1991); Ben Freudenburg and Rick Lawrence, *The Family Friendly Church*

Some of the leaders may in fact want to read this entire text in order to understand more fully; also the Vanderwell text is a good supplement.[10]

Spiritual/affective (heart). The heart is the key. New knowledge and authentic experience by themselves will not initiate radical change; only when the heart is captured will real change be possible. This step in the process focuses the heart of those in leadership on the love they feel toward those in their spiritual care and helps them see how intergenerationality can offer their beloved brothers and sisters new and unique ways to be formed like Christ. Basic guidelines for engaging the heart include the following:

- First, lead a big-picture discussion among the leadership that revisits the fundamental goals or purposes of Christian spiritual formation for this body of believers. Ask: Why does this faith community exist? What is the hope for each person who is part of this community—for the children, the teenagers, the young adults, the middle adults and the oldest adults?

- Follow this discussion with other questions: How are we meeting those goals? How is our worship together meeting those goals? Our Sunday school (or other learning venues)? Our youth group? Our small groups? Our outreach? Our ministry to the poor or marginalized?

- Then, asking participants to draw on recently acquired information from biblical, theological, empirical, sociological and theoretical fields, ask: How might a more intergenerational approach enhance how we reach the goals just mentioned? To help prime the pump, share stories from this book, from personal experience or from other sources that illustrate keenly how intergenerational worship and ministry can foster spiritual growth and development.

- Last, lead a discussion contrasting and comparing the spiritual needs of children, teens and adults. Ultimately this comparison/contrast process will illuminate the surprising similarities of the spiritual needs among

---

(Loveland, CO: Group, 1998); Merton P. Strommen and Richard A. Hardel, *Passing on the Faith: A Radical New Model for Youth and Family Ministry* (Winona, MN: St. Mary's Press, 2000). Appendix B offers a number of other helpful intergenerational resources.

[10]Howard Vanderwell, ed., *The Church of All Ages: Generations Worshiping Together* (Herndon, VA: Alban Institute, 2008).

BOX 13.1

"We Are All Beggars"

Ministry leaders, and particularly the catalyst leader, must nurture their own spirits. Reformation leader Martin Luther had a single well-worn note in his pocket when he died. It read: "Wir sind alle bettler" ("We are all beggars"). Luther spoke of how we come to worship with an empty sack and throughout the service God drops grace, mercy and forgiveness into our sack.[a] We hear the very Word of God read and grace is dropped in; we hear of Christ's forgiveness and forgiveness is added. When we leave worship, we go out into the world with a full bag. Pastor Matthew Harrison explains what we do with the full bag as follows: "We leave [the worship service] with the sack over our shoulders and quickly find ourselves in need of what the Lord has given us. Our spouse sins against us, and we sin against our spouse. What do we do? We open our sack: 'Here, I have a sack full of grace, mercy, and forgiveness. Take some. In the name of Jesus take it.' . . . We encounter a person in need and cannot turn away, 'Friend, I have received mercy from the Lord. Please receive the Lord's mercy and love from me.'"[b]

Allowing God to give His gifts to us and nurture us in Christ Jesus through reading Scripture and worshiping together with the body of Christ is essential for any church worker; otherwise they have nothing of God's to share with others. How much more necessary when one needs extra ability to teach something new in a gentle and patient manner. The steadfastness and patience of our Lord Himself will enable us to remain steadfast in our newfound passion for five, seven, nine years—however long it takes—to help others embrace the understanding that intergenerationality inherently shows us how to live together as God's children.

---

[a]Martin Luther, *Dr. Marin Luthers Sammtliche Schriften*, ed. Johann Georg Walch, 2nd ed. (St. Louis: Concordia, 1881-1910), 19:802, cited in C. F. W. Walther, *The Proper Distinction Between Law and Gospel* (St. Louis: Concordia, 1929), p. 19.
[b]Matthew C. Harrison, *Christ Have Mercy: How to Put Your Faith Into Action*, (St. Louis: Concordia, 2008), pp. 22-23.

all age groups. This discussion alone can be a profound *aha* moment for those considering intergenerationality.

As these discussions are held, ask God's blessings upon the process, that hearts will be open to bringing the generations together. The stories and these discussions will gradually open hearts to gaps in current practices and to strengths of intergenerational approaches.

Experiential/behavioral (hand). The last aspect of the head-heart-hands reorienting process is the experiential part; new *experiences* can light the fire for change. An excellent experiential introduction to intergenerationality would be to plan a spiritual retreat for the ministry staff, including all family members—babies, toddlers, elementary children, teens, emerging adult children (if they are in the area) and spouses, along with all senior staff and the board or elders of the church. This one event should be planned to have a powerful positive impact on all the participants, so that each catches a deep sense of the essence of intergenerationality. The retreat should incorporate stories from the old and young, worship including all ages, cross-age games, service activities, and short teaching times that illustrate the biblical practice of including all the generations, along with role-play or drama to demonstrate some of these principles.[11] The Wagon Train episode and discussion or the family rewriting of Psalm 136 found in Appendix A ("Forty Intergenerational Ideas") may also be used here. When small groups are used in this setting, ensure that groups are cross-generational (don't expect attendees to form themselves into such groups); preplan the formation, and frequently remind participants of the goals of the retreat.

IMPLEMENTING INTERGENERATIONALITY: CONGREGATIONAL LEVEL

As leaders begin to grasp the essence and the significance of cultivating a more age-integrated community, they may wish to implement sweeping

---

[11]Specific biblical passages offered throughout this text but especially in chapters five and nine could be utilized here. For example, read Deut 6:6-9 and act out (intergenerationally, of course) the indicated behaviors literally: "Talk about [the commandments] when you *sit at home* and when you *walk along the road*, when you *lie down* and when you *get up. Tie them* as symbols *on your hands* and *bind them on your foreheads. Write them on the doorframes of your houses* and *on your gates.*"

changes immediately. However, it is crucial that they winningly invite everyone else to join the journey they have been traveling. For the believing community as a whole to adopt an intergenerational outlook, all will need to join the leaders on their head-heart-hands journey into a commitment to bringing the generations together. Thus, the process that was followed in drawing the leaders into a more intergenerational paradigm should be implemented with the whole congregation—children through seniors.

As mentioned earlier, Snailum's panel of experts offered a variety of recommendations for churches that wish to move toward a more age-integrated approach to Christian formation. Snailum groups their recommendations into seven categories:

- Establish intergenerational community as a core value.
- Keep intergenerational values in balance with age-specific ministry.
- Leadership must be fully vested.
- Begin where you are.
- Educate the congregation.
- Be intentional and strategic.
- Include all generations and ministry venues.[12]

Allan Harkness, a Christian educator and specialist in intergenerational issues, offers guidelines for facilitating movement toward intergenerational activities in a Christian community that sound similar to the recommendation from Snailum's team of experts: (1) raise the subject with interested people and decision makers; (2) raise the level of congregational intergenerational consciousness; (3) find entry points in your own faith community; (4) recognize factors that enhance intergenerational involvement, such as the use of variety, thematic programs and the five senses; (5) review prayerfully.[13]

One recommendation from Snailum's panel of experts—valuing *age-specific* ministry as well as intergenerationality—calls for further comment.

---

[12]Snailum, "Implementing Intergenerational Youth Ministry," p. 168.
[13]Allan G. Harkness, "Intergenerational Education for an Intergenerational Church?" *Religious Education* 93 (1998): 443-44.

As Harkness[14] notes, these two values are not opposed; that is, they are not mutually exclusive. Some ministry venues indeed flourish better in segregated settings—by age, gender or need; for example, learning the books of the Bible, group sleepovers, discussions regarding pornography, and issues concerning the apocryphal books certainly call for age-appropriate settings. Churches that embrace an intergenerational culture also deeply value the unique and important place of age-graded learning settings, the appropriate bonding fostered in youth groups, and wonderful blessings of fellowship with those in shared seasons of life. "Everyone needs to be part of a 'web' or network of relationships that includes peers as well as members of other generations."[15] It is a *both/and* proposition, not *either/or.*

Another recommendation that needs further unpacking is the intergenerational experts' suggestion that faith communities should begin where they are.[16] In other words, intergenerationality is not a new program that must be added on to everything else the church is doing; rather, it is a way of being that can be woven into the fabric of already successful activities and ministries. One of Snailum's participants said: "Church communities that have been successful have often started with what they are already doing well in one of the ministries of the church. Then [they] ask the question, 'Since this is already good (or even great), what would it take to move to the next level and use this to become [more] intergenerational?'"[17] In addition, recognizing that some of the ministries of the church are already cross-generational (at least occasionally) can encourage the process, as people realize that intergenerationality is not a foreign concept, but one that they have experienced.

Christine's research participants suggested many of the same ideas that Snailum's experts offered.[18] In addition to the previously mentioned recommendations, Christine's participants also suggested that congregations transitioning to more intergenerational practices should consider facility

---

[14]Allan G. Harkness, "Intergenerational and Homogeneous-Age Education: Mutually Exclusive Strategies for Faith Communities?"*Religious Education* 95 (2000): 51-63.
[15]Snailum, "Implementing Intergenerational Youth Ministry," p. 169.
[16]Ibid., p. 170.
[17]Ibid.
[18]Ross, "A Qualitative Study Exploring Churches"; Ross, "Four Congregations."

needs, evaluate new interage ministries and activities, and publicize and highlight successes.[19]

Church facilities must enhance intergenerational relationships by providing spaces large enough and/or suitable for people of all ages to meet together. Although service, mission and fellowship events can occur outside of the church building, once relationships are built there must be a place where all the generations may join for fellowship.

As soon as the first intergenerational activity occurs, evaluation needs to begin. The ministry team can ask participants for feedback and discuss among themselves how well the activity met the goal of bringing the generations together in a positive manner that promotes faith maturity as well as serves the church mission.

Leaders must discern the best means for publicizing successes. When nonparticipants read a generational peer's comment describing the positives of an intergenerational mission trip, they are more likely to join a future event. When parents whose first response to being asked to attend confirmation with their child is "That's the church's job" hear other parents discussing the benefits of studying faith formation with their child and building relationships with both their child's and their own peers, these parents may begin to look forward to the opportunity. The authors of *Youth Ministry Management Tools* state that an activity must be publicized seven to nine times through various venues.[20] Continuous and encouraging publicity will be needed for people to become positive about a new philosophy of ministry.

The four ministry experts cited in this chapter are convinced of the spiritual benefits of cross-age ministry. According to one expert, the end goal is not to "just have generations rub shoulders . . . but the goal is maturity in Christ while fulfilling the 'one another' commands together."[21] The fifteen ministry leaders in intentionally intergenerational faith communities in Christine's research are similarly convinced and are excited about the benefits they have seen in their congregations. They have seen

---

[19]Ibid.

[20]Ginny Olson, Diane Elliot and Mike Work, *Youth Ministry Management Tools* (Grand Rapids: Youth Specialties, Zondervan, 2001).

[21]Snailum, "Implementing Intergenerational Youth Ministry," p. 172.

children and youth involved in church-wide activities; families ministering together and being ministered to; singles and older adults building
healthy relationships with various church members; and the biblical
themes of the body of Christ and family of God being lived out on a daily
basis. Yet all of these intergenerational leaders recognize the challenges
inherent in embracing such a countercultural ministry paradigm.

One challenge noted by almost all who recommend intergenerational
approaches is the lack of available resources to assist ministry leaders. The
remaining chapters of this book seek to address that paucity. These
chapters describe and explore dozens of ways to bring the generations together for service, for worship, for missions, for education, for story
sharing. Though it is true that "'intergenerational' is not something
churches *do*—it is something they become,"[22] *becoming* intergenerational
nevertheless entails actually bringing the generations together for cross-
age activities, events and experiences. The next seven chapters paint a
plethora of intergenerational scenes.

---

[22]Quote from research participant in Snailum's research reported in, "Implementing Intergenerational Youth Ministry," p. 168.

14

INTERGENERATIONAL WORSHIP

Worship is the single most important activity that brings one generation of saints into contact with another in the life of a congregation.

James Frazier, in *Across the Generations: Incorporating All Ages in Ministry*

Young men and women,
 old men and children.
Let them praise the name of the LORD,
 for his name alone is exalted;
 his splendor is above the earth and the heavens.

Psalm 148:12-13

FOR THIS CHAPTER, INTERGENERATIONAL WORSHIP will refer to the regular (usually weekly) gathering when the body of Christ as a community meets together to praise and honor God, to hear from God's Word, and to encourage one another. Though a good case can be made that *worship* may entail one's whole life—that is, that everything a believer does is lived before God as an act of worship (Rom 12:1)—this chapter will focus rather on faith communities as they gather to worship together on (usually) Sunday mornings. In America this hour or two has become a very age-segregated aspect of life in Christ.

The chapter will discuss in particular integrating children and adults in the worship gathering, but it will also address the larger issue of musical worship styles that has contributed substantially to generationally divided worship gatherings. The chapter will offer some general guidelines for moving toward intergenerationality in worship as well as some specific ideas for inviting worshipers of all ages to actively participate together in the weekly worship gathering—a formative and empowering facet of Christian life.

Research Congregation: Canadian Church[a]

In 1987 a pastor with a heart for intergenerational faith formation arrived at a small urban Canadian church with predominantly elderly members. Prior to moving to the new parish, the pastor had been considering how a congregation can best model the biblical metaphors of the church as the body of Christ and the community of saints. Upon accepting the call, he realized that he would be moving his children from their biological grandparents. These combined thoughts persuaded him to implement an intergenerational philosophy of ministry at the Canadian church. He believed that intergenerationality would best enable Christian community as well as provide surrogate grandparents for his children. Thus, he slowly began incorporating intergenerational practices into worship and education by adding children's messages in the worship service, by starting a family confirmation program in which at least one parent attended classes with their middle-school youth, and by intentionally expressing during the worship service the joy that seeing children in worship brought him.

After reading Strauss and Howe's book on generational theory,[b] he presented the material to the church council members through Saturday workshops. During these workshops the pastor and church leaders discussed how each generation perceived God or faith and what each generation valued about church. After the church's lay leadership agreed to shift to an intergenerational philosophy of ministry, the pastor openly introduced intergenerationality to his congregation during worship services. He designed four distinctive liturgies, each one created to appeal to a different generation. Throughout the worship services he explained

why a certain type of music and liturgy style might be attractive to a spe-
cific generation. Generally he heard positive comments from the older
church members such as, "If we would have had music like this when my
children were growing up, they might still be attending church." The
pastor took the few resistant members to lunch and carefully explained
the theological and generational benefits of having a multigenerational
church that worships together. The majority of resistant members
became supportive of the ministry change, although a handful of couples
left for other churches.

Although the congregation lost members who didn't like multigener-
ational worship, it also attracted new members who liked the intergen-
erational philosophy of ministry. Believing that an intergenerational
model of ministry created a healthier congregation, the church leaders
established a vision statement that included the phrase "[we] will be a
multifaceted, intergenerational ministry." In 2000 the congregation
moved to a larger space, and by 2006 the church was offering two
blended Sunday morning services as well as a casual Saturday evening
service. At this casual service parents with infants and toddlers sat on
the side aisles and children played on the floor with toys. Each service
included all ages as greeters, ushers, Scripture readers and members of
the music team.

Outside of worship, Sunday school was adapted to enable increased in-
teraction of ages; various generations served together to visit homes of
new members or the elderly; and the church started an intergenerational
baseball team. In 2005 the sanctuary was in the process of being remodeled
to enlarge the side aisles to create space for young children to "toddle" and
space for rocking chairs to enable parents to better care for a fussy baby
while remaining in the worship service.

---

[a]Christine M. Ross, "A Qualitative Study Exploring Churches Committed to Intergenerational Ministry" (doctoral dissertation, Saint Louis University, St. Louis, MO, 2006). See
note two of our introduction earlier in this book.
[b]William Strauss and Neil Howe, *Generations: The History of America's Future, 1584 to 2069*
(New York: Quill, William Morrow, 1991).

WELCOMING CHILDREN

Philip (age eleven) attends a church where he has worshiped primarily in children's church since preschool. However, in Holly's interview with him,[1] when he described his mother worshiping, the following conversation ensued:

Interviewer: So you go in big church with [your parents] sometimes?

Philip: *Yeah 'cause I don't really like the kids' church. It's okay but it's not the best.*

Interviewer: So what is it you like about being in big church?

Philip: *Well, in big church you get to sing more adult songs . . .*

Interviewer: What else?

Philip: *You get to be with your family.*

Other children in this research mentioned specifically worshiping with their families as they responded to various interview questions. In the recorded conversations below, the children were responding to the question, "Who do you know who knows God?"

Tabitha (age ten): *My mom and my dad.*

Interviewer: All right, let's start with your mom. . . . What [is it] about your mom makes you think your mom knows God?

Tabitha: *When I see her worshiping she is not worried about everybody else around her. She really connects with God and she closes her eyes.*

■ ■ ■

Interviewer: What is it about your Dad that makes you think he knows God?

Lydia (age eleven): *For Dad, the way he loves to worship. Also the way he talks about God.*

■ ■ ■

---

[1]The interviews were part of the field research for Holly's dissertation (Holly C. Allen, "A Qualitative Study Exploring the Similarities and Differences of the Spirituality of Children in Intergenerational and Non-Intergenerational Christian Contexts" [doctoral dissertation, Talbot School of Theology, Biola University, La Mirada, CA, 2002]). See chapter 12, note 19.

Interviewer: What about your mom?

Philip (age eleven): *Well my mom, she sometimes comes in and helps with the Sunday class and in the big church, when I've been in there, she's always praising God, lifting her hands in the air and everything.*[2]

These children have worshiped with their parents. That statement may not be surprising to some, but to many Christians in America, parents and children worshiping together has become an uncommon experience.

Families need to be worshiping together. Children in Old Testament times worshiped with their families on feast days, special celebrations and on Sabbath. Children in the early church worshiped in house churches with their families. Eddie Prest recommends particularly including children in worship, saying, "The optimal spiritual impact upon children will take place in a warm, belonging, caring and concerned interaction with the gathered people of God, particularly in worship."[3]

In *Right from the Start: A Parent's Guide to the Young Child's Faith Development,*[4] early-childhood expert Shirley Morgenthaler recommends including infants in worship so that they become comfortable with the style and rhythm of worship from the start of their lives. Throughout her book, Shirley provides parents and congregational leaders with ideas regarding how to integrate infants into the congregation.

Both John Westerhoff and James Fowler[5] strongly advocate intergenerational worship in which children are welcome, and a few books over the years have focused specifically on this idea; for example, *Parenting in the Pew: Guiding Your Children into the Joy of Worship, Children in the Worshiping Community* and *Creative Designs with Children at Worship.*[6]

---

[2]Ibid., pp. 309-10.

[3]Eddie Prest, *From One Generation to Another* (Capetown, South Africa: Training for Leadership, 1993), p. 20.

[4]Shirley Morgenthaler, *Right from the Start: A Parent's Guide to the Young Child's Faith Development* (St. Louis: Concordia, 2001).

[5]John Westerhoff III, *Will Our Children Have Faith?* rev. ed. (Toronto: Morehouse, 2000); James Fowler, *Weaving the New Creation: Stages of Faith and the Public Church* (New York: HarperCollins, 1991).

[6]Robbie Castleman, *Parenting in the Pew: Guiding Your Children into the Joy of Worship* (Downers Grove, IL: InterVarsity Press, 2002); David Ng and Virginia Thomas, *Children in the Worshiping Community* (Louisville, KY: Westminster John Knox, 1985); Roger Gobbel and Philip Huber, *Creative Designs with Children at Worship* (Atlanta: John Knox Press, 1981).

Prest in particular insists that as children worship in intergenerational settings, they are "assimilated . . . with a deep sense of belonging into the body" of Christ.[7] Prest eloquently and poignantly creates a vision for intergenerational *koinonia,* which should be quite appealing to faith communities seeking to integrate the generations. Prest summarizes, "The contention of intergenerational Christian experience is that it provides the best environment for a child to be helped to find faith and internalize Christian values. Its requirements are a context of warm acceptance and belonging to the family of God's people and the restructuring of worship to incorporate all members and relevantly meet the spiritual needs of each age group."[8] In intergenerational worship settings children will see their parents and others worship, they will make sense of their experiences with God, and they will come to know God better.

When Christine received notification of permission to use a song from the band Lost and Found (chapter eleven), she also received a personal note from one of the band members. Michael wrote:

> I have *long* believed that a key to the worship life of the Church serving the whole family and congregation is keeping the whole family and congregation together. And, of course, the worship life of the Church is the center of the Church's life.
>
> Oddly, even shockingly, we've been to hundreds of congregations over the years that literally segregate the congregation by age when it comes to worship. The larger congregations might even have a separate BUILDING for the younger members. And, then, while the adults are singing these extraordinarily catchy and singable songs, full of scriptural content and theological meaning, the kids are off in another room singing entirely separate songs. Then, when the kids find themselves in "adult church," they don't know the songs, or the meaning of what is going on. But if one just said to the children, "Here is a new song, called 'This is the Feast,' and here is how it goes . . ." the kids would be all over it.
>
> Congregational worship has to be a time when there is something for everyone. It is a truer picture of God and a truer picture of the Church. My three-year-old daughter sits (or stands on my lap so she can see) happily

---

[7]Prest, *From One Generation to Another,* p. 25.
[8]Ibid., p. 22.

engaged in the two-hour Easter Vigil, because it is full of dramatic liturgy from the starting of the new fire, the individual candles, the baptizing of the new members, the asperges, the music, the celebration at the alleluia, the walking around for the Eucharist, and so on. There is never a dull moment! Thank goodness, she isn't forced into a nursery, but is learning the traditions of the Church.

We've been playing concerts for twenty years. And we have ALWAYS seen them as intergenerational events. But the hosts generally say, "Oh Lost and Found are coming. Call the kids!" And they mean well. But the adults who find themselves there saying afterwards, "You know, I think I enjoyed it as much as the kids."[9]

Until recent decades, all generations, including infants, children and teens, worshiped together as a matter of course. Why then have faith communities in the last few decades created alternative worship opportunities for children rather than continuing to welcome them into communal worship? One answer to this question is that developmental concerns and spiritual concerns came to be seen as essentially synonymous; therefore, ministry leaders began to create more *developmentally* appropriate worship opportunities for children in order to bless them *spiritually*.[10] The problem here is that spiritual development is not fundamentally cognitive development. That is, the way children (and adults) grow in their understanding of math or science is not fundamentally the way they (and we) grow spiritually. Other factors are at work in spiritual development, not all primarily age related. The unique spiritual benefits of all ages worshiping together are lost when segmented populations worship exclusively; among these spiritual benefits are a deep sense of belonging and the blessing of participating in the spiritual journeys of those across the age spectrum (see chapter three for a fuller discussion of these spiritual benefits).

WORSHIP WARS

Some churches, besides having age-specific children's and teen worship services, offer a Millennial worship service (sometimes on a Saturday

---

[9]Personal email communication between Christine Ross and Michael Bridges, January 21, 2012, used with permission.

[10]A more global, comprehensive and nuanced response to this question is offered in chapter two of this text.

evening), a traditional worship service at 8:00 or 8:30, and a contemporary worship service at 10:30 or 11:00, in effect dividing the church into five generational cohorts. Is it really possible to bring all the generations together to worship as one, with the needs and desires of each generation being met? John Ortberg says, only slightly tongue-in-cheek, "Effective intergenerational worship would be a congregation of diverse ages sitting through a service of mixed styles that *displeases* everyone equally."[11] Is he right? And even if the benefits of intergenerational worship are deemed worthy of the effort and "cost," *how* can this be done?

Though the style of music is only one piece of the current generational "worship wars," it is a volatile piece. Churches are navigating the issue of traditional vs. contemporary worship styles in basically three ways: (1) by maintaining steadfast loyalty to traditional hymns; (2) by adopting fully contemporary approaches; or (3) by attempting to blend the two.

It seems self-evident that becoming fully and intentionally intergenerational will call for some degree of blending styles. To insist on traditional hymnody entirely, ignoring all worship music written in the last several decades, assumes an elitist historical stance that ignores the fact that God is still at work among twentieth- and twenty-first-century believers, pouring out new songs about old truths. However, insisting that the exclusive use of contemporary music and lyrics is necessary to keep churches vital overlooks inescapably the needs of one or two generations as well as the powerful theological and aesthetic contributions of past spiritually gifted musicians and poets. It also unavoidably limits the worship music repertoire of future generations.

A Chinese-German couple lives in Holly's small town. Mei's first language is Mandarin, Kurt's is German, and they speak English as well. Their preteen children are trilingual—fluent in all three languages. A person's first language is considered that person's "heart" language. Mei and Kurt's children have *three* heart languages—that is, languages through which they can express their deepest, most profound feelings and understandings.

Perhaps it can also be said that one's first music "language" is one's heart music. What a blessing it would be if the next generation were to

---

[11]John Ortberg, "The Gap: The Fractured World of Multi-Generational Church Leadership," *Leadership* 30 (Summer 2009): 50, emphasis ours.

become "multilingual" musically from childhood—that is, they would be able to express their spiritual praise, lament, adoration, petition and love through a wide range of musical worship styles. For this blessing to occur, it is keenly important that the worship music of our children and youth tap into the depth and breadth of theologically sound, melodically memorable, profoundly true songs, hymns and spiritual songs not only from the ages but also from the last several decades—and last week. And generational theory indicates that *now* is the right time to move toward such a vision as the millennial generation has relationships with its elders and as the Silent generation is more disposed toward change (than was the G.I. generation), seeing change as one way to keep their grandchildren in church.

John Brown University (JBU) in northwest Arkansas, where Holly teaches, is an interdenominational Christian university that draws students from forty other states and around forty foreign countries (including about a hundred missionary kids and sixty "Walton scholars" from Central America). Most of these students are "emerging adults" (ages eighteen to twenty-nine) from a broad spectrum of evangelical Christianity—from nondenominational churches to highly liturgical churches. Those who plan JBU's twice-weekly chapel worship are committed to incorporating both traditional hymns and contemporary Christian music, integrating worship styles and languages from around the world, and including gospel and other forms from nonwhite American churches. The hope and intention is that JBU's emerging adult students will feel at home with a range of worship music when they leave college—that the repertoire of songs, hymns and spiritual songs they know and love will be not only theologically powerful, poetically beautiful and melodically strong, but also historically and stylistically broad and diverse.

BROADENING THE SCOPE

Embracing intergenerational worship is more complex than simply including the children and successfully negotiating the worship wars. Being intergenerational in outlook means that all generations, from toddlers to seniors, will feel welcome and included when the body of Christ gathers together; they will be intentionally received; they will belong. Besides inviting the children and youth back into the community and singing songs from both contemporary and traditional sources, how can faith communities become more intergenerational when they gather for praise and worship, for prayer, to hear the Word, to break bread? The remaining sections of this chapter will suggest some general guidelines as well as some specific suggestions.

General guidelines. Becoming more intergenerational when the faith community gathers together for worship is a process that will require intentionality. The first step is simply grasping the concept that *"the church is all generations.* From the . . . infant to the homebound, aged widow—all are members of the faith community. . . . And all are members of the Body."[12] Glassford also utilizes the body metaphor: "Fostering a climate that is conducive to intergenerational worship means that both the leadership and the congregation must endorse [the] truth *that they are the body of Christ."*[13] Just as each member of the physical body (liver, ear, hamstring, big toe) is engaged actively in the very *living* of that body, so each worshiper is to be engaged actively in the worship life of the body of Christ. Grasping this crucial concept can unite a faith community around the construct of intergenerationality. (For further guidelines, chapter thirteen in this text offers a fuller explanation of the processes necessary for moving toward an intergenerational culture.)

Worship in historically liturgical churches typically includes an invocation or call, a period of praise through song or prayer or responsive reading, congregational confession, a declaration of forgiveness in Christ, the hearing of the Word, a sermon or homily, a response to the Word (which might entail reciting a creed, Eucharist/Communion, responsive readings, prayer or a baptism), an offering and the benediction. Churches that are not historically liturgical nevertheless follow some form of informal liturgy that typically includes an opening prayer, several songs of

---

[12]George Koehler, *Learning Together: A Guide for Intergenerational Education in the Church* (Nashville: Discipleship Resources, 1977), p. 10.

[13]Darwin Glassford, "Fostering an Intergenerational Culture," in *The Church of All Ages: Generations Worshiping Together,* ed. Howard Vanderwell (Herndon, VA: Alban Institute, 2008), p. 79, emphasis ours.

praise or thanksgiving (including perhaps a choir presentation), Scripture reading, a sermon, Communion (occasionally, weekly or quarterly) and an offering, with other prayers intermingled. Drama, testimonies, dance and other activities may also be a part of worship in these churches as well as in the more historically liturgical worship settings. Leaders who want to nurture an intergenerational culture must consider each element of the typical worship liturgy with one question in mind: How can children, teens, emerging adults, young adults, middle adults and older adults be drawn in more fully?

Once the conceptual work has been done, one key to implementing more intentionally intergenerational worship gatherings is to find those who are most committed to the concept to be part of the worship planning team. And planning worship should indeed be a *team* effort—even in smaller churches. If there is only one planner, he or she will become stale, perhaps even burned out, and inevitably, a worship gathering that should be fresh, enlivening and spiritually rich may become repetitive and mundane. Even a worship planning team can allow worship to fall into predictable patterns or reflect only a narrow perspective since these teams are typically composed of only one or two generations—either mostly young to middle adults, or middle to older adults, depending on which group or groups hold sway in the community. Thus, the planning team of staff and volunteers should intentionally include persons from across the generations, so that insights, desires and ideas from the entire life cycle will be reflected in how the faith community worships. When the elderly, the retired, the emerging adults, the teens and even the children also have a voice in planning worship, a richness and diversity enlivens a process that might otherwise reflect the insights of only a small band of permanent planners.[14]

Specific suggestions. Once a faith community has decided to become more intentionally intergenerational, there are dozens of specific ways to include all ages by design. In recent years, as we have worshiped in a broad

---

[14]Some of these ideas for an intergenerational worship planning team come from Norma de Waal Malefyt and Howard Vanderwell, "Worship Planning in a Church of All Ages," in *The Church of All Ages: Generations Worshiping Together,* ed. Howard Vanderwell (Herndon, VA: Alban Institute, 2008).

range of churches, we have noticed that the historically liturgical churches have been more deliberate about engaging all ages in their worship times together. Children and teens light candles, older and younger men and women lead prayer and read Scripture, and all ages participate in the choir and cantatas. The reciting of the creeds and the responsive readings elicit active participation from all readers, first graders through the oldest present. And even preschoolers can (and do) respond to the greeting "The peace of Christ be with you" with "And also with you," and join with everyone after the reading of the Word in saying, "Thanks be to God." Adopting some of these more participatory practices at least occasionally would offer specific ways for other churches to foster more active involvement across the entire life span.

Beyond these embedded opportunities, worship planners can consider every element or activity of worship as an opportunity for intergenerationality. For example:

- Recruit both older and younger greeters to welcome everyone.

- Verbally welcome specific generational cohorts on a regular basis (see appendix A, "Forty Intergenerational Ideas," for examples).

- Foster cross-age drama.

- Encourage father/son-led prayers (or mother/daughter if allowed in the setting), and other cross-generationally led prayers.

- Allow gifted artists of all ages to share the work God is giving them to do.

- Look for ways the older generation in particular can share stories of their faith journey (see chapter sixteen for specific ideas).

- Seek recent versions of older hymns—for example, the new versions of "Amazing Grace"—encouraging the choir, the praise team, the cantor, the pianist to integrate the well-known older hymn with a newer incarnation.

- In a song such as "Be With Me, Lord," suggest that the congregants sing "us" in place of "me"; this one change can create a tangible sense of cross-age community.

- Encourage cross-generational worship leaders. Often, depending on the tone of the church, the worship leaders are heavily drawn from the younger generations, typically the twenty- or thirtysomethings. Make a concentrated effort to draw on older members, even the oldest members who desire it, to be a part even if only occasionally. Also, mentoring teens, and even preteens, into this role can allow these younger members to listen in on the process, to hear the hearts of those who lead, to be included as equal partners and to contribute.

Other suggestions regarding intergenerational leadership and preaching to a cross-generational gathering are offered in chapter twenty.

A NEW WORSHIP IDEA

In recent years emerging churches have experimented with "worship stations"—multisensory, experiential opportunities for meditating, praying, listening to God, reading the Word or praising God. Not long ago, a small nondenominational church created eight worship stations one Sunday morning. The gathered body of Christ met as one for a few minutes for greeting and blessing, then the eighty-plus worshipers were formed into cross-generational groups of about ten each. Each group was directed to a station, with the general instruction to process that station in about twelve to fifteen minutes, then the groups would rotate to another station for twelve to fifteen minutes, and then to one more station for twelve to fifteen minutes; each group experienced three worship stations. A description of a worship station is given in box 14.2.

Worship stations offer rich opportunities for fostering spiritual relationships across the generations. Families can experience worship stations as family units, and intentionally formed cross-generational clusters can experience worship stations together.

Three to five people of various ages can *create* a worship station. To facilitate this process, leaders may want to offer a few guidelines along with suggestions for themes (e.g., stubbornness, fear, God's omnipresence, trusting God) or a scriptural passage (e.g., Gen 1, Ps 23, Lk 15). Key principles for creating worship stations include the ideas that they should be participatory, should focus on one biblical/spiritual concept, must utilize the senses and must be kept simple. Some churches offer worship stations a few times a year in place of their regular worship service. Two

BOX 14.2

The Trinity

Print a color copy of Andrei Rublev's fascinating depiction of the Trinity. Mount the color print on a small table-top tripod so that those who visit the station can observe it and discuss it (or pull up the image on a computer screen). Have a Bible marked at 2 Corinthians 13:14 and Matthew 28:19, or print out the verses. Provide crayons or markers and blank paper. The facilitator will guide the group using the following directions:

- *Explain: "Look at the picture on the table. It is a painting created by a man named Andrei Rublev a long time ago; he titled it 'The Trinity.' It is his idea of what God the Father, God the Son and God the Holy Spirit might be like. We are going to think about this today. For a few minutes we will just look at the picture."*

- *After several quiet minutes (or when younger members seem to get restless), read 2 Corinthians 13:14 and Matthew 28:19.*

- *Ask any of the following questions (rest easily with silence if no one responds): "Is this what you think the Trinity might be like? Which figure do you think is God? Why? Jesus? Why? (etc.)." Encourage children or others to point to parts of the painting that are particularly interesting or to make their point.*

- *Ask: "How else might the Trinity be shown?" Point out the crayons or markers and paper; allow a few minutes for participants to think about the Trinity and draw an idea if they wish to.*

- *Close by reading the words of the chorus of Keith Green's song, "There Is a Redeemer." If the group knows the song, you may wish to sing the chorus:*

  > *Thank you, oh my Father, for giving us your Son*
  > *And leaving your Spirit 'til the work on earth is done.*[a]

---

[a]Lyrics from "There Is a Redeemer" by Melody Green. Copyright 1982, Birdwing Music/Cherry Lane Music Pub. Co., Inc. Used by permission.

more worship station descriptions are included at the end of appendix A: "Forty Intergenerational Ideas."[15]

INTERGENERATIONAL WORSHIP AS CHRISTIAN FORMATION

Under the leadership of Caroline Fairless, the associate for intergenerational worship, St. Andrew's Episcopal Church in New Hampshire is transitioning toward a more age-integrated approach to its traditional worship service. Fairless says the process hasn't been easy, and she describes the transition as "a work in progress."[16] Currently, one Sunday a month the historical Episcopal elements of worship, built around the lectionary and the *Book of Common Prayer*, are recreated in a way that purposely engages all ages.

Fairless describes a recent worship service that focused on the story of Philip baptizing the Ethiopian in Acts 8. The story was enacted with an adult playing Philip and a young person playing the role of the Ethiopian. At the close of the story, "Philip" baptized the "Ethiopian" in a small pond that had been hand-built in the worship space for this purpose. After the retelling of the story, all worship participants were invited to renew their baptismal vows and share Communion. "The pond was stunning and beautiful, the drama was simple, and it was intergenerational," Fairless summarized.[17]

Fairless says that mixing the generations is "about an entire community being involved in the design and offering of worship, from adults to the smallest children. More than education, it is *spiritual formation*."[18]

---

[15]Logistically worship stations work well in smaller churches, that is, those with fewer than 150 participating. Ten or fifteen different worship stations can be set up, and each small group of five to eight could choose three to visit during the typical worship time period; or one station can be replicated and set up in ten or fifteen different places around the sanctuary or in fellowship halls or even classrooms, and everyone in the church spends half an hour at one station then joins together for closure and blessing. Meeting and greeting visitors and facilitating their participation in the worship stations is a crucial aspect of this novel approach. Larger churches and megachurches would find it difficult to create enough worship stations to accommodate hundreds or thousands. However, most larger churches foster the formation of small groups. Worship stations such as those described can be implemented in small group settings in homes. Rather than replace their weekly scheduled worship opportunities, historically liturgical churches may wish to offer worship stations on a Sunday evening, a weekday evening or during a holiday season.

[16]Angie Ward, "Let the Little Children Come," *Leadership* 30 (Summer 2009): 57.

[17]Ibid., p. 57

[18]Ibid., emphasis ours.

15

INTERGENERATIONAL LEARNING EXPERIENCES

When the whole community learns the same things at the same time, it strengthens the sacred nature of the whole community.

Mariette Martineau, Joan Weber and Lief Kehrwald,
Intergenerational Faith Formation

An intergenerational educational method that brings both adults and children together to explore God's [presence] . . . span[s] a gap in the fabric of the congregation and, therefore, in ministry to the world.

Dorothy Probst, *Worshipping God*

WHEN EITHER OF US SPEAKS on the topic of intergenerational learning, we often sense almost breathless interest among some in the audience; on the other hand, among others we detect intense skepticism, which shows itself in questions such as: How can you make *any* material interesting to adults and yet accessible to children? What biblical or theological material do you recommend for people from age four to eighty? We don't know how to do this; can you recommend any intergenerational curriculum? How do you find *anyone* willing and able to teach preschoolers, children, teens, young and older adults all at the same time? Usually someone in the audience states flatly, "We tried that. It doesn't work. The children don't like it; the teens don't like it; the parents don't like it; the seniors don't like it."

Teaching across the life span is indeed a challenging undertaking, one that is not popular and not easily accomplished well. If all of this is true, then why do it at all?

WHY INDEED?

Biblical precedent. When Moses gave his last address to Israel, all of the Israelites were there to hear and participate; when Joshua was preparing the children of Israel to enter the Promised Land, everyone was there to hear and participate; when Sennacherib was threatening Judah, the king called everyone together to pray; when Ezra read the word, everyone listened. Of course, these were large-group gatherings more akin to, say, our primary worship gatherings on Sundays. (In this context, see chapter fourteen on intergenerational worship.)

However, we have good historical evidence that when Paul's letters arrived and were read in the early house churches, all were present—men, women, slaves, children—to hear Paul's guidelines in Ephesians and Colossians: "husbands, love your wives," "wives, respect your husbands," "children, obey your parents" and "slaves, obey your masters."[1] These house churches would resemble our small groups perhaps. One might object to this connection by suggesting that first-century gatherings were intergenerational due to the cultural mores—that all ages were always present for everything; it simply wasn't an option to drop children at the babysitter's, or leave them at the building with the teens, or plug them into a video. Nevertheless, there is the biblical precedent that all ages can and did listen, eat, pray and learn together, and thus at least occasionally we can and perhaps should emulate this pattern. And there are other reasons to consider as well.

Hearing from the marginalized. In her enlightening chapter "Learning Together," written from an Anglican perspective, Judith Sadler shares that all-age learning has become a significant feature of education in the Church of England. One key point she makes is that "children are marginalized in churches as much as in society as a whole."[2] Children are

---

[1]Robert Banks, *Paul's Idea of Community: The Early House Churches*, rev. ed. (Peabody, MA: Hendrickson, 1994), p. 53.

[2]Judith Sadler, "Learning Together: All-Age Learning in the Church," in *Learning in the Way: Research and Reflection on Adult Christian Education*, ed. Jeff Astley (Leominster, Herefordshire, UK: Gracewing, 1999), p. 120.

often unseen and unheard, not unlike the children of Jesus' day (Mk 10:13-16). Sadler has found that adults in all-age learning settings "come to recognize the value of opinions that are held by those who have traditionally been regarded as having views of lesser worth. Such perceived worth-lessness rests in powerlessness. . . . All-age events might be regarded as a means of bringing about a shift in power toward previously under-valued groups of people."[3] Welcoming children and teens into the adult learning environment is one way to bestow value on them, to affirm them as worthy parts of the body, to publicly recognize their legitimate contribution to the adult educational enterprise.

After a long history of Wednesday evening age-graded Bible classes, the (very) small church plant that Holly worships with recently decided to meet intergenerationally for twelve weeks—about forty-five adults, teens and children with ages ranging from two to seventy-six. The pastor is leading this effort, though he confessed he has no prior experience; each week he has asked for feedback and suggestions.

One week we discussed the contest on Mount Carmel. We had a spoon-egg contest to begin with, which (naturally) drew in the children (as well as the teens and adults). He asked questions primarily of the children along the way, and their eyes were with him for the entire forty minutes; they were attuned, interested and engaged, as were the youth and adults. It was delightful to hear the children's responses, to participate in their enthusiasm, to note how pleased they were to be among the adults and with the teens. The adults and teens were the readers and the occasional participants in discussion. Several adults asked good extemporaneous questions that attested to their engagement with the material.

For a few weeks, the focus was on the Lord's Prayer, initially looking at the prayer as a pattern. The pastor asked Jenny, one of the "crafty" members, to bring a sewing pattern; on the floor in the middle of the circle, she demonstrated how to use a pattern. There followed a discussion across the ages of what a pattern is and is not, and what it might mean to have a pattern for prayer. Again the children were very engaged, as were the teens and adults.

---

[3]Ibid., p. 118.

Churches in our religious traditions have offered relatively few opportunities for women to take a more public role in the sharing of ideas and in leading. This approach affords ongoing opportunities for the men, teens and children to hear from their mothers, wives, daughters, sisters, grandmothers and aunts. It also offers more opportunities for the little ones to hear the older members share, and for the adults to be blessed by the children.

Pedagogical considerations. It is well established that when teaching children, one should utilize all the senses—seeing, hearing, touching, tasting and smelling—as well as a variety of learning styles (e.g., collaborative, analytical, commonsense, dynamic).[4] When all generations are present, *all* benefit when those teaching keep these pedagogical principles in mind. That is, adults *also* learn through their senses; that they *can* and often *do* learn primarily aurally in public settings doesn't mean that they don't also learn well through all their senses. For example, if an intergenerational group is studying the role and importance of the tabernacle, burning incense, lighting a small seven-armed candelabra and serving a loaf of unleavened "shewbread" would make the study more interesting and memorable not only for the children, but also for the teens and young, middle and older adults.

The same principle holds for learning styles; there are many adults whose primary learning style is not analytical (the common learning style adult teaching tends to accommodate). Many adults are collaborative, commonsense or dynamic learners.[5] When teachers intentionally create learning activities for all types of learners, adults as well as children are better served. For instance, if an intergenerational group is studying the book of Esther, a basic historical and geographical foundation will need to be established, probably *analytically* (and with the aid of maps and timelines); an experiential understanding of Esther and Mordecai's marginalized position in society could be best gained *collaboratively* (with all

---

[4]For discussions of the importance of utilizing the senses when teaching children, see, for example, Marlene LeFever's *Creative Teaching Methods* (Colorado Springs: Cook Communication Ministries, 1996) and Lawrence O. Richards's *A Theology of Christian Education* (Grand Rapids: Zondervan, 1975).

[5]For an excellent discourse on learning styles, see Marlene LeFever's *Learning Styles: Reaching Everyone God Gave You to Teach* (Colorado Springs: Cook Communication Ministries, 2001).

ages—teens, adults and children—sharing times when they have felt marginalized in work, school or social settings); grasping the whole plotline of the story can best be captured *dynamically* through an intergenerational enactment of the storyline (with props); ultimately the theological essence of this story—that God is at work in the world on behalf of his people—needs to be made relevant for all present. Doing so will especially bless the *commonsense* learners.

In sum, many basic pedagogical principles that are intentionally employed with children enhance learning at *every* age. Therefore, accessing these principles can strengthen adult learning as well.

HOW MIGHT INTERGENERATIONAL LEARNING BE IMPLEMENTED?

Quite often we hear of congregations who have attempted an all-age learning series at some point (for example, the research congregation described in chapter twelve). These experiences might take a variety of forms; for example, a summertime intergenerational Sunday school class, a whole congregational event or a small group Bible study.

Drew Zahn describes an intergenerational undertaking called Generation Bridge he remembered from his young adult years. The class, made up of participants from diverse age groups, met for three months and studied the book of James; an older person and a younger person shared the teaching task each week. "In time, friendships and mentoring relationships were built that last to this day."[6]

A Bible church in Holly's city has offered an all-church, all-age summer Sunday school several times in the last decade. It is a labor-intensive undertaking, but apparently a memorable and important piece of the church's traditions. Two of Holly's university students who attended that church as children chose to include a description of that cross-age summer learning experience in a reflection paper entitled "Five Memorable Spiritual Experiences from My Childhood." One of the students, Sarah, wrote: "Growing up, I always looked forward to summer. For one thing, summer meant family Sunday School at church. Instead of going to our own individual

---

[6]Drew Zahn, "Connecting the Generations: How Churches Are Building and Sustaining Age-Integrated, Multi-Generational Ministry," *Leadership* 23 (Spring 2002): 37.

classrooms, my brothers and I got to go to the sanctuary with Mom and Dad. There we got to sit in the pews and learn cool lessons. Each Sunday, a different family got up and taught." Sarah concluded her comments about the cross-age Sunday school with, "Church was not just for the adults, or just for the kids. It was a time for all of us, for all of us to learn together about God and his Word and work."[7]

Creating positive, effective, enjoyable intergenerational learning opportunities is a daunting undertaking. To implement a successful intergenerational learning experience, we recommend the following:

1. Offer the intergenerational learning setting as an option. That is, have other good learning options available for those who do not wish to join. It is vital that those who attend wish to be there; naysayers can kill enthusiasm and dampen the spirits of others.

2. Suggest an age limit; for example, first graders and up or, for more complex material, ten-year-olds or sixth graders and up. Including preschoolers is quite difficult due in part to their more limited attention span, though some have successfully incorporated ages four to eighty.

3. Limit the study to six to ten weeks with a finite topic. Examples would be the fruit of the spirit, the ten commandments or a specific passage to unpack such as Isaiah 61:1-4.

4. Enlist the most creative and experienced adult, youth and children's teachers to collaborate in constructing the teaching/learning materials. George Koehler, who wrote intergenerational curriculum in the 1970s, recommends the best approach to intergenerational curriculum is "to take a unit for younger learners and adapt it upward. . . . It is easier to add information, concepts, and activities for adults than it is to adjust adult-oriented material to children" [because] "adults can learn more from an approach for children than children can learn from an adult-oriented approach."[8]

5. Recruit a team of enthusiastic teachers (including those who constructed the materials).

---

[7]Sarah Cowles, used by permission.
[8]George Koehler, *Learning Together: A Guide for Intergenerational Education in the Church* (Nashville: Discipleship Resources, 1977), pp. 61, 55.

BOX 15.1

What makes it work?

In 2007 participating parishes in the intergenerational faith formation Generations of Faith project were asked to complete a survey requesting that they identify what is needed "to ensure good intergenerational learning." [a] *The 276 responders identified the following factors:*

- *A welcoming environment to all ages*
- *Clarity of goals*
- *Variety*
- *Being open to the Spirit*
- *Good timing (no one activity is too long)*
- *Good facilitators (enthusiastic, know the audience)*
- *Engage all learners (active, not passive engagement)*
- *Meaningful learning experiences (with theological depth)*
- *Pastor support and presence.* [b]

[a]Ibid., p. 80.
[b]Ibid., pp. 80-85.

Publishers are currently producing more intergenerational curricula than in the past. Some materials are listed in appendix B in this text. For example, the publisher Children Desiring God offers two intergenerational series, one on the Ten Commandments and one on prayer.[9] Materials for *families* learning together are also available; these focus specifically on parents with children in the home, and thus are somewhat limited in full cross-age settings. However, they can be adapted. Some of these materials are also listed in appendix B (e.g., Karyn Henley's excellent series as well as *Family 'Round the Table* curriculum from GenOn Ministries[10]).

---

[9]Sally Michael, *The Righteous Shall Live by Faith: A Study for Children and Adults on the Ten Commandments* (Minneapolis: Children Desiring God, 2005); Sally Michael, *Lord, Teach Us to Pray: A Study for Children and Adults on Prayer* (Minneapolis: Children Desiring God, 2006).

[10]GenOn Ministries (formerly known as The LOGOS Ministry) is endorsed by prominent minis-

For about a decade, over 1500 parishes of the Catholic Church have been doing something quite ambitious and radical; they have been using an intergenerational catechesis approach called *Generations of Faith*. Martineau, Weber and Kehrwald have followed this project and examine and explain the theory and practice of this intergenerational faith formation catechesis in their book *Intergenerational Faith Formation: All Ages Learning Together*.[11] The basic learning format in the *Generations of Faith* approach includes an opening prayer, an all-ages learning experience, an in-depth learning experience (either as a whole group, divided into age groups or through learning centers), a whole-group sharing experience, a personal or household reflection time, and closing prayer.

PERCEIVED BARRIERS TO INTERGENERATIONAL LEARNING OPPORTUNITIES

One concern of educational developmentalists is that children and adults are typically at different cognitive developmental stages; that is, they *think* differently. In Piagetian terms, preschoolers are intuitive (nonlogical) thinkers, elementary-age children are concrete thinkers, and teens and adults are capable of abstract thinking. Therefore, combining these groups of people in a learning environment could be pedagogically problematic or even unworkable. However, Sadler notes that "people of the *same age* might be at *different stages* (and, of course, that people of different ages might be at the same stage). Educationalists display an unrealistic perception of what is being learned if they assume, for example, that a particular learning programme designed for abstract-thinking adults is appropriate for all adults and inappropriate for all children. Likewise, much is lost when it is assumed that adults cannot learn with and from those younger than themselves."[12]

In other words, even abstract thinkers can learn concretely also, and

---

try practitioners who promote intergenerational approaches to ministry, such as Ben Freudenburg (author of *The Family-Friendly Church*), Gene Roehlkepartain of the Search Institute, Marva Dawn (author of *Is It a Lost Cause? Having the Heart of God for the Church's Children*) and Mark DeVries (author of *Family-Based Youth Ministry*).

[11]Mariette Martineau, Joan Weber and Lief Kehrwald, *Intergenerational Faith Formation: All Ages Learning Together* (New London, CT: Twenty-Third Publications, 2008).

[12]Sadler, *Learning Together*, p. 115.

preschoolers and elementary children need not have everything they learn spoon-fed at their level. A key principle of the sociocultural learning theory is that persons learn best with those in the next stage ahead of them (see chapter seven on learning theory).

Some adults may find learning with children to be unchallenging and boring. This need not be the case. Utilizing a congregation's best teachers can provide strong teaching/learning materials and approaches from which all may benefit. Of course, some segments of the congregation may desire only heavily cognitive, dense or philosophical study subjects. As mentioned earlier, intergenerational settings should be optional, with other learning choices available. However, church leaders may wish to keep in mind that the deepest theological issues are not necessarily so cognitively complex that children and adults cannot participate together in taking them in. The story is widely told that when Swiss theologian Karl Barth came to the United States for the Warfield Lectures at Princeton in 1962, a student asked him: "What is the greatest thought that has ever passed through your mind?" Barth paused, then replied: "Jesus loves me. This I know, for the Bible tells me so."[13] Cross-age learning settings need not focus on the imprecatory psalms or the authorship of Hebrews with children present; nevertheless profound perennial truths of the faith can be rendered teachable (and learnable) across a wide expanse of ages.

And finally, some parents, especially those with children who have short attention spans or behavioral challenges, may not wish to participate in learning settings with their children. Sometimes, the emotional and physical space that age-segregated learning settings offer is a cherished break for such parents. Again, making intergenerational learning opportunities optional is important. However, parents should be encouraged to try an intergenerational learning activity before opting out; an unexpected benefit of an intergenerational confirmation program in one of Christine's research churches was the decrease in discipline problems.[14]

---

[13]James Montgomery Boice, *Foundations of the Christian Faith: A Comprehensive and Readable Theology* (Downers Grove, IL: InterVarsity Press, 1986), p. 331.

[14]Christine M. Ross, "A Qualitative Study Exploring Churches Committed to Intergenerational Ministry" (doctoral dissertation, Saint Louis University, St. Louis, MO, 2006), p. 71.

BLESSINGS FOR CHILDREN

Adults comprehend much more about the human situation than do children and teens. Studying together can bring the life experiences of adults to the learning palette of younger participants. Jerome Berryman says that "death, aloneness, freedom, and meaninglessness are the primary subject matter of religious education"[15] and that we should not avoid these subjects when children are among us. In fact, a cross-generational discussion of these profound issues can be a blessing for all concerned.

Recently one of Holly's colleagues, Jason, mentioned that the intergenerational small group that meets in his home is going to study the subject of death. Among the group's members are a couple in their eighties, a widower in his sixties, a couple in their forties with two teenage boys, a couple in their thirties with two elementary-age girls, another young couple with two preschoolers, and two twentysomething single women. Jason and his family are part of a church that until recently was composed mostly of older couples, widows and widowers; in the last few years, several young families including Jason's family have joined this older faith community. In the last year, three of the congregation's older members have passed away, and it is clear that there will be more funerals in the near future as the oldest members are now in their eighties and nineties. Jason's small group has decided to study the process of grief, dying and death—and what happens afterward. Jason said that though he is especially looking forward to what the oldest members of the group have to share, he is keenly interested in creating this opportunity for his two daughters, ages eight and ten, as well.

BLESSINGS FOR TEENS

The last decade has produced dozens of articles and books from practicing and former youth pastors lamenting the silo nature of youth ministry and advocating a more intergenerational approach to ministering to teens.[16]

---

[15]Jerome W. Berryman, "Teaching as Presence and the Existential Curriculum," *Religious Education* 85: 518.

[16]See for example, Mark DeVries, *Family-Based Youth Ministry*, rev. ed. (Downers Grove, IL: InterVarsity Press, 2004); Jason Lanker, "The Family of Faith: The Place of Natural Mentoring in the Church's Christian Formation of Adolescents," *Christian Education Journal* (series 3) 7, no. 2 (Fall 2010): 267-80; Chap Clark, *Hurt: Inside the World of Today's Teenagers* (Grand Rapids: Baker Aca-

The Search Institute's "Effective Christian Education" study found that intergenerational interaction helps young people grow in their faith in the following ways: contact with older adults is more likely to give young people mentors with mature faith; it builds for young people a sense of community, that is, they feel more comfortable in the church and more like part of the family of God; it fosters mutual respect among the generations; and it creates shared experiences for youth and parents.[17] The following vignette illustrates the power of intergenerational learning opportunities, especially for teens.

> In a recent cross-age study of the prodigal son parable in Luke 15, the discussion leader asked three men in the group to play the roles of the father, the younger son and the older son. The role of the father was played by a fiftysomething man (Jack); the younger brother was played by Jack's nineteen-year-old son (Josh); and the older son was played by a thirtysomething father (Nathan, parent of three elementary-age children in the group). Following the reading of the parable with each "actor" reading his appropriate lines, the discussion leader asked for a short period of silence while the listeners considered the thoughts and feelings of each of the three men in the parable. Then the leader asked, "Do you have any questions you would like to ask the father, the younger son or the older son?" There was a short pause, then Brynna, age thirteen, launched forthrightly into a question for the father. In an exasperated voice, she asked, "Why did you let your son go? Why did you give him all that money?"
>
> Jack (the "father") who had been primed for several likely questions—though not this one—initially looked a bit flustered; then in a piercing yet quiet voice, he responded: "Parenting adult children is really hard, harder than when they were toddlers or school age. So I guess I knew he was going to leave anyway; I thought having the money would provide him with some protection from the world." He paused again. "Perhaps I was wrong. Parents don't always make perfect decisions."
>
> A hush fell over the group. Tears came to Jack's eyes, and then he turned to his real son Josh (the "younger brother"), and their eyes locked for a moment. Some people in the group knew that Josh had been pushing the

---

demic, 2004);

[17]Eugene Roehlkepartain, *The Teaching Church: Moving Christian Education to Center Stage* (Nashville: Abingdon, 1993), p. 145.

boundaries in recent months and that his dad had pushed back pretty hard.

Into the quiet, a high school senior in the group asked the "younger brother" (Josh), "What did you think your dad would do when you got home?" Josh hesitated a moment, then said, "Well, I didn't think he would throw me a party, but I didn't think he would turn me away. Dads always love their kids, even when their kids have acted stupid." Again the group was silent, as each one entered the parable in new ways.

This parable came to life that night in Jack and Josh and in the young people who asked those very real questions. This story movingly illuminates the profound possibilities of intergenerational learning settings.

BLESSINGS FOR ADULTS

In recommending intergenerational Bible study, Allan Harkness says that children have "the capacity to bring to the learning situation their critical openness and questioning of traditional interpretations of biblical texts coupled with the ability to express feelings and experience."[18]

Children often see things in Scripture adults may overlook; they sometimes ask questions in new ways about things that adults think they have long ago settled.

Once when a teacher was telling the good Samaritan story, she concluded by asking the question that Jesus asked, "Which of these three do you think was a neighbor to the man who fell into the hands of robbers?" (Lk 10:36). The children of course responded saying the neighbor was the one who helped the hurt man. But one of the children asked a surprising question: "Who was the robbers' neighbor?" This boy's father works in prison ministry, and apparently the boy had really wondered about who might befriend a robber and become his "neighbor."

Judith Sadler says that children possess some qualities parents may urge them to outgrow; for example, directness and vulnerability, intense curiosity, and even their confidence. Sadler says that in intergenerational learning settings "many adults might now benefit from recapturing the values of such apparently child-like attributes."[19]

---

[18]Allan Harkness, "Intergenerational Christian Education: An Imperative for Effective Education in Local Churches (Part 2)," *Journal of Christian Education* 42, no. 1 (1998c): 45.
[19]Sadler, *Learning Together*, p. 115.

And harking back to her discussion on marginalization, Sadler admonishes: "Those who are not marginalized need to learn from those who are. They may thus discover and appreciate different perspectives on God, the church and worship. The all-age [learning] experience is symbolic of this widening perspective."[20]

BLESSINGS FOR ALL

Learning about prayer with all ages present has been a unique blessing for Holly's small faith community. As they sat in the large circle one recent evening, the teacher asked Allee, age eight, if her daddy ever tells her no when she asks for something. She grinned and blushed a little, then said in a rather small voice, "Yes, he won't let me dye my hair pink." There were a few giggles around her from her friends, and her dad also blushed a bit. The teacher turned to Allee's dad and asked, "Does your Heavenly Father ever say no to you?" Allee's dad paused a moment, then said very thoughtfully, "He does." Then he added, "I think I see now that I should trust him when I ask, because I know that when I say no to Allee, it is because I love her and want what is best for her." That comment hovered in the quiet for a few seconds as children, teens, parents and other adults let it soak in.

"Intergenerational learning . . . mirrors the community. Instead of segmenting individuals into like age groups, we let them experience and witness the learning that takes place among all ages around them."[21] Martineau, Weber and Kerhwald continue: "When a middle-schooler sees that a young adult is genuinely learning and growing in his faith, this provides a powerful witness to the young adolescent. Similarly, when a middle-aged adult sees a youngster have an 'aha' moment of faith, it freshens and enlivens the faith of the mature adult. When the whole community learns the same things at the same time, it strengthens the sacred nature of the whole community."[22]

All ages learning together can be an effective, powerful, life-changing and blessed element in Christian formation.

---

[20]Ibid., p. 120.
[21]Martineau, Weber and Kehrwald, *Intergenerational Faith Formation*, p. 62.
[22]Ibid.

16

INTERGENERATIONALITY AND STORY SHARING

The heart of intergenerational congregational life is to be found in the telling of stories.

Jane Rogers Vann, foreword to *The Church of All Ages*

EVERYONE HAS A STORY TO TELL, and one of the best ways to bring the generations together is through telling those stories. One purpose for sharing narratives is simply to get to know one another. But beyond that, seeing God's story in each other's stories is a key spiritual blessing of story sharing in intergenerational faith communities.

GOD'S STORY

Stories speak to us in ways that nothing else can. When the stage presentation of *The Diary of Anne Frank* played in Dresden and Berlin in 1956, the impact on the German people was profound. Though of course most Germans had been aware that Jewish boys and girls had died in the camps, somehow the telling of Anne's story spoke into their hearts and souls as statistics and even photographs had not.[1]

---

[1]This argument is made in a variety of sources, but particularly well in: Hanno Loewy, "The Universalisation of Anne Frank," in *Marginal Voices, Marginal Forms: Diaries in European Literature and History*, ed. Rachel Langford and Russell West, trans. Russell West, Internationale Forschungen zur Allgemeinen und Vergleichenden Literaturwissenschaft (Atlanta: Rodopi, 1999), pp. 156-74.

In 1956 Gert Kalow in the Frankfurter Allgemeine Zeitung interpreted a common admission of guilt as the sign of a spiritual reunification: "There was hardly a West- or East-German theatre that didn't advertise, or make part of the season's programme this call to reflection on the past: an

About half of Scripture is made up of story. God made us and knows that stories speak uniquely to us. As Eugene Peterson says so eloquently: "It is significant that God does not present us with salvation in the form of an abstract truth, or a precise definition or a catchy slogan, but as *story*."[2] The Bible is the record of God's story—the story of how he preserved human life and prepared a nation in order that he might have a relationship with humankind through the life and death of his Son, the Savior of the world. Scripture is, in essence, one story (Lk 24:27; Jn 5:39; Acts 10:43; 2 Tim 3:15).

Every semester for several years, Holly taught one or two sections of Old Testament Survey at John Brown University. There were usually forty-five students in each section, most of whom had been raised in Christian homes and had worshiped faithfully in their home congregations; some had been homeschooled, some were missionary kids, some had attended Christian schools. On the first day of class each semester, Holly placed the students into groups of four or five and asked them to construct a list of five things they hoped to learn in this course. Every semester in every class on virtually every list was some version of, "We know the stories in the Old Testament, but we want to understand how the Old Testament fits with everything else—how it all fits together." They knew the *stories* but they didn't grasp the *story*.

---

element of reunification, spiritual reunification, conferred by a thirteen year-old Jewish girl who was murdered by us in Belsen concentration camp (let us not say 'by the evil Nazis', as if we could place the burden of guilt upon an authority which has already become part of the past, but rather let us say 'by us'). No-one, not even the old anti-fascist resistance-fighter, not even the former Nazi, can look into this mirror reflecting bottomless suffering borne without hatred, without being deeply shocked. No-one, however energetically he might deny it, comes away from the performance unchanged." Taken from Gert Kalow, "Lob eines Zimmerspiels," *Frankfurter Allgemeine Zeitung*, 28 December 1956.

In terms of its public impact, says "Nazi hunter" Simon Wiesenthal, the Anne Frank diary is "more important than the Nuremberg trials" (The Washington Post, April 1, 1979, p. H3). . . . As the British monthly *History Today* noted in its March 1985 issue: "The impact of the Diary has been immense, especially on younger generations, school children, adolescents and students. In Germany, a type of Anne Frank cult developed in the fifties similar to movements started by St. Teresa and St. Bernadette. In 1957, mass emotion was channelled into a pilgrimage of two thousand young people, mainly from Hamburg, to Bergen-Belsen where, in pouring rain during the course of a ceremony, flowers were placed on the mass graves—in one of which Anne Frank was buried."

Mark Weber, "Anne Frank," Institute for Historical Review. Retrieved from <www.ihr.org/jhr/v15/v15n3p31_Weber.html>.

[2]Eugene H. Peterson, "Introduction to Exodus," in *The Message: The Bible in Contemporary Language* (Colorado Springs: NavPress, 2002), p. 105, emphasis in original.

The past decade has produced several books that emphasize this ancient truth, newly rediscovered by some traditions, that the Bible is one story. Bartholomew and Goheen's *The Drama of Scripture: Finding Our Place in the Biblical Story*[3] speaks eloquently to this new/old truth. Robbie Castleman's recent Bible study guide is titled *The Story of Scripture.*[4] Zondervan markets *The Story: The Bible As One Continuing Story of God and His People.* What these books have in common is the proclamation of the unity of Scripture as story. These more popular-level works have emerged from the earlier theological work of N. T. Wright and others who have been making the case for Scripture as the one overarching story, or metanarrative, out of which Christians live their lives. As Wright says, "The whole point of Christianity is that it offers a story which is the story of the whole world."[5]

In perceiving Scripture as the story of God's work in the world, and in light of the biblical indication that God's work is not done until Christ returns and God reconciles all creation to himself, one is left with the realization that this story is *continuing;* that is, the fulfillment of Revelation 22 is still to come. And this realization can lead to the recognition that God's story is continuing today; that is, God is still showing his power and working wonders among his people even yet.

OUR STORIES

Throughout Scripture God tells his people to remember his mighty acts and to tell the next generations of his power and the wonders he has done (e.g., Ps 78:4). Several times in Scripture, specific illustrations of how to do this are laid out. For example, when the Israelites crossed the Jordan into the Promised Land, Joshua instructed that a stone altar be built with twelve stones, representing the twelve tribes. Then Joshua said, "When your children ask their fathers in times to come, 'What do these stones mean?' then you shall let your children know, 'Israel passed over this Jordan on dry ground.' For the LORD your God dried up the waters of the

---

[3]Craig G. Bartholomew and Michael W. Goheen. *The Drama of Scripture: Finding Our Place in the Biblical Story* (Grand Rapids: Baker, 2004).

[4]Robbie Castleman, *The Story of Scripture* (Downers Grove, IL: InterVarsity Press, 2008).

[5]N. T. Wright, *The New Testament and the People of God* (London: SPCK, 1992), pp. 41-42.

Jordan for you until you passed over . . . so that all the peoples of the earth may know that the hand of the LORD is mighty, that you may fear the LORD your God forever" (Josh 4:21-24 ESV).

The way that the Israelites were to tell the next generations about God was to describe for them what God had done in their lives. Those stories were written down—they are the Bible stories we tell today—and as Sandage, Aubrey and Ohland say, "An essential purpose of the church is to be a community of memory that tells and retells God's larger transcending story."[6] However, we are not only to be telling the stories of how God worked in the past; we are also to tell our children and the next generations about God's ongoing work in the world today. One of the best ways to do this is to tell about God's mighty acts in our own lives: "The Christian community is . . . a place where the stories of 'ordinary saints' are made meaningful. . . . Embedding one's personal story in a larger story is [an important] . . . dimension of community."[7]

In a chapter titled "The Power of Telling a Story," Jeff Barker explains, "One of the beautiful things about stories is that the best ones function across generations. The event structure of a story, like falling dominoes, attracts and holds everyone's attention, even young children's, while the values housed within a protagonist's conflicting motivations provide nuance and mystery for those most experienced in life."[8]

Behling and Rask, a mother-daughter writing team, share of a memorable intergenerational storytelling event:

> In preparation for All Saints' Day we invited people to write things they remembered about life in the congregation on a time line posted in the narthex. They were hesitant at first, assuming their personal memories were insignificant. People just don't tell their stories automatically; but gradually, people felt free to add their words. Someone remembered a baptism when the heat went out, so it was held at home. Over the next two weeks our composite story began to appear. On All Saints' Sunday after worship, we held a potluck meal and then walked through the time line,

---

[6]Steven Sandage, Carol Aubrey and Tammy Ohland, "Weaving the Fabric of Faith," *Marriage and Family: A Christian Journal* 2, no. 4 (1999): 393.
[7]Ibid.
[8]Jeff Barker, "The Power of Telling a Story," in *The Church of All Ages: Generations Worshiping Together,* ed. Howard Vanderwell (Herndon, VA: Alban Institute, 2008), p. 101.

as we encouraged one another to tell stories so others could hear them. Most people have lived here their whole lives, but we all heard new stories that day and gained a deeper appreciation of our roots in this community of faith.[9]

GOD'S STORY, OUR STORY

Five years ago Holly was speaking to about a thousand women about *story*—God's story and our metanarrative. Between the morning and afternoon sessions, Holly realized a new way to make this message very real to the women in attendance. During the hour-long break, Holly made the props she would need—about thirty twelve-by-eighteen-inch (the size of large construction paper) posters with a biblical name on each: Adam, Eve, Abraham, Sarah, Jacob, Leah, Tamar, Shiphrah and Puah (the midwives who spoke to Pharaoh), Jochebed, Moses, Joshua, Deborah, Rahab, David, Esther, Mary, Jesus, John, Mary Magdalene, Paul. Then she added other names, including Perpetua (early Christian martyr, mother of an infant), Teresa of Avila (Spanish contemplative nun of the sixteenth century), Martin Luther and Lottie Moon (nineteenth-century missionary to China). Before the break ended, Holly found about thirty women from among the attendees to hold each of the posters. She also found three additional women to participate: a woman whose recently deceased mother had been a well-loved sister in this faith community, a young mother who had her nursing infant with her, and a pregnant woman.

When the next session began, women were lined up across the stage area in "chronological order," holding their poster with the name hidden. As Holly orally and quickly walked through the story of God's work on earth, the names on the posters were revealed. Along the way, she mentioned that these were people God had used throughout the ages to accomplish his work on earth (Adam, Abraham, Esther, Mary, etc.). When the poster with Perpetua's name was flipped over, Holly paused—since all of the previous names had been people in Scripture. Then she said, "You may not remember Perpetua from Scripture. The reason you don't is that Perpetua died a

---

[9]Karen Rask Behling and Carol Rask, "Ordinary Time: Intergenerational Ministry," in *Ordinary Ministry, Extraordinary Challenge: Women and the Roles of Ministry*, ed. Norma Cook Everist (Nashville: Abingdon, 2000), p. 78.

couple of centuries after Christ lived. She was a Christian martyr." Then she went through the other names of those who have continued to be part of God's story here on earth, those God has used to do his work and his will.

Then Holly came to the woman who held the poster with her mother's name on it. Holly asked her to turn the poster over. It said, "Lorene." Holly said, "Those of you who are part of this church knew Lorene well. She was well known and well loved here. She served those in need here and taught you what God had taught her. She too is part of God's continuing story here on earth."

The next woman's poster displayed the name of the child she was holding, Carlos. "God's story is continuing through Carlos; already his mother is singing over him, telling him who God is, bringing him with her when she joins this body of believers in worship."

Then the last woman turned over her poster. It had "Baby Tabitha" written on it. And Holly said, "God's work is continuing into the future. Tabitha is already part of the story."

For a few seconds, there was a pause as everyone scanned the displayed names that represented God's story, their stories and how God is continuing to work in this world. Then Holly said to the 950 women still in the audience, "I want each of you to visualize yourself in this line. God is writing you into his story even today."

Holly has used this activity in many settings since that surprising moment five years ago. In small gatherings, she asks everyone present to actually take their place in the line. This bodily movement—getting up, walking to the line, standing physically in line following David, Esther, Paul, Perpetua—is always a stirring moment; it visibly affects those who participate. It is especially moving in broadly intergenerational settings as the oldest present and the youngest present take their places in line, and see in each other the story of God at work in his kingdom.

FOSTERING INTERGENERATIONAL STORY SHARING

Barker notes that "people in our culture tell stories to each other far less than people in other cultures and in previous generations."[10] We watch

---

[10]Barker, "The Power of Telling a Story," p. 95.

movies and read novels, but we all crave *real* stories, stories from those we know and love. Stories are the universal language of all ages.

Stefanie Germanotta has a tremendous following of fans; they hang on her every word as she tells stories of her childhood and teen years when she felt rejected and out of step with her peers. Children, teens and emerging adults in our faith communities would love to hear the childhood, adolescent and young-adult stories of older believers who survived bullying, failure and loneliness when they were younger. These stories are as powerful as Stefanie's (better known as Lady Gaga) and have the added benefit of attributing to God his role in delivering and redeeming.

Due to the isolation of the generations, children don't know the seniors—the elderly may seem old and scary; the seniors don't know the youth—teenagers may seem young and scary; emerging adults may not know anyone except other emerging adults. If we do not know one another, how can we be community? How can we be brothers and sisters? How can we encourage one another on this pilgrim journey? One of the best ways to get to know one another across the generations is to listen to one another's stories.

David Kinnaman tells a story about inviting a very elderly member of his church for Sunday dinner in his home; his elementary-age children were fascinated by this woman in her mid-nineties. After dinner, David asked her, "What would you say is one advantage of living to a very old age?" After she paused for a few seconds, she replied, "Well, most of my friends have passed on." She paused again. "I guess I would say . . . that there is less peer pressure." What a fabulous story for these children to have heard; it will be repeated for years to come—perhaps to their own children.[11]

John Williams's small study of intergenerational storytelling found that hearing each other's stories and participating in intergenerational ministries together brought the teens and senior adults in the study closer together and they grew in appreciation for one another.[12] Grefe reports that the benefits of intergenerational narrative sharing include coming to un-

---

[11]David Kinnaman, speaking at LOGOS Live, First Presbyterian Church, San Antonio, TX, October 6-7, 2010.

[12]John T. Williams, "If You Build It, They Will Come: Using Storytelling as an Intergenerational Bridge" (D.Min. thesis, Wesley Theological Seminary, Washington, DC, 2006).

derstand both the common and unique aspects of different stages of life and opportunities to resolve intergenerational misunderstandings.[13] But even more importantly, hearing the stories across the generations is a way of chronicling God's work among us, a way of tracing God's ongoing story.

EMBEDDING OUR STORIES IN GOD'S STORY

Behling and Rask, the mother-daughter writing team, remind us that "we all have stories. It is a matter of being intentional about sharing them. It's a matter not of finding the time, but claiming the time, making the time, naming the time as God's time to share the . . . Word of God at work in the world."[14] One way to claim this time is through prompted intergenerational storytelling.

BOX 16.1

Guidelines for prompted intergenerational story sharing:

- *Choose a passage and create a prompt. In the example below, the prompt was drawn from 1 Samuel 17:37 and read: "God who delivered David from the bear, and the lion, and from Goliath, has delivered me from . . ."*

- *Prayerfully consider whom to ask, then ask three or four persons from different generations to share a story from their lives that illustrates the prompt.*

- *Request written responses and choose those that fit; if someone you ask is unable to recall such a story, ask another.*

Other prompts are located in appendix A: "Forty Intergenerational Ideas."

Storied responses to the 1 Samuel prompt follow:

- *A forty-year-old self-made millionaire: God who delivered David from the bear, and the lion, and from Goliath, has delivered me from greed. I intended to make my first million by*

---

[13]Dagmar Grefe, "Combating Ageism with Narrative and Intergroup Contact: Possibilities of Intergenerational Connections," *Pastoral Psychology* 60 (February 2011): 104.

[14]Behling and Rask, "Ordinary Time," p. 79.

the time I was thirty; I succeeded in that goal, but it brought me no joy until God delivered me from greed. As I have worked in our church's recovery ministry, God has replaced my greed with his spirit of compassion and generosity.

- A twenty-four-year-old single woman: God who delivered David from the bear, and the lion, and from Goliath, has delivered me from hopelessness. I was trapped in a life of promiscuity, seeking from men what only God could give. As I have studied the word of God in the lives of Rahab, Esther, Tamar, Ruth, Deborah, Lydia and Mary, God has brought me to a place of hope and peace—a place I thought I could never be.

- An octogenarian: God who delivered David from the bear, and the lion, and from Goliath, has delivered me from my fear of death. I have been paralyzed for two decades by my fear of growing old and of dying. But in recent months as I have comforted those in Blue Willow HospiceCare, God has replaced my fear with a place of contentment, a quiet calm, a joy in each day and an acceptance that I will soon be with him forever.

We are a story-formed people. As God has been at work through the ages, bringing about his good purposes, delivering his people from their enemies, he is still at work. Sharing the biblical narrative and our personal spiritual narratives across the generations will form our identity as God's people as perhaps nothing else can do.

Everyone has a story.

BOX 16.2

When Rod was in middle school, he became aware that he was quite different from the other boys in sixth grade: he loved to learn, he delighted in math, he participated wholeheartedly in all projects and all class discussions. He said to his dad one day, "I think I'm a nerd. Mostly I don't care, but sometimes I know that the other boys think that's not cool." Not long after that, a middle-aged NASA engineer spoke in chapel at Rod's Christian school. This engineer said,

> I was a bona fide geek in school. I thought calculus and trigonometry were amazing; I loved chemistry lab. But it wasn't cool in my school for guys to like to learn; I was very uncool. I asked two different girls to the prom my senior year; they both turned me down. But I had a teacher who said that God uses even uncool people for great things in his world, and that there is good work for someone who loves math and science. The work I am privileged to do today builds directly on the math and science foundation that was laid in middle and high school. I have loved being part of the awesome feat of putting astronauts into space and bringing them back. God has indeed used for good the gifts he placed in me.

The personal story by the NASA engineer altered Rod's sense of the present and the future; he is now a computer programmer who still loves to learn.

17

INTERGENERATIONAL SERVICE AND MISSIONS

One of the best ways for multiple generations within a church to develop relationships is by becoming externally focused and serving together. When the various generations corporately serve others, the focus is off generational differences and on working and cooperating together.

Peter Menconi, *The Intergenerational Church*

DURING THE LAST YOUTH GROUP service trip Christine led, she found herself wishing for an *intergenerational* service team. As two adults and seven youth spent a weekend serving in an urban homeless shelter, Christine observed that the children in the shelter received lots of attention while the adults of the shelter sat on the sidelines. Christine and the other adult in the group attempted to talk with adults at the shelter and ensure that their needs were met, but questions by or issues with the youth group often interrupted those opportunities to serve; the two adults on the trip functioned primarily as chaperones for the youth rather than as co-servants alongside them. This experience paved the way for Christine's first attempt at an intergenerational mission trip.

The intergenerational Vacation Bible School (VBS) trip to Alaska consisted of fifteen participants aged seven to seventy-two. The trip was publicized as an intergenerational opportunity for all members of the church; ultimately the service team consisted of one family of five, two Silent generation couples, a Boomer single woman, a Gen X single woman and four Millennials. As soon as the team arrived at the VBS congregation,

Christine began to observe the benefits of an intergenerational service team: People of all ages greeted them with a welcome dinner and, while the youth played with kids and began building relationships with other youth, the adult team members began building relationships with adults in the community. They had been told beforehand that only children would attend VBS, but due to the relationships built during meals, a few older youth and adults served with them on various days. They became particularly close with one family whose husband-father had recently left, leaving mom with a farm and four children to manage. This mother verbally expressed her thankfulness that the team could build relationships with every member of her family and spiritually encourage each one, including herself.

In an informal, verbal evaluation of the mission trip, youth noted the following benefits of an intergenerational team:

> "It is better to have people of different ages working together. It brings more experience and different views."

> "You learn a lot about yourself and how to treat other people, and you also grow a lot in your faith because everyone is at different places in their faith."

> "We energized the adults, and the adults helped us become more responsible and focused."

> "I think intergenerational was a lot stronger witness to the families of Alaska. We modeled the body of Christ rather than just taught it."[1]

World Servants is a mission-sending organization that provides opportunities for intergenerational and family short-term mission trips. World Servants' online literature describes intergenerational mission trips in the following manner: "There is no better way to understand the 'Body of Christ' than through sharing work and life together in another culture with a variety of people. It is a time of learning, teaching and growing together as you serve a community each using your own set of skills, talents, life perspectives and experiences."[2]

The majority of benefits noted in literature regarding intergenerational

---

[1]Christine Ross, *Intergenerational Christian Education: Opportunity for Building Community* (River Forest, IL: Lutheran Education Association Monograph Series, Spring 2003).
[2]World Servants, retrieved August 28, 2011, from <www.worldservants.org>.

service focus on what the serving team members learn from each other. However, we chose to begin this chapter as we did to highlight what we believe is the key benefit: An intergenerational service team is more likely to meet the needs of those who are served.

SPARSE LITERATURE

Each of the churches involved in Christine's dissertation research[3] discovered that service activities and mission trips were the most natural means of uniting the generations, as such activities enable people of different generations to work together toward the common goal of serving others. The congregations were involved in service or mission activities, such as all ages working on funeral meals together, young people volunteering to play games with older adult day-care participants, and all generations participating in local service activities or national or international mission trips hosted by the congregation.

Peter Menconi's book *The Intergenerational Church*[4] includes a brief chapter entitled "Intergenerational Outreach and Service" that describes potential all-age service and mission activities that faith communities could initiate. Other authors mention intergenerational service and mission only in passing. For example, James Gambone[5] notes that churches that are intentional about intergenerationality will look for ways to bring all generations of Christ's body together in a variety of avenues within the church ministry, including within worship, fellowship, discipleship and *service*. In an article about transgenerational churches[6] another church leader indicates that his congregation is involved in intergenerational activities such as worship, prayer services and *building projects*. Other churches tout intergenerational small group options, one-on-one mentoring opportunities, weekend camps and *monthly service projects* as means

---

[3]Christine M. Ross, "A Qualitative Study Exploring Churches Committed to Intergenerational Ministry" (doctoral dissertation, Saint Louis University, St. Louis, MO, 2006).

[4]Peter Menconi, *The Intergenerational Church: From WWII to www.com* (Littleton, CO: Mt. Sage Publishling, 2010), pp. 207-11.

[5]James V. Gambone, *All Are Welcome: A Primer for Intentional Intergenerational Ministry and Dialogue* (Crystal Bay, MN: Elder Eye Press, 1998).

[6]Garth Bolinder and James Emery White, "Two Pastors in a Demographic Debate: Should the Church Target Generations?" *Leadership Journal* 20 (Spring 1999): 104.

of building relationships between people of various generations.[7] Though intergenerational service and mission projects are recommended, there is very little focused literature written regarding *why* or *how* to create successful intergenerational service or mission activities.

A NATURAL MEANS OF STRENGTHENING GENERATIONAL RELATIONSHIPS

The ministry leaders interviewed in Christine's dissertation research confirmed the premise that intergenerational service activities naturally strengthen relationships between the generations. Following an intergenerational China mission trip, a pastor commented that the trip helped the generations appreciate one another and understand how each generation brought gifts to the team. In particular he noted that the youth's perceptions of older adults changed for the better as they all worked together as a team and saw how each age group has something to offer the service project. A youth leader made a similar comment and added that the bonds between the ages seem to grow stronger after mission trips in which the generations are equal team members compared to bonds created between youth and adult chaperones on a youth trip. Other leaders mentioned that service and mission activities were the easiest ways to introduce intergenerationality into a congregation both because all congregations have service opportunities within them and because giving people something to do together will naturally produce conversation among the participants. A junior high boy who attended an intergenerational fellowship event excitedly talked about Operation Christmas Child, a church-sponsored service activity that his family had worked on together. He said he especially enjoyed the summer intergenerational mission trips because they enabled his family to interact in a unique way.

Enabling the generations to work together also provides an opportunity for generational strengths to be positively utilized. The Silent generation is known for its generous financial giving to God's mandate to serve and share Christ with those in need; thus it is likely that this generation would provide the needed funding for a church service activity or mission trip. If people of

---

this generation participate in such an activity, their work ethic and their ability to mediate between people who view a situation differently can bless the service team. Boomers are known for both the desire for and ability to maintain professional standards in ministry. These characteristics, along with the Boomers' zest for life, will be an asset to any ministry venture. Gen Xers' willingness to think out of the box to get the job done in creative ways is crucial for a mission team serving in a culture different from their own. Millennials can assist in bringing the various generations together as well as use their global perspective to more easily build relationships with people who are different from themselves. Intergenerational service and mission activities provide the generations with opportunities to come together under a single purpose to live out scriptural mandates in a way that also enables individual giftedness and generational characteristics to be used to serve others and experience being the body of Christ.

INTERGENERATIONAL ADVANTAGES

In many congregations service projects and mission trips are activities usually reserved for the youth. However, Scripture indicates that loving one's neighbors and serving them is the response of *all ages* of Christians to the incredible love experienced daily through God. Not only does inviting older generations increase the team's ability to minister more broadly, it has the added advantage of simultaneously breaking down generational barriers and nurturing generational relationships, which may create a more positive environment within the congregation after the event. Another youth who was part of the Alaska VBS trip remarked, "I look forward to going to church because I *now have relationships with all those people*" (emphasis added).[8]

In a period of time when the term *missional* is used to describe congregations that focus on reaching out beyond the church building to create relationships with those who do not know God, and in a time when faith communities are updating mission statements to reflect the change from a predominantly churched to a predominantly unchurched culture,[9] it is

---

[8]Ross, *Intergenerational Christian Education*, p. 3.
[9]Milfred Minatrea, *Shaped by God's Heart: The Passion and Practices of Missional Churches* (San Francisco: Jossey-Bass, 2004).

time for the congregational body to move away from service projects and mission trips being something that "the youth do" to being a focal ministry for the whole faith community.

Taken together, the comments of the VBS mission trip youth highlight the advantages of intergenerational mission trips:

• Bringing together people of differing experiences enhanced the ability to adequately serve the local needs and the needs of the team members.

• Bringing together the generations increased the potential of having a breadth of faith maturity from which to learn.

• The youth energized adults while concurrently the adults assisted in focusing the youths' energy.

Search Institute researcher Eugene Roehlkepartain refers to a study indicating that the greatest impact on faith development of youth stems from family activities. Youth from families that talk about faith together, that participate in family prayer or devotions, *and that participate together in service projects* are more likely to have a mature faith than youth whose families do not partake in any of these activities.[10] Intergenerational service projects can provide youth with all of these assets in one activity. Intergenerational trips, which are open to all members of a congregation, provide a family with the opportunity to serve together. Any service activity, but particularly mission trips, should provide the family with an opportunity to participate in prayer and devotions and faith discussions. After an extended intergenerational event a father mentioned that before the event he had thought about starting family devotions but he was afraid his kids would laugh at him. The intergenerational activity provided his family with a model for devotions and helped them become comfortable praying together so that he now felt comfortable suggesting to his family that they begin a family devotion time during meals.

A common struggle of students who attend the mission trips sponsored by both of our universities is the difficulty of knowing how to talk to their family members about the life-changing experiences they have had. It seems that the more a mission trip has matured their faith and changed

---

[10]Eugene C. Roehlkepartain, *The Teaching Church: Moving Christian Education to Center Stage* (Nashville: Abingdon, 1993), p. 170, emphasis ours.

their worldview, the greater the difficulty explaining to parents what the trip meant to them. After a mission trip, youth can feel alienated from family; they may simply put aside their new and life-changing spiritual insights in order to fit back into their previous comfort zones. Providing whole families and "faith families" with opportunities to join the same mission trip can create common ground for discussion and understanding and could thus increase and extend the spiritual growth. Teens or adults whose family members don't attend the trips can build other relationships that provide them with surrogate family members who can remain accountability partners and talk about the common experience for many years. For example, after the Alaska mission trip some youth began calling one of the single women "aunt" and discussed among themselves that they now viewed the older adults from the trip as grandparents. The "aunt," who previously did not see herself as someone who could work with youth, became an active leader in ongoing youth and intergenerational activities as a result of the relationships she built with young people through the mission activity.

Intergenerational service activities provide intense moments of faith and relationship building as the attending children, youth and adults all are stretched spiritually and emotionally. Peter Menconi writes: "Short-term mission trips are one of the quickest ways to build solid, long-lasting relationships between generations. When an intergenerational group is together in a neutral—and often uncomfortable—environment, conversations are more easily initiated. Mission trips afford wonderful teachable moments for adults, youth and children."[11]

At such times, people tend to cling to Christ and to one another. Not only is it good for adults to see the faith of children, but it is good for younger generations to see adults challenged and vulnerable. Especially after several long days in a new culture performing unusual tasks, people tend to become more authentic. When this occurs, humans are often more open to the work of God's Spirit. In some way, the Holy Spirit works through the team members to encourage and support one another. Prayer and faith discussion often become more insightful and free than is typical

---

[11]Menconi, *Intergenerational Church*, p. 209.

for the Sunday morning fellowship time or committee meeting discussion times. This openness can build a sense of community that can be taken into the greater faith community and be "caught" by others. Meaningful relationships between people of various generations can serve to break down generation gaps, can alleviate ageism and can enable youth to see themselves as part of the church rather than youth group members only.

INCLUDING CHILDREN

> At that time the disciples came to Jesus and asked, "Who, then, is the greatest in the kingdom of heaven?"
>
> He called a little child to him, and placed the child among them. And he said: "Truly I tell you, unless you change and become like little children, you will never enter the kingdom of heaven. Therefore, whoever takes the lowly position of this child is the greatest in the kingdom of heaven. And whoever welcomes one such child in my name welcomes me.
>
> "If anyone causes one of these little ones—those who believe in me—to stumble, it would be better for them to have a large millstone hung around their neck and to be drowned in the depths of the sea." (Mt 18:1-6)

Intergenerational service activities provide a unique forum for adults to observe a child's faith in action, to gain understanding of childlike faith and humility, and to enable children to use their God-given gifts in service to Christ's church. Christine remembers struggling regarding how to answer a mother who wanted to bring her seven-year-old daughter on a week-long house-building project that would take place near a garbage dump in Tijuana, Mexico. Even Christine's love for intergenerational activities didn't remove the qualms and questions. How young was too young for this type of service project? The team was too small to babysit one of their own. Would bringing this child diminish their ability to serve well? Might a child among a group of senior high youth, college young adults and Boomers disrupt the unity of the group? Mainly because the mother couldn't participate unless the daughter came, Christine agreed. Ultimately, her qualms were unfounded as the seven-year-old (called Kate here) was an incredible blessing to the house-building team.

After days of being told she couldn't use the hammer and nails, her persistence finally wore them down and they let her try. Wanting to succeed in her venture, she took instruction well and very carefully started pounding nails. After a few bent nails, Kate began to drive nails as well as the adults and ended up finishing some roofing that required a light and nimble body. When not pounding nails, Kate was building relationships with the local children. Her inability to speak their language didn't stop them from playing together. Kate initiated the team's taking time out from building to lead impromptu VBS-like activities with the local children. She also invited the children to help build the home alongside the team. What could have turned out to be a mission trip in which the "wealthy Americans just come in and do for others" became an opportunity to build relationships with the community and to enable children to be a part of their community. Desire to please, willingness to learn, persistence, ability to build relationships with people who are different from oneself and the ability to play are all attributes the adults observed in Kate. It was a blessed opportunity for a child to teach adults.

INTERGENERATIONAL CHALLENGES

The adage "birds of a feather flock together" applies when planners are attempting an intergenerational activity. The activity leader must intentionally restructure the flock in order to form intergenerational teams. The Alaska VBS group was divided into small teams. The skit, music, teaching, crafts and snack teams were composed of three people, each from a different generation. Not only did these smaller teams work together on their specific task, but they also remained together for some prayer times and team-building activities during pretrip team meetings, which enabled them to be comfortable praying together later in Alaska. Before van rides, passengers were assigned to each van using various methods such as having everyone choose a gumball; those who chose green gumballs rode in one van, and those who chose red ones rode in the other van. There were also times of the trip that the ages or genders separated out naturally; for example, sometimes after dinner the women would end up talking together in the kitchen while the men were outside looking at the host's new golf clubs, or sometimes in the evening the youth would go outside and the adults would remain inside together. Everyone needs time to process and relax with people whose life experiences are similar as well as opportunities to work and learn with or from members of Christ's body who are at a different stage in life. A service activity leader will need to plan ahead for ways to intentionally and naturally connect the generations together in meaningful ways.

Another required aspect of intentional intergenerationality is to teach and explain the biblical as well as sociological benefits for intergenerational service activities. One leader of a research congregation commented that she "felt like a broken record" as she taught the benefits of the generations working together on congregation activities. She felt that she said and wrote and prayed the same message over and over, but that this was needed to ensure everyone was willing to try an intergenerational activity. We have discovered that the first intergenerational activities are the most difficult, but as those who joined the activities discover the benefits for themselves they become advocates for future activities.

When churches begin to form intergenerational mission trips, the youth may be the first to object: "We've never done it that way before!" They may express an unwillingness to allow the "adults to take over their mission trips." Although the Alaska VBS team was the first mission trip for that particular congregation, the youth were still skeptical about the adults' ability to *work with* them rather than *watch over* them. Again, sharing the rationale and purpose behind such a radically new approach can sometimes win over some at least for an initial attempt.

And the adults need to understand the difference between being chaperones and being a team member. Adult chaperones tend either to stand back allowing the youth to serve (only stepping in when their help is needed) or, on the other hand, to actively direct the youth regarding what they should be doing and how they should be doing it. Neither role is appropriate for an adult who is part of an intergenerational service or mission team. Teaching regarding spiritual gifts and Christ's body working together in unity will assist this intellectual and behavioral transition. Also, team building exercises and activities prior to an intergenerational service activity can help team members learn how to work together and experience how gleaning ideas from various team members can be better than any one member working alone.

Another potential challenge in an intergenerational activity is how a teen can hold an adult team member accountable and how the team leader can discipline an adult with youth nearby. Prior to a mission trip or any ongoing intergenerational service, it is important to work with the team to create a team covenant that addresses how disputes or differences of opinions will be handled. The covenant may also address what adults and youth need from each other in order to feel loved and respected by members of a different generation.

SERVICE AND MISSION SUPPORT AGENCIES

How does an intergenerational leader know where to start? If a church already has service activities or mission trips, it is good to begin by adapting some of these to incorporate intergenerational teams.

Some organizations and mission trip providers are willing to work with intergenerational groups. World Servants[12] hosts intergenerational trips

---

BOX 17.1

Potential Local Service Activities for Intergenerational Teams

- *Food pantries and kitchens*
- *Habitat for Humanity home building*
- *Urban gardens to distribute food to poor*
- *Yard work or home repair for homebound senior citizens*
- *Leading worship or games at a local retirement community*
- *"Parents' night out" for church or neighborhood*
- *Sending care packages and letters to missionaries, college students or deployed military persons*
- *Bread baking and taking bread to shut-ins or new members*
- *Making cards and visiting a children's hospital, asking families what you can pray for*
- *Graffiti and trash cleanup around your congregation's neighborhood*
- *An intergenerational thirty-hour famine*

---

[12]World Servants <www.worldservants.org>.

designed for mixed-age groups and for families with young children, and children eight years old or younger qualify for reduced rates. Adventures in Mission[13] provides family mission trips for ages six and up, which can be adapted for general intergenerational mission trips. The Center for Student Mission[14] leads weekend to week-long service activities in ten cities in the United States. The Center provides the logistics of the activities (service events, housing) while the participating church organizes its own Bible studies and team times; this plan adapts easily for an intergenerational team. While Habitat for Humanity[15] does not specifically lead intergenerational teams, it does allow youth and adults to work together on a home build. (Check the minimum age for the Habitat in your area to ensure that all members of the intergenerational team will be welcome.)

Intergenerational service projects and mission trips enable cooperation between the generations as the team members work toward fulfilling a common purpose. And, as Menconi says, "one of the best ways for multiple generations within a church to develop relationships is by becoming externally focused and serving together."[16]

The Great Commandment (Mt 22:37-40) and the Great Commission (Mt 28:19-20) provide a biblical foundation for going beyond the walls of our church buildings, even going to other countries, in order to love people through acts of service and simultaneously share the gospel of Jesus Christ through word and deed. When people of various generations are united under a single purpose, they are more likely to focus on completing the purpose together rather than focus on their generational differences. Even more importantly, they are more likely to bless *all* they have gone to serve.

---

[13]Adventures in Mission <www.adventures.org/choose/>.
[14]The Center for Student Missions <www.csm.org>.
[15]Habitat for Humanity <www.habitatforhumanity.org>.
[16]Menconi, *Intergenerational Church*, p. 207.

18

INTERGENERATIONAL SMALL GROUPS

There is no life that is not in community.

T. S. Eliot, "Choruses from 'The Rock,'" *Complete Poems and Plays*

Small groups are microcosms of God's creation community. . . . Wherever the person of Jesus calls together two or more other persons, male or female, young or old, Jew or Gentile, there is the divine-human community in microcosm, the ecclesia, a Christian small group.

Gareth Weldon Icenogle, *Biblical Foundations for Small Group Ministry*

AS HOLLY MENTIONED in the introduction of the book, her family worshiped for four years with a church that promoted intergenerational small groups every Sunday evening. Her experiences in those intergenerational groups changed her understanding of children and her understanding of Christian education and spiritual formation for children *and* adults. Ultimately these new understandings led to a career change. The work she does now grew out of those life-changing intergenerational small groups and is the work that she believes God has called her to do.[1]

Forming intergenerational small groups is the most comprehensive recommendation we will make in this book—and consequently the most challenging to implement. This chapter will describe in detail *one form* that these small groups can take.

---

[1]Parts of this chapter were adapted from or previously published in Allen, "Nurturing Children's Spirituality" (2003); Allen, "Nurturing Children's Spirituality" (2004); and Allen, "No Better Place" (2010). See permissions, page 4.

For the four years that the Allen family participated in cross-generational small groups, the adults and children stayed together for about half of the time, about an hour. During this time the children, youth and adults participated together in an icebreaker, worship, prayer and the Lord's Supper. After these activities, the children were dismissed for the children's learning time, while the adults studied and prayed together.[2]

ICEBREAKERS

The first thing that happens in an intergenerational small group is the icebreaker. A question is asked to which all—adults and children—can respond.

One icebreaker was: "What are you afraid of?" Some of the responses were:

- Gaining too much weight in my pregnancy
- That I will die young like my dad did
- That I won't be able to finish my thesis
- That I won't pass fourth grade
- That my cancer will return
- That Ben won't get his parole

Then it was Jeremy's turn. He was a second grader at the time. He put his head on his arm and began to cry, and he said in a small, jerking voice, "I'm afraid to go to sleep because I have nightmares." One of the dads in the group immediately came over to Jeremy and put his arm around his shoulders. He held him for a minute, then prayed with him and over him, that God would take away the nightmares. Then one of the older elementary girls in the group came over and said to Jeremy, "You know, Jeremy, I used to have nightmares, but I prayed to God and he took them away." A new Christian in the group, a graduate student, said with surprise and delight in her face: "I was reading the Psalms this morning, and I found a Scripture for you, Psalm 4:8: 'I go to bed and sleep in peace. Lord, you keep me safe.'"

---

[2]Many of the stories and illustrations shared in this chapter happened in the intergenerational small groups the Allens participated in during the 1990s. However, the Allens have continued to participate in intergenerational small groups, and other illustrations in the chapter are taken from those more recent settings.

This story illustrates the kind of intergenerational ministry that can and does happen even in the lightweight part of the evening, the icebreaker. Of course, often the icebreaker is simply light and fun. In a recent intergenerational gathering, the icebreaker question was, "What year did you (or will you) graduate from high school?" That night about thirty people were present; the youngest child was six and the oldest person was eighty-three. The graduation years ranged from 1945 to 2022. Another time the question was, "What is your favorite ice cream flavor?"

Each week, every person who attends—preschooler, grandparent, graduate student, young mom, teenager, tween, fortysomething or second grader—gets to say, "My name is _____, and my favorite ice cream is . . ."

And what happens cumulatively is that the participants come to know each other by name, they acquire interesting pieces of information about each other and they simply enter each other's lives—the funny parts, the sad parts, the hopeful parts, the fearful parts. Children see adults as whole, multidimensional people, and adults see children as complex, growing *people*.

WORSHIP

Following the icebreaker the group usually enters into a period of praise. Sometimes a child chooses the songs; sometimes a teen or college student leads the songs. Sometimes a parent and his/her child will have chosen the songs together. The praise time may last a few minutes or half an hour, depending upon such factors as the song leaders' choices, the spirit of the group, response to the Sunday morning experiences or the needs of the evening. Sometimes the praise time turns into a time of lament if some or many in the group are suffering through difficult times.

One evening the Allens' small group sang "Jesus, Lamb of God," and in the stillness that followed, kindergartner Justin called out in his tiny, high voice, "Can we sing it one more time?" Of course, the group sang it again, this time with a new sweetness, knowing anew that Justin was absorbing this beautiful message. Another time Holly's twelve-year-old son (who ordinarily seemed somewhat disengaged during the worship time) asked if the group could sing Dennis Jernigan's "While You Sing Over

Me." The Allens owned a copy of this song on CD, but Holly had never noticed that Daniel paid any attention when it was played. She certainly didn't know he knew the composer or the name of the song. From that moment on she began to see her son with different eyes. Worshiping together in a close and intimate setting reveals our inner spiritual lives to our children and theirs to us.

PRAYER

In Holly's experience with intergenerational small groups, the groups didn't usually have long periods of prayer while children were present, but each week the group did pray with and for each "family" present. A family is defined as a household; it can, of course, be a nuclear family with parents and children, but it can also be a widow, a college student, a single parent and her/his children, a teen attending without parents, or a married couple with no children or with adult children.

There were dozens of special moments of prayer in those small groups. Holly remembers especially one thirtysomething couple who had been married about two years; they had both been married before and the wife had two daughters by a previous marriage. When this couple became pregnant with their first child, it was a time for the whole group to rejoice together. The group began praying for this new baby, a child who would represent the blending of the two families. Holly's daughter, Bethany, who was about eight years old at the time, always joined in as the group prayed for this new little one forming in Teresa. Sadly, after about three months, Teresa miscarried. The family's loss was deeply felt by the whole small group. Bethany especially was devastated; she had felt a kinship with this new life. A few months later, Teresa became pregnant again. Once again Bethany and the whole group began praying for this little one. As the pregnancy progressed, Teresa allowed her two daughters as well as Bethany to place their hands on her growing abdomen each week as the group prayed. The three girls marveled at the firmness of the swelling belly and the movement they occasionally felt. In a deeply meaningful and personal way, these girls experienced the passage, "I am fearfully and wonderfully made" (Ps 139:14).

Other transition times for families were important prayer times. One time a man in his early forties who had owned his own business for twenty years decided to take a job working for someone else; he felt he would be less stressed and have more time for family and those he cared for in the church. The adults had prayed for him (and his wife) for some weeks as he was making the decision, but as they were now facing the transition, the group prayed together for the whole family.

All transitions are important opportunities for prayer in the group. When a child graduates from high school and goes to technical school, or joins the military forces, or gets a job or goes to college, the group prays for the whole family. When a child enters kindergarten, goes to middle school or junior high, or high school, this is a big deal, and the group prays with and for that child. No child should enter middle school without massive amounts of prayer!

Other prayer times that involved children specifically included the dreaded achievement tests that were administered every spring in the schools. For some of the children in the groups over the years, this was a very stressful time. Each spring several children would ask for prayer for concentration, clear-mindedness, peace and good sleep. Sometimes teens asked for prayer about the upcoming ACT or SAT tests they were preparing to take, and college students were pressed on all sides with papers due, relational issues and coming to adulthood, for which the groups prayed.

Early in the forming of a group, most were willing to gather around someone as the group leaders prayed for that person. Gradually more and more of the adults would begin to voice prayers. Early on some of the children were willing to pray, and gradually most of the children would say a prayer especially for other children, but it was not uncommon for children to pray for the adults as well. Interestingly it sometimes took about six months before some of the children and even some of the adults felt comfortable enough to be prayed *for* by the whole group.

One story keenly illustrates the changes that were occurring in everyone over those months of praying for one another. In preparation for the doctoral program, Holly was required to take several graduate courses in Bible, Christian education and theology. The first course she took was New Testament Theology with one of the most challenging professors in the graduate school. She rose very early one morning to study for the initial test of the semester. When Daniel (about thirteen at the time) rose around 6:30, he found his mom working through her notes and asked her what she was working on. She told him how worried she was, that she had stayed up until midnight and had risen at 5:00 to study; she said she seemed to be forgetting more than she was remembering and that she was fearful that she would make a poor showing. When she finished explaining how she was feeling, Daniel looked at her for just a moment, then asked, "Do you want me to pray for you?"

Daniel had been learning experientially in the small groups that the first thing to do is pray. And that is what he did. He sat beside his mom on their blue couch and prayed for her. It was a deeply moving moment for them, a bonding moment, a memorable event in their relationship.

LORD'S SUPPER

The Allens' small groups met on Sunday evenings, and they found that observing the Lord's Supper[3] in small, close settings brought new meaning and depth to what can become a rote ceremony, especially for children. The children in the small groups partook of the Lord's Supper with the adults; doing so offered opportunity for children to hear their parents and other adults they knew talk about their feelings and thoughts as they took of the bread and the cup.

There are dozens of ways to observe Communion, and each way surfaces a different facet of Christ's death: the Passover, the crucifixion itself, the resurrection, the sacrifice, the atonement, the substitutionary Lamb. Here is a partial list of the multiplicity of ways that a small group might observe the Lord's Supper:

- Ask two fathers to read the passage in Genesis 22 in which God asks Abraham to sacrifice his son Isaac. Then ask the father who read Abraham's part to describe how Abraham must have felt. Then ask the father who read God's part to describe how God felt when he sacrificed his son.

- Ask three adults to recall a particularly meaningful Communion service and tell why it affected them so much.

---

[3]Those from a more sacramental tradition may not choose to offer Eucharist in this less formal setting.

- Ask each person to say what moment of the crucifixion they think was most difficult for Jesus.
- Reenact the Last Supper, assigning members of the group to portray Jesus and his apostles.

These ways of partaking of the Lord's Supper elucidate the spiritual concepts surrounding it. The children begin to discern the many facets of the sacrifice of God and Christ. An added benefit for parents is that it becomes more and more natural to discuss spiritual things in their families.

There is at least one other benefit of taking the Lord's Supper in a small group with children participating. In the four years that Holly's family was with this church, they were a part of five small groups. They always went with the new group when the old group "birthed." In all five small groups, the children wanted to serve the Lord's Supper. They took great delight in carrying the loaf of unleavened, whole wheat bread to the other participants. The children also viewed with solemnity the task of toting the tray of juice-filled cups; then they enjoyed taking up the used paper cups. (Though these groups never experienced a massive tray spill, many individual juice spills occurred—thus they discovered the efficacy of white grape juice.)

Celebrating the Lord's Supper in these intimate intergenerational settings provided spiritually formative opportunities for all involved. The children participated in the spiritual life of the Christians around them; they were taught; they actually served. The adults participated more interactively in this central Christian practice; they were given opportunities to express their spiritual understandings and insights; and parents and children became more comfortable discussing spiritual things.

BLESSINGS FOR ALL

More recently, the icebreaker in Holly's current intergenerational small group was, "When you daydream or imagine, what do you see yourself doing?" Among the responses were:

- I see myself in college, loving it, having a boyfriend. (Jennifer, a teenager)
- Oh, I like to imagine myself as an NFL quarterback, winning the Super Bowl! (Ed, fortysomething)

- I'm in the World Series and I hit a homerun with bases loaded in the bottom of the ninth and win the game! (Chris, a graduate student)

- I'm always a ninja turtle. (Tristan, a fourth grader)

- I'm back in Vietnam, saving the buddies in my platoon. (Sergio, sixty-something)

- I imagine Reese living with us again; he has a good job. We have another baby, a girl. (Jan, thirtysomething, husband in Afghanistan)

Then it was Cora's turn. Cora is eightysomething; Ralph, her husband of fifty-five years, died a decade ago. She whispers, "I imagine myself in heaven with Jesus. Ralph is there, James [her deceased son] is there, my mother and dad and my sister, Robbie, are there, and then . . . our other children start to join us and then, their children. And it just goes on and on. I greet each one with open arms and homemade cookies!"

There was a quiet pause. Then Tristan said, "I'll be there too."

Jennifer said, "Me too."

And everyone joined in.[4]

---

[4]See box 18.1 for additional ways to do intergenerational small groups.

BOX 18.1

Three Alternate Approaches for Intergenerational Small Groups

Intergenerational small groups can be formatted and conducted in a variety of ways.

- *Some faith communities offer opportunities for children, teens and adults to study Scripture together. As suggested in chapter fifteen, it is feasible and, in fact, commendable for cross-age groups to learn together. The guidelines offered in chapter fifteen could be useful in initiating such groups, and a few sets of curriculum exist that support this approach (see appendix B).*

- *Building cross-generational interest groups is another approach. Some churches have asked senior adults to sponsor interest groups for younger generations based around particular skills such as quilting, basic car maintenance, baking, fishing, scrapbooking, gardening, etc. On the other end of the spectrum, emerging adults and teens have been asked to generate interest groups around social networking or even basic computer skills that older adults may wish to learn. These cross-age interest groups create occasions not only for learning skills but also for mentoring relationships to develop, and for stories to be shared (see chapter sixteen).*

- *Another approach to intergenerational small groups has been developed by GenOn Ministries (previously known as The LOGOS Ministry). GenOn's Family 'Round the Table is a complete curriculum for holistic cross-generational gatherings; these weekly gatherings (each volume contains fifty-two sessions) involve eating together, playing together, studying together and praying together (for more information, go to www.genonministries.org; also see appendix B).*

Intergenerational small groups offer unique opportunities for the generations to share each other's spiritual journeys. The particular format may vary, but intergenerational Christian formation is the ultimate goal.

19

CROSS-GENERATIONAL RELATIONSHIPS IN MULTICULTURAL CHURCHES

Chinese (Cantonese): "Dui niao tan qin."
  "(Intergenerational communication is like) playing music to a cow."

Japanese: "Oite wa ko ni shitagae."
  "When you become old, you should obey your child."

Matthew S. Kaplan, "Using Proverbs to Explore Intergenerational Relations Across Cultures"

WHILE RESEARCHING TO LEARN what Eastern cultures might teach Western Christians about intergenerational relationships, Christine discovered that the "generation gap" extends beyond Western culture, a fact that may surprise many Westerners.

Many Eastern cultures are based on the Confucian system of "filial piety," which means that the worldview of most Asian elders is founded upon "family ties, an obedient spirit, submission to elders, and [a] hierarchical order in relationships."[1] Min Ho Ko, focusing on intergenerational differences in Korean congregations, explains that in the Korean mind, the self initially emerges in an I-*We* relationship, in which the parents are *We*, and "know own parents" is the foundation of self-identity. In Western culture the self emerges from *differentiating* oneself from one's parents such that becoming independent is a sign of maturity.[2] In *Growing Healthy*

---

[1]Danny Kwon, "Spiritual Formation in the Lives of Korean-American Youth," *The Journal of Youth Ministry* (Spring 2005): 81.
[2]Min Ho Ko, *Recognizing and Bridging Common Intergenerational Differences in a Korean American Congregation* (Doctor of Ministry project, Drew University, Madison, NJ, 2010): 3.

Asian American Churches, Cha, Kim and Lee indicate that the system of filial piety can both strengthen and undermine intergenerational ties.[3] The opening Chinese and Japanese quotes are from a research study that examined different cultures' proverbs about aging, finding that "filial piety can be a factor that can exacerbate the relationship between younger and older generations."[4] As technology and rising economies bring changes to Eastern societies, the ancient Confucian system is being challenged by the younger generations who are growing up in this new environment.

GENERATIONAL DIVIDES IN ASIAN AMERICAN CULTURES

While Cha, Kim and Lee acknowledge the intergenerational challenges of Caucasian North Americans, they also believe that "some of the unique aspects of Asian American cultures and immigrant life dynamics make generational conflict within Asian immigrant churches particularly complex and challenging."[5] While Americanized second- and third-generation Asian youth progressively function within American cultural norms, their first-generation parents or grandparents function primarily within their Asian birth culture. Researching specifically Korean churches in America, Reverend Key Young Han notes that such churches

> experience enormous gaps between the first generation and the second generation members mainly with language and cultural differences. The gap is unavoidable as the first generation church members speak Korean and the second generation members use English as their daily language. The problems of the gap become more complicated as the cultural background they bring in varies depending on what period of the lives they are in and how long they have lived in America. As these gaps stay untreated, they may threaten the unity of the congregation today and endanger healthy Christian living for the growing second generation Korean-Americans in the future.[6]

[3]Peter Cha, Paul Kim and Dihan Lee, "Multigenerational Households," in *Growing Healthy Asian American Churches: Ministry Insights from Groundbreaking Congregations*, ed. Peter Cha, S. Steve Kang and Helen Lee (Downers Grove, IL: InterVarsity Press, 2006): 147.

[4]Howard Giles et al., "Intergenerational Communication Across Cultures: Young People's Perceptions of Conversations with Family Elders, Non-Family Elders and Same-Age Peers," *Journal of Cross-Cultural Gerontology* 18 (2003): 27.

[5]Cha, Kim and Lee, "Multigenerational Households," p. 147.

[6]Key Young Han, *Implementation of Multi-Generational Ministry Activities and Worship for a Korean-*

That such generational-cultural-language differences create division within the church community is also acknowledged by church leaders in other cultures[7]; however, as the majority of present multicultural research projects examine Asian cultures, this section will center upon Asian, and even more specifically, Korean intergenerational relationships.

A consequence of the Asian generational divisions is that many second-generation Asians are leaving the church. Han explains that many second-generation Koreans bear grudges and resentment due to the first-generation-led church's attempt to "pass on" the Korean heritage. Such attempts are often viewed by the younger generation as oppressive and hypocritical. "Consequently, the unity of a Korean church is diminished when attempts to sustain Korean history and heritage leaves one section of the congregation estranged and belittled [the second generation], while simultaneously leaving the other portion convicted that their personal culture has not only been rejected, but eroded [the first generation]."[8] Ko adds, "There is no more I-*We* relationship at home and in the church . . .; [there is] an I-*It* relationship between the generations,"[9] meaning people of differing generations look at one another as objects for examination rather than people with whom to build a relationship. Additionally, first-generation Korean pastors are often ill-equipped to nurture the spiritual development of the English-speaking and Americanized second and third generations, resulting in shallow spiritual nurture of youth.

ATTEMPTS TO BRIDGE THE GENERATIONAL DIVIDES

Due to the conflicts between generations described above, many congregations have chosen to provide an English ministry for the younger generations, which results in a church with two separate congregations, one in English and one in Korean. Over time, the gap between them widens; they begin to meet at different times and in different spaces with fewer opportunities for interaction and fellowship. The family comes to a di-

---

American Church (Doctor of Ministry project, Golden Gate Baptist Theological Seminary, San Francisco, CA, 2009): Abstract.

[7]Daniel A. Rodriguez, *A Future for the Latino Church: Models for Multilingual and Multigenerational Hispanic Congregations* (Downers Grove, IL: InterVarsity Press, 2011).

[8]Han, *Implementation of Multi-Generational Ministry*, p. 9.

[9]Ko, *Recognizing and Bridging*, p. 3.

vided church, and the opportunity to worship as one faith community almost ceases to exist. Due to the resulting generational divide, prejudices and stereotypes arise, which are not helpful in building a strong church.

Churches need to adapt new strategies for unifying all age groups within the congregation in order to counteract the mass departure of second-generation members from ethnic churches—a trend that is identified as the "Silent Exodus." [10] Korean American churches have existed long enough to realize that offering options by age or language has not slowed this migration of young adults from the church. Given this "silent exodus, developing healthy intergenerational ties is a critical task for Asian congregations in North America. . . . In short, the wellness and survival of most Asian immigrant churches are greatly dependent on their ability to form healthy intergenerational ties." [11]

THEOLOGICAL RATIONALE

The contributors to this discussion cited thus far provide theological rationale for intergenerational unity. Reverend Han explains that our God is and loves diversity and unity; therefore, we are to teach this basic truth about God. In our diversity we are to worship God in unity, and we are to carry out ministry in a manner that represents God's diversity and unity. We ascertain that God is diversity and unity through the doctrine of the Trinity, and we understand that God loves diversity and unity as we imagine the body of Christ, "from every nation, tribe, people and language, standing before the throne and before the Lamb" (Rev. 7:9), giving worship to God. [12]

Cha, Kim and Lee point out that Paul tells the Ephesians, "*You are no longer* foreigners and strangers, but fellow citizens with God's people and also members of his household" (Eph 2:19, emphasis ours). Paul didn't tell the early Jewish and Gentile Christians to work out their differences in order to achieve Christian unity. Instead, "he simply reminds them that Christ has already achieved their unity as he broke down the dividing wall of hostility when he died on the cross. In light of what the Savior has al-

[10]Ibid., p. 12.
[11]Cha, Kim and Lee, "Multigenerational Households," pp. 147-48.
[12]Han, *Implementation of Multi-Generational Ministry*, pp. 14, 25.

ready accomplished, Paul then calls Christians to appropriate this new reality, to enjoy a life of reconciliation and unity with all God's people."[13]

Danny Kwon, focusing less on intergenerational relationships than on the spiritual formation of Korean American youth in general, describes how using church mainly as space for social services, fellowship and maintenance of Korean culture results in a lost view of the church and ministry, as well as the biblical role of parents: "Church can become a place for youth and parents simply to be with other peers. Hence, there is a loss of priority of 'seeking God,' and faith can become secondary to culture. For youth, they often see the hypocrisy of this and can in turn become confused or alienated about their faith. Youth and their parents must be taught the importance of church, worship, and seeking God first in one's life, all of which is rooted in and motivated by God's grace and love, not social activities."[14]

In addition, due to the great expectations placed on youth by their parents, youth must be taught the unconditional love and grace of God in Christ as well as their identity in Christ as loved sons and daughters.

RESEARCH SUMMARIES

The three Christian Korean American researchers cited above studied Korean American church projects that aimed to unite the first generation with the second generation as well as with the "1.5" generation (that is, youth born in Korea but who immigrated to America at a young age). Reverend Han's project included preactivity surveys of twelve English speakers made up of six 1.5-generation youth and six second-generation youth, as well as surveys to ten first-generation members all from the same congregation. The surveys, which focused on perceptions of the "other" generations, were followed by five Sundays of united worship and two intentional intergenerational activities—a service event and a Bible quiz game and fellowship time—followed by interviews of each previously surveyed person.

Ko's intergenerational project included an initial meeting with a group of seventy- to ninety-year-old first-generation adults and a separate

---

[13]Cha, Kim and Lee, "Multigenerational Households," p. 149.
[14]Kwon, "Spiritual Formation," p. 83.

meeting with a group of fourteen- to eighteen-year-old 1.5 and second-generation youth in order to ascertain each generation's view of the other. The interviews were followed by two intergenerational activities—a game in which youth taught adults to play with a Nintendo-Wii and an activity in which adults shared the history and traditions of the Korean celebration of a child's first birthday. These activities were followed by an intergenerational group discussion of how perceptions of one another changed due to the relationship-building activities.

Last, Cha, Kim and Lee examined a church that has worked to build intergenerational unity between its first- and second-generation congregations, which had previously been meeting in the same complex with little interaction.

RECOMMENDATIONS FOR MAINTAINING RELATIONSHIPS BETWEEN FIRST AND SECOND GENERATIONS

Although the language and cultural complexities between first- and second-generation Asian Americans may increase the difficulty of uniting the generations, the means of building healthy crosscultural intergenerational relationships are surprisingly similar to those suggested for Caucasian American churches.

1. Recognize that uniting the generations so that they become a healthy multigenerational "household of God" will not be achieved overnight. It can be costly and requires long-term commitment, sacrifice and concerted efforts from both generations.

2. Intergenerational unity begins with building a unified pastoral team of first-, 1.5- and second-generation leaders. Relationships are built through weekly meetings, prayer and worship, regular lunches, and joint recreational activities. Cross-generational planning and modeling of the leadership facilitates participation of members from the various generations.

3. All generations, even when the Korean- and English-speaking congregations remain autonomous, must share the same mission statement, vision and core values, thus enabling the generations to serve one another and serve with one another in their shared mission.

4. Service projects are especially good ways to integrate disparate generations. One research congregation served the local homeless shelter together,[15] while another sent an intergenerational team to serve in an African country.[16] Both activities enabled the building of relationships and the diminishing of language as a barrier; such benefits were magnified as the generations worked side by side in a third culture and language.

5. Start slowly with joint worship services. Although the researchers avowed the importance of intergenerational worship for faith formation, the research indicated that people prefer to worship in their "heart language," which increases the complications of joint worship. Reverend Han concluded that unity through worship can be achieved when time, energy and monetary resources are put into high-quality earphones, training music and interpretation teams, so that all members can hear the full sermon and sing in their heart language as well as be able to easily learn music in their second language. Participants in this project preferred monthly intergenerational worship,[17] while another research congregation began with special services such as Thanksgiving, Christmas, Easter and baptismal celebrations.

6. Provide common meeting spaces where members can come together regularly to deepen fellowship ties. Both first- and second- generation participants in Ko's project initially spoke of how members of the other generation do not visit their generation's meeting spaces. Youth, especially, verbalized that the adults had never set foot in their rooms, and the youth interpreted this as a lack of concern toward them. Ko interpreted the varied comments regarding space and lack of cross-generational interaction within even shared spaces to indicate that such comments were "not just about a visible meeting place but about an emotional place for interacting together. It was the response from the unconscious level. . . . The generations do not feel intimate with each other."[18] Thus, congregational leaders must work intentionally to

---

[15]Han, *Implementation of Multi-Generational Ministry,* p. 74.
[16]Cha, Kim and Lee, "Multigenerational Households," p. 159.
[17]Han, *Implementation of Multi-Generational Ministry,* p. 74.
[18]Ko, *Recognizing and Bridging,* p. 49.

encourage interaction between the generations, which will enable the development of mutual understanding and intimacy.

7. Church leaders must nurture the 1.5 generation as bridge-makers between the first and second generations. This Korean-born yet Americanized generation is often more likely to respect the values of the first-generation's heritage and also be a positive influence on second-generation members. This generation "can play key roles in how people engage in and adhere to both Korean and American culture. The more we know about the 1.5 generation, the better prepared we will be to approach intergenerational differences."[19]

8. Take heart that generations will become more positive toward each other through efforts to build intergenerational relationships. Through cross-generational service projects, second-generation young people saw qualities in the first-generation members that they desired to emulate, such as dedication, servanthood, hard work, commitment, discipline and diligence. "Some [youth] also joined in the early morning prayer meetings to experience the fervor and the passion the first generation members have toward God in serving others in need and submitting their prayer concerns."[20] First-generation participants also responded more positively regarding the younger generation. They enjoyed getting to know these younger members of their congregations and enjoyed learning about their interests, opinions and thoughts. They also enjoyed being greeted by the youth when they met outside of the research activities. Adults verbalized their desire to participate in more activities with the younger generation to get to know them better; they also expressed their desire for the second generation to have more ownership of the church. They believed that the second generation can "offer flexibility, open-mindedness, willingness to change, compromise, and tight fellowship, which is generally lacking in the first generation ministries."[21]

Reverend Han is so optimistic about the role of intergenerational unity that he believes "if Korean American churches can successfully unify the first and second generations, it is not unreasonable to claim that these

---

[19]Ibid., p. 66.
[20]Han, *Implementation of Multi-Generational Ministry*, p. 81.
[21]Ibid., p. 67.

churches may ultimately possess the potential to play a major catalytic role for church revitalization in the United States."[22]

DRAWING CONNECTIONS TO OTHER CULTURES

Other Asian cultures are dealing with generational disconnects among first- and second-generation cohorts in their faith communities. Recently Holly and her young adult daughter Bethany attended a Chinese American church worship service. This congregation is facing all the issues that researchers have described. About thirty older adults were gathered in the small sanctuary; about the same number of young adults with small children were among the worshipers; and a dozen or so college-aged students and teens were also part of the gathering. Holly and Bethany were greeted at the door by a twentysomething woman who asked if they needed earphones for translation—as the sermon would be given in Chinese. Most of the worship service was conducted in both English and Chinese. The hymns were sung in both languages simultaneously as the lyrics in both English and Chinese were projected on the screen. A ten-year-old girl read the biblical text in English before the congregation; an older Chinese man then read the same text in Chinese. During the sermon, the biblical texts that were quoted were projected on the screen in both English and Chinese. About a third of the congregation wore earphones, and a high school girl translated the sermon for those with earphones. At the close of the service, the announcements were given in both English and Chinese, and as visitors, Holly and her daughter were greeted and introduced. They were also invited to join the whole church for the potluck downstairs—where traditional Chinese dishes were in abundance, as well as hot dogs and macaroni and cheese. Many welcomed Holly and Bethany, even older members who spoke very little English.

This congregation is making every effort to bond the generations together despite the presence of first-, 1.5- and second-generation members. At this point, those efforts seem to be working very well.

In *A Future for the Latino Church*,[23] Daniel Rodriguez writes that Spanish-speaking American churches are also struggling to keep their

---

[22]Ibid., pp. 11-12.
[23]Rodriguez, *A Future for the Latino Church*.

English-speaking [second] generations engaged. Rodriguez's text highlights multigenerational Hispanic churches that have recently begun to offer two services, one in English and one in Spanish, with the goal of enabling families to worship within the same church complex while being spiritually fed in their heart language. If these congregations follow the Korean congregations' pattern, then in another decade or so they may sense a divide and possibly estrangement—perhaps even hostility—between the split congregations and may seek ways to join together again. We can't help but wonder if these Latino multigenerational church leaders might adapt their present approach if they knew of the past and present direction of their Korean American brothers and sisters.

If typical English-speaking churches continue the trend of separating worship by generations and styles—children, youth and younger adults enjoying contemporary worship and older adults enjoying traditional worship—will these congregations find themselves later returning to intergenerational worship to counteract the ensuing rift between the generations of the body of Christ? It seems that they too could learn from and with the Korean brothers who are attempting to create unity amid diversity rather than estrangement within their churches. The previous chapters may themselves be the answer to this question: church leaders in typical English-speaking faith communities *are* already discovering that when youth do not build relationships with church members of other generations, they are unlikely to feel comfortable transitioning from youth to adulthood in the same congregation, or perhaps in any congregation. Church leaders *are* sensing that dividing the church predominantly by age and personal music preferences does not reflect a biblical understanding of the bodily unity. Church leaders *are* discovering that each generation needs others both older and younger to see what it "looks like" to practice faith at various ages and to be spiritually formed by the whole community of Christ.

Despite language and cultural differences, there are many similarities between the earlier recommendations in this text from intergenerational research and the recommendations from the Korean American church research: changing attitudes takes time and energy, intergenerational relationships are built slowly, and church leaders must fully embrace and be role models of intergenerationality. The Korean American church researchers discovered that the 1.5 generation may be the bridge to uniting younger and older generations, while generational theory indicates the relationships that Millennials have with both their Silent grandparents and Boomer parents may be a bridge to unity. The similarities indicate that churches from different cultures can learn from one another regarding ways to enable cross-generational Christian formation within our faith communities.

20

INTERGENERATIONALITY AND MEGACHURCHES

A large church isn't a small church with more people; it's fundamentally a different organization.

John Erwin in Helen Lee, "Age-Old Divide"

Relationships—relationships between and among generations— are paramount.

"Intergenerational Teams," in *Christian Management Report,* August 2006

IN OUR EXPERIENCES, churches of two hundred or fewer seem like a big family: children know the teens, the teens know the adults and the seniors know everybody. When an elderly member dies, everyone—including children and teens—attends the funeral; determining when to have a baby shower takes place after church as a few women clump together, drawing others in as they walk by. Everyone knows that the Kim's baby has an ear infection; that Sean, the ninth grader, made the varsity team; that Christa didn't make the drill team; that the Rankins are struggling financially; and that Linda's chemo treatment went well this week.

On the other hand, churches of two thousand or more seem a bit like corporations: children know a few other children their own age; teens know some of the other teens; senior adults know the other senior adults. When an elderly member dies, few children or teens or young adults attend the funeral; determining when to have a baby shower takes place after consulting the church calendar and rooms available, and clearing it with the powers that be; Linda is one of the dozens (or hundreds) on the online prayer list (along with the Kim baby); a few in the youth group will know about Sean's honor; perhaps no one will know about the Rankins' financial struggles or Christa's sense of failure and loss. Creating authentic opportunities for relationships— even relationships *within* age and stage levels—is a daunting challenge for those who lead megachurches. Fostering opportunities for cross-generational relationships may seem unrealistic. Church growth specialist Lyle Schaller affirms our experiences as he describes characteristics of churches.[1] Schaller titles a church over seven hundred members an "autonomous nation" with a pastor running this entity as a CEO may run a business.

However, recently Holly visited a megachurch in the Dallas area. The Sunday she visited, the church hosted an old-fashioned Sunday noon whole-church intergenerational potluck. Emails had been sent, RSVPs for about a thousand people had been received (and respondents had signed up to bring macaroni and cheese, potatoes, green beans or dessert), fried chicken was ordered, and a thousand babies, children, teens, young adults, middle adults and older adults ate Sunday dinner together; everyone was served in thirty minutes with eight food lines open. It was quite amazing. After the potluck, the church hosted a variety/talent show with participants ranging in age from four to seventy-nine. This faith community also has an intentional intergenerational small groups program that has been operational for two years.

DESEGREGATING THE MEGACHURCH

Desegregating megachurches generationally is a challenge, says John Erwin, pastor to families at Yorba Linda Friends Church, a megachurch in Yorba Linda, California. Erwin notes that a "large church isn't a small church with more people; it's fundamentally a different organization."[2]

---

[1]Lyle Schaller, *Looking in the Mirror: Self-Appraisal in the Local Church* (Nashville: Abingdon, 1984).
[2]Helen Lee, "Age-Old Divide: How Do You Integrate the Generations and Life Stages at Your Church? Five Church Leaders Respond," *Leadership* 27 (Fall 2006): 46.

Most megachurches offer a full hour of well-planned energetic children's church while the parents worship elsewhere. Logistically it is not feasible or safe to allow the children to stay with parents until time for the sermon, and then dismiss hundreds of children simultaneously for their own learning time, so megachurches must offer the full hour—or none. Erwin accepts that parents are accustomed to having their hour of worship without the kids present to distract, and he recognizes that changing that cultural expectation is too difficult. So Erwin recommends seeking other avenues for integrating the generations.

Erwin describes several ways Yorba Linda Friends Church has been attempting in recent years to create intentional intergenerational opportunities. The church offers family worship opportunities several times a year; for these special worship services, children five years old through sixth grade join the adults. Also several special events have been incorporated into the calendar year; for example, a father-son weekend called Passage for teen boys and their dads, as well as an annual family camp.

Beth Kenyon at Fellowship Bible in Northwest Arkansas faces some of the same issues Erwin describes. Fellowship is a megachurch that utilizes the Celebration/Cell approach to structure: large-group worship (Celebration) on weekends and small-group (Cells) meetings through the week. Originally only adults met in small groups; now, however, emerging single adult groups, teen groups and junior high groups meet in homes during the week also, and children's small groups meet during the Celebration worship hour on weekends. To foster intergenerational relationships, the church purposely brings together cell groups from different age/stage groups for service and mission activities: "We have adults, teen, and child small groups working with each other, serving together, going on mission trips," says Kenyon.[3] Fellowship also offers family worship opportunities once a month on Sunday evenings, which, Kenyon says, have been enthusiastically endorsed and well attended.[4]

One large church in Tennessee has bucked the age-segregated trend

---

[3]Angie Ward, "Let the Little Children Come," *Leadership* 30 (Summer 2009): 56.
[4]Beth Kenyon, personal conversation, April 15, 2010.

among megachurches. Twelve years ago Second Presbyterian Church in Memphis offered a strong children's church program, but when the children's minister stepped down, the church temporarily invited the children back into the adult worship services. It was a difficult transition. "Parents had gone hands-off with teaching their kids about worship," says Sandy Hazelwood, the children's minister who facilitated the transition.[5] Nevertheless, eventually the church leadership decided that it was better spiritually for the children to worship with their parents and the rest of the faith community, and the temporary decision became permanent.

The largest megachurches may not be able to emulate Second Presbyterian. Reversing the long-entrenched, homogeneous, age-based approaches in megachurches will be difficult. Erwin explains, "It's a challenge going against the tradition of age-segregated ministry that churches have done for several decades now."[6] However, they can continue to actively seek other ways to bring the generations together.

When the leaders of a megachurch truly embrace an intergenerational outlook, one excellent way to draw others into this paradigm shift is to challenge every ministry leader and every program director to incorporate into each planned activity the key step of asking the following two questions: *How can this activity/study/event include at least two generations?* and *Who else can we invite to join us for this opportunity?*

When the preschool Easter egg hunt is planned, extend a gracious invitation to the older congregants to come and participate; when the youth group forms a clean-up crew to help tornado victims, ask parents to come—not as "sponsors" or drivers, but as fellow workers; when the seniors decide to plant a garden in the back lot, invite the younger elementary children to bring trowels and gloves and help plant seeds and dig; when the emerging adults plan a worship service, ask for input from the oldest members of the faith community or invite two or three specific older members to join the planning team for this event.

This powerful challenge will disseminate the age-inclusive perspective throughout the entire faith community, and the ongoing spiritual blessings that intergenerationality affords will be poured out abundantly.

---

[5]Ward, "Let the Little Children Come," p. 54.
[6]Lee, "Age-Old Divide," p. 46.

INTERGENERATIONAL PREACHING

If a faith community commits to fully intergenerational worship, that is, welcoming *all* generations, those who are charged with speaking to these generations will surely find the prospect daunting. Five or six generations are present when entire faith communities gather together:

- children (twelve years of age and under)
- teens (ages thirteen to eighteen, in junior high and high school)
- emerging adults (ages nineteen to twenty-eight or so, often single)
- young adults (young marrieds; pre-children or with young children; may include young singles as well, divorced or never married; may overlap with emerging adults)
- middle adults (still working; teenage and emerging adult children; may include single middle adults also, divorced or never married)
- older adults (retired and older; married, divorced, single, widowed).

Rick Richardson acknowledges that preaching to five or six generations is a challenge; in fact he calls it a "cross-cultural" challenge.[7] Richardson says that anyone who preaches is communicating crossculturally in a variety of ways: navigating gender barriers when preaching to men and women; navigating ethnic barriers when preaching to Asian Americans, Latinos, African Americans, whites and others; and navigating generational barriers when preaching to all ages. Richardson offers several principles to aid when teaching/preaching across cultural divides. The following pertain especially to generational divides.

Acknowledge trust issues. Richardson describes a specific trust issue among some of the younger generations. "They mistrust anyone who, while claiming to know truth, discredits other ideas as wrong. This makes preaching to postmoderns a challenging cross-cultural experience."[8] Postmoderns are typically the twenty- and thirtysomethings, but some fortysomethings find problematic the message that Jesus is *the* way. Richardson says that when preaching in a setting with all ages present, he tries "to

---

[7]Rick Richardson, "Preaching Across the Great Divide: Seven Means to Communicate When Facing Today's Ethnic, Gender, and Generational Gaps," *Leadership* 26, no. 2 (2005): 47.
[8]Ibid., p. 48.

acknowledge where the bridge is broken before I try to cross it. I identify with people's fears. I talk about how uncomfortable I am with people who reject others. Then I talk about the hope and love that Christ gives."[9]

Use their heart language. Richardson says music is the heart language of many young people and that therefore "referencing their music shows you are trying to understand their world."[10] And every generation has its own heart music; mentioning popular tunes from the 1940s, the 1960s, the 1980s and so on will connect with those who came of age during those eras as well. Richardson said that the speaker need not be steeped deeply in a particular type of music (or art, or film genre) to reference it; the attempt to connect and genuine interest are sufficient to build communication bridges.

Become a good storyteller. All ages appreciate stories. Stories about life, family and struggles typically translate well across cultures and ages. "Narratives help us relate to each other. Through story-telling we share pain, apply truth, express humor, and build trust. Becoming fluent in the universal language of story is essential if we want to reach across cultures."[11] Good cross-age communicators tell stories from across the life span: kid stories, school stories, dating stories, first-job stories, newlywed stories, midlife crisis stories, aging stories. Everyone loves stories.

Cultivate connections. Richardson recommends cultivating friendships with people from all generations. If the preacher is a Boomer, spending time with Millennials and with those from the Silent generation will broaden and deepen understanding on both sides. But more importantly, according to Richardson, these friends can also "translate" the needs and perceptions of their generations for the preacher. Likewise, checking in with a key teen occasionally to ask what the youth group might like to hear could be invaluable. Mike Breaux, teaching pastor at Heartland Community Church in Illinois, recommends including youth "in preaching illustrations or challenge points ('whether you're at work or by your locker'). It means learning about their culture and addressing their issues."[12] To do this well will mean making intentional connections.

---

[9]Ibid.
[10]Ibid.
[11]Ibid.
[12]Mike Breaux, "A Mad Multi-Gen Strategy that Works, Dude," *Leadership* 26 (Spring 2005): 45.

A general truism is that all communication is crosscultural. Being heard across generational divides is especially challenging, but Richardson says the speaker is more likely to be heard if he or she acknowledges and honors the cultures of those listening; in this case, the younger, the older and those in between.

INTERGENERATIONAL LEADERSHIP

In the preface, Christine mentioned that the small rural congregation of her youth welcomed youth into leadership positions. Mainly due to the need for leaders, junior and senior high youth became Sunday school and VBS teachers, children's choir leaders, members of the worship committee or property committee. As churches grow, there are more adults to assume leadership, and ministry *to* youth becomes an adult responsibility. Currently, the adults in leadership positions are most often middle-aged Boomers and those from the Silent generation, although hundreds of new churches are now being planted by Gen Xers. What has been unusual historically is for a larger church to have a working, healthy, *intergenerational* leadership team.

The North Way Community Church in Wexford, Pennsylvania, has intentionally crafted an intergenerational ministry team: a fifty-nine-year-old senior pastor, a forty-seven-year-old executive pastor and a thirty-year-old teaching pastor. The senior pastor, Jay Pasavant, recognized a couple of years ago that it would be wise to have a teaching pastor who represents Gen Xers (called Mosaics in this setting), since that generational cohort is a substantial portion of the church (though the church also has substantial middle-aged and older adults).[13]

Don Neff, associate/executive pastor of a church called The Worship Center in Lancaster, Pennsylvania, says that when The Worship Center was twenty-five years old, he realized the leadership was composed of people forty-five to fifty-five years old. He had begun to notice that when a church reaches the twenty-five-year mark, it "will intentionally connect with the next generation, or it will become a one-generation church and

---

[13]"Intergenerational Teams: How One Ministry Shows They Can Work," interview with Jay Pasavant, Dan Chaverin and J. R. Kerr, *Christian Management Report* 30 (August 2006): 17-20.

slowly decline."[14] The Worship Center began to bring younger people into leadership roles; they invited some to lead worship, others to join planning teams for church-wide events and others to be on the board.

Mike Breaux, former teaching pastor at Willow Creek Community Church in Illinois, also recognizes the importance of cross-generational direction. He recommends "including teens and twentysomethings in visible ways: worship, drama, testimonies, and *even leadership*."[15]

Why is it difficult for older ministry leaders to invite younger generations into leadership?

Neff admits that "the older generation can get very comfortable and not be as open to change."[16] Also, older leaders recognize that the forty- to seventy-year-olds are the financial support base, so Neff says leaders must walk a fine line: they don't want to alienate the older members of the church, but they also want to build relationships across all the generations.

Interestingly, it is sometimes as difficult for younger generations to join an older ministry team as it is for the older to welcome them. Pasavant remarks that "a substantial number of Mosaics [Gen Xers] have predetermined that Boomers are incapable of relinquishing control."[17] Pasavant goes on to say that young leaders "marvel at how dense and thick and organized and linear and driven and productive we Boomers can be. We, on the other hand, marvel at how nonlinear, abstract, creative *they* are."[18] Boomers tend to have a "come and see" mentality; Mosaics tend to have a "go and do" mentality.[19]

In general, intergenerational faith communities are blessed when the leadership is made up of young, middle and older adults. Pasavant concludes his advice on building intergenerational teams by saying that older and younger generations must have a learner mentality; that is, leaders must be willing to learn and grow. A learning and growing leader will welcome new people with fresh ideas.

---

[14]Lee, "Age-Old Divide," p. 44.
[15]Breaux, "Mad Multi-Gen Strategy," p. 45, emphasis ours.
[16]Ibid.
[17]"Intergenerational Teams," p. 18.
[18]Ibid.
[19]Ibid.

RESEARCH CONGREGATION:
AN INTERGENERATIONAL MEGACHURCH

In the early 1990s a pastor and lay minister began a new congregation in the Mountain Time region. The two leaders' vision for the new church was central to the initial mission statement of the congregation, "Caring about and for the body of Christ through relationships." When Christine visited, the church was 2600 members strong with fifteen full- or part-time ministry staff members.[20]

Four years into establishing the new congregation, the founding lay minister read Strauss and Howe's book regarding generational theory.[21] Though the book did not immediately change his ministry philosophy, as the lay minister watched the dissension within the multigenerational congregation, he realized that some of the conflict stemmed from the clash of values and needs of the different generations. He recognized the importance of teaching the congregation about the different values, gifts and needs of the various generations in order to provide understanding and unity. As the lay minister grew in his comprehension of the importance of cross-generational relationships within the church, he came to believe wholeheartedly that intergenerational relationships are an important biblical concept and that each generation has much to offer the others. He believed that all of life, especially church life, is more meaningful and more purposeful when the generations share and work together.

The lay minister discussed his new vision with the senior pastor. As the senior pastor was already convinced of the importance of building strong relationships within the body of Christ, it was not difficult to persuade him about the importance of building intergenerational relationships. The senior pastor encouraged the lay minister to consider how to share the philosophy with the congregation. Over the next few months, the lay minister planned a series of sermons in which representatives from each

---

[20]Christine M. Ross, "A Qualitative Study Exploring Churches Committed to Intergenerational Ministry" (doctoral dissertation, Saint Louis University, St. Louis, MO, 2006). See note two of our introduction earlier in this book.

[21]William Strauss and Neil Howe, *Generations: The History of America's Future, 1584 to 2069* (New York: Quill, William Morrow, 1991).

generation shared what it was like to grow up in their respective genera-tions; each described the unique gifts her generation had to offer, and each shared how he believes God spoke to his generation. Afterward, the lay minister preached about unity and diversity. These messages "hit a re-sponsive chord with the staff," and they began talking together about how to implement intergenerational ministry into the congregation. Soon after, the senior pastor developed three ministry values that he called the staff and elders to embrace: be interdepartmental (ministry leaders must coordinate events so they do not compete with one another); be intergen-erational (ministry leaders consider how to connect all ages together); and be interdisciplinary (ministry leaders will implement a variety of spiritual disciplines into programming).

With intergenerationality as a congregational value, the large min-istry staff vigorously worked together to integrate the value into the main activities of the church. They made an intentional effort to ensure that all adult generations were included on boards. The youth ministers and the women's minister worked together to encourage junior through senior high youth to join women's activities, and they brought a high school girl onto the women's ministry board. Youth ministers also worked with the men's minister to create intergenerational mentoring relationships between boys and men. All ministry staff brainstormed regarding which current church activities could easily adapt to inter-generationality. Other means of building intergenerational relation-ships included: choirs of junior high youth through senior adults to-gether; Sunday school having three or four grades combined with male and female high school and adult leaders; young adults leading junior high and high school classes; adult Sunday school topics chosen for the likelihood of being of interest to a range of adults; the Operation Christmas Child project designed to enable families to box and wrap gifts immediately after church; intergenerational mission projects; quarterly intergenerational activities such as a barbeque dinner and square dance, or a picnic and fishing at a nearby lake.

As the church continued to grow, plans were made to enlarge space for fellowship. The fireplace room was decorated to resemble a coffee shop. The beautifully painted room included cozy couches, round tables surrounded by comfortable chairs, artwork and the enticing aroma of brewing coffees and hot chocolate. Hallways were also enlarged and nicely decorated with artwork, plants and scattered comfortable chairs to promote conversation. The intergenerational philosophy of ministry was—and still is—carried out in this congregation.

CONCLUSION

The best way to be formed in Christ is to sit among the elders, listen to their stories, break bread with them, and drink from the same cup, observing how these earlier generations of saints ran the race, fought the fight, and survived in grace.

James Frazier, in *Across the Generations: Incorporating All Ages in Ministry*

THE PROCESS OF BECOMING CHRISTLIKE in one's attitudes, values, beliefs and behaviors—that is, Christian formation—does not happen alone. The premise of this book has been that intergenerational faith communities are God-designed places for Christian formation.

The situative-sociocultural theory promotes the idea that persons learn the ways of a community of practice as they participate authentically and relationally with "more experienced members of the culture."[1] No better place exists for the most number of people to learn Christian ways from more experienced members of the culture than intergenerational Christian communities. People of all ages and maturity levels are present, actively carrying on the very essentials of Christianity. In intergenerational communities, children learn from each other, younger children, older children, teens and adults. And adults learn from teens and children as well as older adults. All benefit from each other with a sense of mutuality; in essence, they grow each other up into Christ.

But for intergenerational Christian formation to happen, the genera-

---

[1]James Wertsch and Barbara Rogoff, eds., *Children's Learning in the "Zone of Proximal Development": New Directions for Child Development* (San Francisco: Jossey-Bass, 1984), p. 1.

tions must *be* together; they must *know each other;* and they must experience life in the body of Christ *together.*

Creating an entire culture or ethos of intergenerationality will require wise leaders who will remind the faith community often of the strengths, benefits and joys of intergenerational experiences. These leaders will share encouraging cross-age stories in person and through Facebook and blogs: eightysomething Charlie and five-year-old Slade pulling weeds together; the youth group and their parents serving Thanksgiving dinner at the shelter; older members inviting all the elementary-aged children to an evening of "Stories from the Dark," where the seniors shared memories from their childhood when the lights went out—or even tales of life before electricity.

These wise leaders will welcome all the generations when the faith community gathers; they will communicate in their bearing a sense that the babies, children, teens, emerging adults, young adults, middle adults, older adults, singles, divorced, widowed, married—all—are family in this body of Christ, that is, they all *belong.* They will foster settings where, when their young men see visions and their old men dream dreams, the young men and the old men will be there to hear each other; they will create cross-age learning occasions; they will seek opportunities for service projects where seven-year-olds can hammer nails with septuagenarians. They will remind the community that each generation brings gifts that encourage spiritual formation.

And these wise leaders will read often Jesus' words, calling for his followers to oneness and unity: "My prayer is . . . that *all of them may be one,* Father, just as you are in me and I am in you. May they also be in us so that the world may believe that you have sent me. I have given them the glory that you gave me, that they may be one as we are one—I in them and you in me—so that they may be brought to complete *unity.* Then the world will know that you sent me and have loved them even as you have loved me" (Jn 17:20-23, emphasis ours).

And finally, these leaders will exhort the saints in their care to "consider how to stir up one another to love and good works, not neglecting to meet together, as is the habit of some, but encouraging one another, and all the more as you see the Day drawing near" (Heb 10:23-25 ESV).

As the day of Christ's return draws near, let us not be found in faith communities divided by age, but let us unwaveringly take hold of the fact that in Christ Jesus:

> We are the family of God
> And he has called us together to be one in him
> That we might be formed into the likeness of his Son,
> Enabled to worship him in unity
> And be the light of Christ in this dark world.

To God be the glory.

Appendix A

FORTY INTERGENERATIONAL IDEAS

MOST CHURCHES HAVE five or six generations. When guidelines say "two or more generations," they are referring to the generations listed below:

- children (twelve years of age and under)
- teens (ages thirteen to eighteen, in junior high and high school)
- emerging adults (ages nineteen to twenty-eight or so, single)
- young adults (young marrieds; pre-children or with young children; may include young singles as well, divorced or never married; may overlap with emerging adults in age)
- middle adults (still working; teenage and emerging-adult children; may include single middle adults also, divorced or never married)
- older adults (retired and older; married, divorced, single, widowed)

TEN IDEAS FOR DRAWING THE GENERATIONS TOGETHER THROUGH UTILIZING THE SENSES:

1. Share a loaf of whole wheat bread and a loaf of white bread in an inter-generational setting. (Perhaps ask two people from an older generation and a younger generation to make the bread.) Discuss how the whole wheat bread is different from white bread (more substantial, more nutritious, more filling, healthier, etc.). Discuss how Jesus is our "whole wheat bread of life." How is whole wheat bread like spiritual food?
2. While reading Genesis 1, play Smetana's "The Moldau." Ask: Does this sound like music that goes with creation? What other music that you know would go beautifully with reading Genesis 1? (If you wish, look up the background on this symphonic composition; the Moldau is the river that flows through Prague.)

3. Ask someone who knows sign language to teach an intergenerational group (or the whole gathered faith community) the signs for *God, Lord, glory* and *holy*. Then pray the prayer, "Lord, you are holy; God, we give you glory" with everyone signing the words that were taught.

4. Encourage two from different generations make a recipe together for a potluck or a small group gathering.

5. Ask participants to bring a favorite blanket, stuffed animal, afghan, pillow or other favored textured item from home (children especially will participate proudly). As each person shares his or her favorite touchy-feely item, ask *why* this item is so important. After all have shared (or along the way if it works), discuss the importance of texture, the comforting nature of some textures and why we are comforted by them. Then ask: Why might God have made us in such a way that these soft, warm items comfort us? How are they like him?

6. Organize an intergenerational art event; encourage young to old to bring their drawings, paintings and other artistic creations to share.

7. After a meal together, discuss how studying from Scripture is like eating (it nourishes us; we must eat/study regularly, not just sporadically; when we study together, we bring different insights to the "meal," and can thus share the food; when one hasn't had time to study, she or he can "eat off another's plate").

8. Ask a willing person from each generation—all six generations if possible—to share with the gathered faith community how they would "make a joyful noise" to the Lord (Ps 95:1 ESV). Encourage them to bring props if needed.

9. Call two specific generations to set up for a potluck meal (e.g., teens and middle adults); call two specific generations to clean up after a potluck meal (e.g., emerging adults and [active] older adults).

10. In any cross-generational setting, bring three aromatic herbs or spices (e.g., cinnamon, lavender, chili powder) in unmarked containers. Let participants catch a whiff of each scent, discuss special memories associated with those aromas, then ask: What will be the aromas in heaven? Why?

TEN IDEAS FOR ENGAGING THE GENERATIONS WHILE READING SCRIPTURE:

1. Ask three individuals (from three different generations) to share a time when a particular passage became *life* for them.

2. Read Psalm 136 antiphonally; all, even nonreaders, can repeat the phrase, "His love endures forever."

3. Ask three people from three different generations to share their favorite memory verse—and why it is important to them.

4. Show Michelangelo's *Pietà* (sculpture of Mary holding Jesus after his death); read about Mary's standing at the foot of the cross when Jesus died. Discuss how she may have felt. If you wish, ask a mother who has an adult child to share how hard it would be to watch her son or daughter die.

5. Share a story from Jesus' life that carries deep meaning (ask individuals from different generations).

6. Ask three people from three different generations to share an important psalm in their life.

7. Ask: Where do you go in Scripture when you are lonely, sad, hurting, wounded, thrilled, thankful? (Ask someone from three different generations to share.)

8. While reading Luke 15:11-32, show a picture of *The Return of the Prodigal Son*, Rembrandt's famous painting of the father receiving the son. Ask who the different people are in the painting. Note the young brother's appearance. Point out the expressions on the faces of the father and the older brother. What is most touching about the painting? Do we have stories like this among us? How do we receive those who return?

9. Locate six to eight people of various ages in the faith community who speak different languages. While reading Acts 2, ask them to begin saying several phrases in their non-English language: "How is it we understand in our own language?" "Aren't these men unlearned Galileans?" "I speak only Spanish and she speaks only Chinese; how are we understanding what is being said all at once?" "Who are these men?" "What is happening here?"

10. Read Psalm 78:1-8 aloud with everyone listening for how many generations are mentioned. Ask how many generations were named (people usually find four generations, though it is possible to name five). Read it again, noting the different generational references as you go. See if you have five generations represented in your group (possibilities: child, teen, emerging adult, young adult, middle adult and older adult). Then enact the following scene: the oldest generation representative tells something powerfully true about God (e.g., "God is good" or "God loves you") to the next generational representative, then that person turns to the next person and tells that same truth, and so on to the child. (This will work even if only three generations are present.)

FIVE WAYS TO DRAW THE GENERATIONS TOGETHER THROUGH WORSHIP IN SONG

1. When singing "Be with me, Lord," suggest singing "Be with *us*, Lord." (Note that Paul used the expression "our Lord" fifty-three times in his letters, but used "my Lord" only once.[1])
2. Ask two from different generations to choose the songs occasionally or frequently.
3. Sing pairs of themed songs from two (or three) different generations (e.g., a song on thankfulness from the 70s or 80s and a current one, or a Reformation-era hymn and a contemporary song on grace).
4. Choose a song all generations know and enjoy, then ask a younger person and an older person to share what this song means to them (ask ahead of time).
5. Include a teen or child on the worship planning team occasionally or regularly; so doing will affect the choice of songs/hymns and spiritual songs chosen.

FOUR ACTIVITIES FOR GETTING TO KNOW EACH OTHER

1. Ask in mixed-age setting: Where were you when . . .
   • JFK was killed?

---

[1]Joseph Hellerman, *When the Church Was a Family: Recapturing Jesus' Vision for Authentic Christian Community*. (Nashville: B & H Academic, 2009), p. 177.

- Apollo landed on the moon?
- the Challenger exploded (1986)
- the Berlin Wall fell (1989)
- you heard of Princess Diana's death?
- 9/11 occurred?
- you heard the news that Osama Bin Laden had been killed?

2. Bring an item from your past and share a story:
   - Christmas ornament
   - Card received
   - Picture of a special day in your life

3. Share:
   - Saddest day of life
   - Most victorious day of life
   - Good move to another city or place; or a hard move to another city or place
   - Favorite room in childhood home
   - Favorite meal your mother used to prepared (or still prepares)
   - Show and share about a body scar (talk about it, if you can't show it)

4. Movement
   - Ask the youth group to create a labyrinth (see guidelines on page 282); walk the labyrinth in generational pairs.
   - Sing "Deep and Wide" together with motions (or other song with traditional movement); discuss what it means.
   - Go as a large group to a park with play equipment; once there, team cross-generational pairs and have fun.
   - In generational pairs or groups, cut snowflakes together and decorate windows.

FIVE PROMPTS FOR INTERGENERATIONAL STORY SHARING

1. Passage: Genesis 29:31-35 (as Leah shifts the focus of her trust from Jacob to God)
   Prompt: Share how you learned not to depend on human approval and to rest in God's approval alone.
2. Passage: Philippians 4:8: Whatever is true, right, noble, pure, admi-

rable, praiseworthy, lovely, excellent, "think about such things."

Prompt: Share a time when you were dwelling on harmful, destructive thoughts, and God taught you how to focus instead on "these things."

3. Passage: Joshua 4:1-7 (where the children of Israel build a twelve-stone marker to memorialize the miraculous crossing of the Jordan River)

   Prompt: Bring a physical reminder of God's work in your life and share the story that goes with it.

4. Passage: Isaiah 61:1-2 (Jesus applied these verses to himself in Luke 4:16-20. He is the one who has come to bind up the brokenhearted, set captives free and comfort those who mourn.)

   Prompt: Share a time when Jesus bound your broken heart, set you free or comforted you.

5. Passage: Isaiah 61:3-4 (Jesus applied these verses to himself in Luke 4:16-20. He is the one who has come to bestow a crown instead of ashes, a garment of praise instead of a spirit of despair, and to rebuild, restore and renew.)

   Prompt: Share a time when Jesus replaced your ashes with a crown, exchanged your despair for thanksgiving, or has rebuilt, restored or renewed in your life.

SIX MORE EXTENSIVE IDEAS FOR BRINGING THE GENERATIONS TOGETHER

1. Share the learning. Ask children's classes to share what they have been learning in a brief way when the whole church gathers.

For example, Holly's elementary-aged class had been studying the "I am" passages regarding Christ. On the week they looked at "I am the bread of life," they made whole wheat bread loaves and discussed what it means for Jesus to be their "whole wheat" bread of life (versus their white bread of life). Their ideas included that he fills us up, that he is more nutritious, that he tastes good, that he is more robust and substantial. After they made their small whole wheat bread loaves, the children took them home to their families (though Holly noticed that some were nibbled during the worship service). The next week the children asked if they could make whole wheat bread loaves for every family unit (including singles) in the congregation—about twenty-five loaves for their small church. So two weeks later they did this; they mixed and formed the loaves during class and baked them during the worship service, and then at the end, the elders asked the children to come up and share what they knew about Jesus as their "whole wheat" bread of life. They each shared a sentence or idea, then stood at the door distributing the loaves to families on the way out the door. It was a fabulous activity, but this activity is transferable with many things children are learning in their Bible classes.

2. Welcome a particular age cohort each week.

- Children or teens: "We are so glad to have our children among us today; our newest member is here today, little Ryan; we are glad Remi is back among us from her illness; we are delighted our high school band members are back in town after their trip to the Rose Bowl." In larger churches where specific events would exclude too many, more generic welcomes can include: "We are glad to have our newly minted graduates among us" (or our new middle schoolers, our new first graders or our new kindergartners).

- Emerging adults: "We are particularly blessed to have among us our twentysomethings who are learning what it means to be part of the adult world. We want you to know that those of us who are older have been through these tough years and are here to support you and mentor you as you figure out the financial world (renting, owning a home, insurance, savings), learn to live with roommates or to live on your own, negotiate the work world of bosses and coworkers, and generally take responsibility for your decisions and your lives; we are here and want to bless you as you move through these challenging years. We are glad you are with us today to worship with us."

- Parents of young children: "We have lots of babies today; we welcome you and your parents who are here to worship. We want you to know that though we have facilities available should you need them, you are welcome among us. We will interpret the occasional cries of these children as representing the cries of the world; it is good to be reminded that there are many calling out in need for what we have here. We are glad you are among us."

- Middle adults: "This church has a number of families with preadolescent children and teens. These are very important years for your families, and we are delighted you are here among us worshiping God together. We want you to know that there are many here who have survived these very busy years when children are going in many directions, jobs are very demanding, finances are tight and families are pulled in different directions. If you need encouragement for not just surviving but thriving in these years, look around and find those who have already traveled the journey you are on. In the meantime, lay aside today's worries and join us as we worship together."

- Older adults: "Today we want to especially welcome our older adults. We are very blessed in this faith community to have among us many who have known God for many decades and have learned from him how to live wisely in his world. We recognize that we need you, and we want you among us; we ask that you embed yourselves among us so that we can learn from you, and so that we can bless you also. We are glad you are among us today as we worship."

3. Faith community as wagon train. In an intergenerational group setting, watch an episode of the old television series "Wagon Train." Divide those who watched into small intergenerational groups of ten to fifteen, with an experienced facilitator prepared to lead the discussion. A few props can make this more accessible to young children (firewood, outdoor cooking pot, picture of a Conestoga wagon, a saddle, a quilt, a burlap sack of beans or flour, a picture of a buffalo, possibly a map showing a common wagon train route). Ask: What was the purpose of a wagon train? Discuss what it was like to be part of a wagon train: What jobs were needed for the train to safely cross the plains? Did children have any jobs? Teens? Young, middle and older adults? What were the wagon train leader's responsibilities? The scout's job? What problems did wagon trains encounter? External enemies? Internal enemies? Key question: How is our church like a wagon train? Possible responses may include:

- We are a pilgrim band, traveling together toward a destination.
- We are all traveling together—everyone is actually traveling; singles, children, teens, young, middle, older adults.

- All are valuable; we are in this together.
- We help one another in order for us to succeed; we need each other.
- We rejoice together and mourn together.
- There are important jobs for all. (Elaborate if desired.)
- We have leaders.
- Who are our scouts?
- We have external enemies and internal enemies.

4. "He is risen!" Around Easter, color dozens of boiled eggs red, and host an intergenerational "He is risen indeed!" event. This is based on a Greek orthodox traditional Easter activity.

Place the eggs in several baskets. Arrange everyone who is participating in a large circle (up to fifty or sixty could work). Give a basket to five people. Each person with a basket of eggs walks along the circle and gives an egg to each person sitting, saying, "He is risen." The person who receives the egg responds, "He is risen indeed."

The Greek Orthodox tradition from which this is adapted follows:

A crowd of people just heard of Christ's resurrection. One of the women refused to believe it, so she said: "If it's true may the eggs in my basket turn red." She looked down and all her eggs had just turned red, so of course she believed. From this event, a Greek Orthodox tradition was established.

Now every Holy Saturday (midnight service before Easter), thousands of Greek Orthodox members attend church. Right at 12:00 the priest announces that "Christ has risen," and he passes the light from his candle to the members; in a few minutes all the members of the church pass the light to each other, repeating the words "Christ has risen" (*Christos Aneste*), and the other person replies "He has truly risen" (*Alithos Aneste*). At the same time, the church bells ring, and red eggs get passed around (the church dyes hundreds of red eggs for everyone).

Each person takes the red eggs home and sits with their family for a light supper and also to break the fasting (by now it is one in the morning). People usually eat lemon and egg soup. Then the family goes around the table and cracks their egg with the person next to them, again saying *"Christos Aneste"* and replying *"Alithos Aneste."*

All day on Easter Sunday people visit each other's homes and are offered red eggs and cookie pastries.[2]

5. Make a labyrinth. European Christians in the Middle Ages would sometimes make the pilgrimage to Jerusalem. This was an exhausting, dangerous and expensive trip, and some would save and prepare for such a trip for years before being able to go. The process was viewed as a three-part journey: (1) releasing of responsibilities in one's life, such as family and job, as one walked to Jerusalem; (2) entering the place of Jesus' earthly existence, walking where he walked, dwelling in a sense in his presence; and then (3) returning: making the long laborious return trip where one would once again take up one's former responsibilities in life.

Few people actually made such a trip because it was so costly and long. Eventually labyrinths were built so that more "pilgrims" could participate in a representation of the journey. The most famous labyrinth is at Chartres Cathedral in France. A person could "simulate" the trip to the Holy Land by walking the labyrinth: (1) releasing responsibilities as one walked toward the center, (2) "entering" into a sacred space (dwelling in the center of the labyrinth that represented Christ), and then (3) returning to one's responsibilities, walking out of the labyrinth.

Making a labyrinth today can represent just such a journey. Holly has done this several times, most often in a large cleared room utilizing masking tape on the floor; other times she has used desks, chairs or other furniture to make the labyrinth. A room full of folding chairs in rows adapts quite easily. Other guided labyrinth experiences might use candles, taped music, written prayers or biblical passages. To read more about labyrinths, simply search online.

The following guidelines outline one possible approach. Holly used this format with a class of students recently.

Releasing. Have participants enter the opening of the labyrinth and sit on the floor—or in chairs or on cushions if needed. Dim the lights and light candles at the entry of the labyrinth. Say:

- The initial part of a labyrinth is the releasing.
- We will sit in silence a while as we release the matters pressing on us.

---

[2]This information was given to me by Dora Weathers, who grew up on the island of Cyprus.

- Let go of the things that are weighing you down.
- Be blessed by the presence of God the Father . . . God the Son . . . God the Holy Spirit.

Wait two to three minutes.

Receiving. Lead the group around the labyrinth walkway to the middle area. Say:

- Sit again. This is the centering part of the labyrinth, the receiving part.
- We will sit here and center our hearts and minds on Christ.
- As we rest here, think of Christ's life on earth.
- While Jesus was on earth, he told his followers several times that he is the Bread of Life. We have here some whole wheat bread.
- He told his followers to partake of him—the Bread of Life.
- This robust, enriching, strengthening whole wheat bread is a powerful metaphor.

(Pass around the bread). Take a nice-sized piece and be filled, receive from Christ.

Rest for several minutes.

Returning. Lead the group to the last candle grouping. Say:

- This is the returning part of the labyrinth, the reentering.
- We will be taking up the things we left when we came in.
- But we go out filled, strengthened to face those tasks, those deadlines, fortified.
- We go out full.

Wait a minute or so.

To experience this intergenerationally, take small groups of children and older adults, families, or teens and middle adults (whatever combination you wish). Afterward, ask one of the groups to facilitate a discussion (while other groups go through the labyrinth). Most labyrinths are set up to be experienced individually and are utterly unguided. If this is done, intergenerational discussions after the activity can still be very beneficial.

6. Rewriting Psalm 136. This passage lends itself to creative rewriting, to which everyone ages five to ninety can contribute. Even four-year-olds can participate, though they will need a teen or someone older to help.

Holly has done this activity with all ages, including college-age students, families and most recently with elementary-age children.

Divide the group into cross-generational pairs (or triads or small groups). Each pair will produce one, or possibly two, four-verse psalms that reflect key aspects of Psalm 136. This process will take about fifteen minutes. Afterward, each new psalm can be shared orally with the group, as the group repeats the phrase, "His love endures forever" after each new verse.

Give the following instructions:

- As a pair or triad, read Psalm 136. If one participant is a nonreader, this person may say, "His love endures forever" after each phrase.

- The psalmist is giving thanks to God because of his nature, his creative powers, his mighty deeds on Israel's behalf and his current care. Using this chart, list in the appropriate column each thing or event the psalmist thanks God for. (Make just one chart for the group; if one participant is a preschooler, simplify as needed).

God's nature vv. 1-3	God's creative power vv. 4-9	God's mighty deeds on Israel's behalf vv. 10-25	God's current care v. 25
		(may note just a few of these verses to get the idea)	

- Next, you will have the opportunity to compose a group psalm to the Lord, patterned after Psalm 136. To help you get started, use the same chart structure for your group's entries.

God's nature	God's creative power	God's mighty deeds in your history	God's current care

For God's nature, write in those aspects of God's nature or character that are especially meaningful to your group. For God's creative power, write down those things in creation that you find particularly awesome. For God's mighty deeds, write down ways God has worked mightily in *your* history. For God's current care, write down the ways he is currently caring for those in your group.

- After you have filled in the chart, use a blank sheet of paper to write your group's psalm of thanksgiving, patterned in some way after Psalm 136. The following shows one family's re-created Psalm 136:

Give thanks to God, for he is boss and father;
his love endures forever.
Give thanks to God who alone made the lakes, woods, fish, ducks and beach;
his love endures forever.
Give thanks to God who has kept us well and has been our provider;
his love endures forever.
Give thanks to God who is in control and guiding our journey;
his love endures forever.

(Composed by Yancy, Tonya, Makenzi [age 13] and Allee [age 9] Sweeten. Used with permission.)

DESCRIPTIONS OF TWO MORE WORSHIP STATIONS (ALLUDED TO IN CHAPTER FOURTEEN)

God as light. This station will offer a display of various light sources; for example, a candle (with safety lighter available), a lantern, a lamp, a penlight, regular-sized flashlight and a powerful large flashlight. Have a Bible open to 1 John 1:5-7. A reader from the group can read the passage. Let each person in the group choose an item to turn on or to light (supervision for younger children would be needed). Ask: How is God our light?

Living by faith today. This station will explore the "by faith" passages in Hebrews 11, and needs a facilitator. Have a Bible open to Hebrews 11, or have Hebrews 11:8, 23 and 31 printed out. Each station will also need a couple-dozen small stick-on stars and a copy of the diagram below (enlarge diagram if you wish). A reader in the group can read Hebrew 11:8 and ask one of the children to place a star on the sheet by Abraham's name; then another person can read verse 23 and ask a child to place a star by the names of Jochebed and Amram (Moses' parents); then someone else can read verse 31 and ask another person to place a star by Rahab's name. You may lead very brief discussions about the faith of each of these persons if you wish.

Next, another reader in the group should read this phrase: "By faith, the Duncans adopted Avah"; then ask, "Are the Duncans in the Bible?" No, actually the Duncans are a family who in 2007 really did adopt a little girl named Avah . . . *by faith*. Ask another member of the group to place a star by the Duncans' name.

Next, ask how we are living by faith today. When this worship station was first experienced, one person said, "By faith, I am going to California to do doctoral work"; another said, "By faith, we are starting a business"; another said, "By faith, I am living my life for Jesus." After giving these examples, ask those in the group to add their names in the blanks in the diagram, state how they are living by faith and then place a star by their name.

When all have shared (who wish to), read Hebrews 12:1a, 2a: "Therefore since we are surrounded by such a great cloud of witnesses, . . . let us fix our eyes on Jesus."

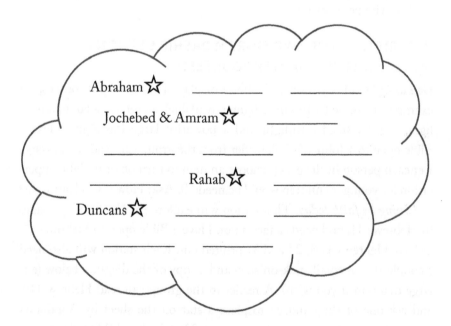

Appendix B

INTERGENERATIONAL MINISTRY RESOURCES

ANNOTATED BIBLIOGRAPHY OF BOOKS ON INTERGENERATIONAL MINISTRY PUBLISHED SINCE 2000

The most recent of these books is Howard Vanderwell's edited volume *The Church of All Ages: Generations Worshiping Together*,[1] published in 2008 by the Alban Institute in cooperation with the Calvin Institute of Christian Worship. Written primarily from the Reformed perspective, the nine authors (pastors, teachers, worship planners and others) address the question, "How can congregations hold the generations together when they worship?"

From the Catholic catechetical world comes *Intergenerational Faith Formation: All Ages Learning Together*,[2] also published in 2008. This small book explains and examines the theory and practice of a current Catholic ten-step intergenerational faith formation approach, focusing primarily on *learning* together. This book was produced as part of the Generations of Faith Project that the Center for Ministry Development has been developing for a decade.

Patty Meyers's book *Live, Learn, Pass It On! The Practical Benefits of Generations Growing Together in Faith*,[3] from 2006, arises out of the general evangelical world (Meyers is a United Methodist deacon and teaches Christian education in the School of Religion at Pfeiffer University in North Carolina). Meyers's text offers general encouragement to churches to be more intentionally intergenerational, with a special em-

---

[1]Howard Vanderwell, ed., *The Church of All Ages: Generations Worshiping Together* (Herndon, VA: Alban Institute, 2008).
[2]Mariette Martineau, Joan Weber and Lief Kehrwald, *Intergenerational Faith Formation: All Ages Learning Together* (New London, CT: Twenty-Third Publications, 2008).
[3]Patty Meyers, *Live, Learn, Pass It On!—The Practical Benefits of Generations Growing Together in Faith* (Nashville: Discipleship Resources, 2006).

phasis on the importance of mentoring and apprenticeships.

In 2001, Augsburg Fortress (publishing house for the Evangelical Lutheran Church of America, ELCA) produced *Across the Generations: Incorporating All Ages in Ministry: The Why and How*,[4] the first major publication on intergenerationality for Christian contexts since James White's 1988 text. Besides offering basic, foundational, biblical and theological support for intergenerationality, the various chapters describe intergenerational approaches to drama, worship, learning and service/ministry. The outstanding chapter on cross-generational learning describes three effective and engaging learning activities.

Three other books consider intergenerational issues by exploring the unique characteristics of the generational cohorts that currently populate faith communities. Carroll and Roof's *Bridging Divided Worlds: Generational Cultures in Congregations*,[5] from 2002, focuses on the three adult generations that have made up religious congregations for a couple of decades: the pre-Boomers, Boomers and Xers. This nuanced, scholarly work is built around qualitative research conducted in the mid-1990s with twenty congregations exploring, among other things, how the generations "contend with one another . . . shaping a religious world, engaging in meaningful religious practice, and in setting priorities of the worshiping community."[6]

Gary McIntosh, in his 2002 book *One Church, Four Generations: Understanding and Reaching All Ages in Your Church*,[7] labels the four generations (from his title) builders, boomers, busters and bridgers, thus adding the latest generation to reach adulthood—those currently in their twenties. Both McIntosh and Pete Menconi (*The Intergenerational Church: Understanding Congregations from WWII to www.com*, 2010[8]) overview and analyze the worldview, key life events, values, popular culture and spirituality

[4]Vicky Goplin, Jeffrey Nelson, Mark Gardner and Eileen Zahn, eds., *Across the Generations: Incorporating All Ages in Ministry: The Why and How* (Minneapolis: Augsburg Fortress, 2001).

[5]Jackson W. Carroll and Wade Clark Roof, *Bridging Divided Worlds: Congregational Cultures in Congregations* (San Francisco: Jossey-Bass, 2002).

[6]Ibid., p. 2.

[7]Gary McIntosh, *One Church, Four Generations: Understanding and Reaching All Ages in Your Church* (Grand Rapids: Baker, 2002).

[8]Peter Menconi, *The Intergenerational Church: Understanding Congregations from WWII to www.com* (Littleton, CO: Mt. Sage Publishing, 2010).

of each generation; offer practical suggestions for minimizing generational conflict; and describe a variety of intergenerational approaches to ministry, worship and leadership.

And last, four books from the United Kingdom (and not widely circulated in the States) also strongly endorse more intentional intergenerationality in faith communities. Gardner's 2008 *Mend the Gap: Can the Church Reconnect the Generations?*[9] focuses on the adolescent/adult "gap" in faith communities. Mounstephen and Martin's 2004 small but substantive *"Body Beautiful"? Recapturing a Vision for All-Age Church*[10] promotes and supports all-age worship, but advocates even more strongly the idea of faith communities as "all-age cultures." Hilborn and Bird's 2002 *God and the Generations*[11] utilizes generational theory as a filter for reintegrating faith communities, similar to the McIntosh and Menconi texts. And finally, Daphne Kirk's book *Reconnecting the Generations: Empowering God's People, Young and Old, to Live, Worship, and Serve Together,* from 2001, is from the charismatic world, thus illustrating that the interest in this topic is quite widespread.

For a fuller discussion of the recent books on intergenerational faith formation, see the Spring 2012 issue of *Christian Educational Journal.* Faye Chechowich overviews and critiques most of the books mentioned here.[12]

INTERGENERATIONAL CHRISTIAN ONLINE RESOURCES

Faith Inkubaters: <www.faithink.com>

- Arts-based children and family Sunday school material
- Faith Stepping Stones material
- Various cross-generational ministry educational material

Youth and Family Institute/Vibrant Faith Ministries: <www.youthand familyinstitute.org>

---

[9]Jason Gardner, *Mend the Gap: Can the Church Reconnect the Generations?* (Nottingham, UK: Inter-Varsity Press, 2008).

[10]Philip Mounstephen and Kelly Martin, *Body Beautiful? Recapturing a Vision for All-Age Church* (Cambridge: Grove Books, 2004).

[11]David Hilborn and Matthew Bird, *God and the Generations: Youth, Age and the Church Today* (Carlisle, UK: Paternoster Press, 2003).

[12]Faye Chechowich, "Intergenerational Ministry: A Review of Selected Publications Since 2001," *Christian Education Journal* (series 3) 9, no. 1 (Spring 2012): 182-93.

- Intergenerational Milestone Events Manual: Helps the congregation celebrate significant highlights of life together.
- FaithTalk™ Cards: Stimulates faith and values conversations among the generations.
- FaithTalk™ Cards for Children: Questions are simpler than in the previously mentioned cards. They are designed for younger children (ages three to eleven) to be able to share their faith with other children and with adults.

INTERGENERATIONAL SECULAR ONLINE RESOURCES

Generations Together: University of Pittsburg project that develops resources for secular intergenerational program and hosts an IG certificate school each summer. <www.gt.pitt.edu>

Generations United, Washington, DC: A national organization promoting intergenerational strategies, programs and public policies. <www.gu.org>

LifeStories™ Game by Talicor: Card deck categories of memories, etchings and valuables lead players to share their life stories with one another. Can be purchased on Amazon or other websites.

Points of View: Intergenerational consulting and other generational material. <www.pointsofviewinc.com>

Public Broadcasting Station (PBS): Site dedicated to intergenerational concerns. <www.pbs.org/americanfamily/gap/>

CURRICULUM/ACTIVITY RESOURCES

AARP. *Intergenerational Projects Ideas Book.* Washington, DC: American Association of Retired Persons, 1993. Variety of ideas that retired people and children can do together.

Bickel, K. *Funtastic Family Nights.* St. Louis: Concordia Publishing House, 1998. Nineteen different topics with Bible study, activities and handouts.

Faith Family Style: Generations Growing Together. Minneapolis: Augsburg Fortress, 2001. Contains plans for ten intergenerational events.

Faith Inkubaters. *Faith Stepping Stones, Generations in Faith Together & Head to Heart Confirmation.* Faith Inkubator educational programs: <www.faithink.com>.

FaithTalk™ Cards for Children, Youth and Family Institute. Cards are designed for younger children (ages three to eleven) to be able to share their faith with other children and with adults. <www.youthandfamily institute.org>.

FaithTalk™ Cards, Youth and Family Institute. Helpful for leading families or faith-families in talking about their faith. From four areas—Memories, Values, Etchings and Actions—people will share stories of God's faithfulness. <www.youthandfamilyinstitute.org>.

Family Crossfires, Inc. Ministries website. A Lutheran Church–Missouri Synod pastor and deaconess write and market intergenerational Sunday school, VBS, retreat and worship materials. <familycrossfires.tripod.com>.

Family 'Round the Table: Year A, Year B, Year C. Designed to help families and other cross-generational groups gather together for Christian formation by sharing a meal, playing together, talking about and reflecting on the Bible, and praying together. Each volume contains fifty-two complete sessions. Available from GenOn Ministries at <www .genonministries.org>.

Gambone, James. *All Are Welcome: A Primer for Intentional Intergenerational Ministry and Dialogue.* Crystal Bay, MN: Elder Eye Press, 1998. Both of Gambone's resources provide ideas regarding how to bring together an intergenerational group that may start your congregation's move toward intergenerationality.

———. *Together for Tomorrow: Building Community Through Intergenerational Dialogue.* Crystal Bay, MN: Elder Eye Press, 1997.

Goings, Nannette. *Fun Family Festivals: 24 Super Celebrations for Family Ministry.* Cincinnati: Standard Publishing, 1999. Designed for bringing several families together for learning and fun.

Henley, Karyn. *Families Learning Together: A Curriculum Resource for Family Ministry.* Cincinnati: Standard Publishing, 1998. Four volumes of fifteen lessons each, covering Jesus' life. Excellent materials for families and easily adaptable for general intergenerational settings. The four volumes are *Jesus' Early Life, Jesus our Teacher, Jesus: Healer and Helper,* and *Jesus' Last Week.*

Johansson, Lois. *Hands and Hearts: Intergenerational Activities Throughout the Church Year.* Harrisburg, PA: Morehouse Publishing, 2006. Lessons for the seven main seasons of the church year; useful for special occasions when all ages of the church come together.

LifeStories™ Game by Talicor. A deck of cards with categories of memories, etchings and valuables lead players to share their life stories with one another. A fun way to get all ages talking and knowing more about one another. Can be purchased through several companies; easy to find using an Internet search engine.

Michael, Sally. *Lord, Teach Us to Pray: A Study for Children and Adults on Prayer.* Minneapolis: Children Desiring God, 2006.

————. *The Righteous Shall Live by Faith: A Study for Children and Adults on the Ten Commandments.* Minneapolis: Children Desiring God, 2005.

CHILDREN'S BOOKS

Crunk, Tony, and Margot Apple. *Big Mama.* New York: Farrar, Straus and Giroux, 2003.

All the neighborhood kids agree that Billy Boyd's grandmother is a wonder.

DePaola, Tomie. *Nana Upstairs & Nana Downstairs.* New York: Putnam, 1973.

DePaola's story of his relationship with his grandmother and great-grandmother who lived with him as a boy; eventually each "Nana" dies, and DePaola describes their passing sensitively from a young boy's perspective.

Fox, Mem. *Wilfred Gordon McDonald Partridge.* Brooklyn, N.Y.: Kane/Miller, 1984.

Wilfred lives next door to an "Old People's Home." When he hears how one woman has lost her memory, he goes to get memories for her and helps her tap into some of her old memories. This would be a good book to use to discuss the importance of mentoring relationships between children and older adults.

Mills, Claudia, and Catherine Stock. *Gus and Grandpa.* Elgin, IL: Sunburst, various dates.

Series of books about an engagingly imperfect boy and his engagingly imperfect grandfather.

Polacco, Patricia. *Chicken Sunday.* New York: Philomel Books, 1992.

A story of cross-generational and crosscultural relationships between Miss Eula and her grandsons and the little girl who lives next door, as well as the elderly Mr. Kodinski.

Appendix C

BIBLICAL PASSAGES THAT REFLECT AN INTERGENERATIONAL OUTLOOK

(Keywords: generations, church, children. All quotations, unless otherwise indicated, are taken from the English Standard Version.)

Genesis 9:12 And God said, "This [rainbow] is the sign of the covenant that I make between me and you and every living creature that is with you, for all future generations."

Genesis 17:7 "And I [God] will establish my covenant between me and you [Abram] and your offspring after you throughout their generations for an everlasting covenant, to be God to you and to your offspring after you."

Exodus 3:15 "God also said to Moses, 'Say this to the people of Israel, "The LORD, the God of your fathers, the God of Abraham, the God of Isaac, and the God of Jacob, has sent me to you." This is my name forever, and thus I am to be remembered throughout all generations.'"

Exodus 12:26-27 "And when your children say to you, 'What do you mean by this service?' you shall say, 'It is the sacrifice of the LORD's Passover, for he passed over the houses of the people of Israel in Egypt, when he struck the Egyptians but spared our houses.'" And the people bowed their heads and worshiped.

Deuteronomy 6:6-9 "And these words that I command you today shall be on your heart. You shall teach them diligently to your children, and shall talk of them when you sit in your house, and when you walk by the way, and when you lie down, and when you rise. You shall bind them as a sign on your hand, and they shall be as frontlets between your eyes. You shall write them on the doorposts of your house and on your gates."

Deuteronomy 7:9 "Know therefore that the LORD your God is God, the faithful God who keeps covenant and steadfast love with those who love him and keep his commandments, to a thousand generations."

Deuteronomy 12:12 "And you shall rejoice before the LORD your God, you and your sons and your daughters, your male servants and your female servants, and the Levite that is within your towns, since he has no portion or inheritance with you."

Deuteronomy 29:10-12 "All of you are standing today in the presence of the LORD your God—your leaders and chief men, your elders and officials, and all the other men of Israel, together with your children and your wives, and the foreigners living in your camps. . . . You are standing here in order to enter into a covenant with the LORD your God (NIV)."

Deuteronomy 31:12-13 "Assemble the people, men, women, and little ones, and the sojourner within your towns, that they may hear and learn to fear the LORD your God, and be careful to do all the words of this law, and that their children, who have not known it, may hear and learn to fear the LORD your God as long as you live in the land that you are going over the Jordan to possess."

Joshua 8:34-35 And afterward he read all the words of the law, the blessing and the curse, according to all that is written in the Book of the Law. There was not a word of all that Moses commanded that Joshua did not read before all the assembly of Israel, and the women, and the little ones, and the sojourners who lived among them.

Joshua 22:26-27 "Therefore we said, 'Let us now build an altar, not for burnt offering, nor for sacrifice, but to be a witness between us and you, and between our generations after us, that we do perform the service of the LORD in his presence with our burnt offerings and sacrifices and peace offerings, so your children will not say to our children in time to come, "You have no portion in the LORD."'"

Judges 2:10 And all that generation also were gathered to their fathers. And there arose another generation after them who did not know the LORD or the work that he had done for Israel.

1 Samuel 2:11 And the boy [Samuel] ministered to the LORD in the presence of Eli the priest.

2 Kings 22:1-2 Josiah was eight years old when he began to reign, and he reigned thirty-one years in Jerusalem. . . . And he did what was right in the eyes of the LORD and walked in all the ways of David his father, and he did not turn aside to the right or to the left.

1 Chronicles 9:23 So they and their sons were in charge of the gates of the house of the LORD, that is, the house of the tent, as guards.

1 Chronicles 16:15 Remember his covenant forever, the word that he commanded, for a thousand generations.

2 Chronicles 20:13 Meanwhile all Judah stood before the LORD, with their little ones, their wives, and their children.

Nehemiah 8:2-3 Ezra the priest brought the Law before the assembly, both men and women and all who could understand what they heard. . . . And he read from it facing the square before the Water Gate from early morning until midday, in the presence of the men and the women and those who could understand. And the ears of all the people were attentive to the Book of the Law. (Cross-references: Nehemiah 8:2; see Deuteronomy 31:11)

Nehemiah 12:43 And they offered great sacrifices that day and rejoiced, for God had made them rejoice with great joy; the women and children also rejoiced. And the joy of Jerusalem was heard far away.

Esther 9:26-28 Therefore they called these days Purim, after the term Pur. Therefore, because of all that was written in this letter, and of what they had faced in this matter, and of what had happened to them, the Jews firmly obligated themselves and their offspring and all who joined them, that without fail they would keep these two days according to what was written and at the time appointed every year, that these days should be remembered and kept throughout every generation, in every clan, province, and city, and that these days of Purim should never fall into disuse among the Jews, nor should the commemoration of these days cease among their descendants.

Psalm 8:1-2

O LORD, our Lord,
　how majestic is your name in all the earth!
You have set your glory above the heavens.
　Out of the mouth of babes and infants,
you have established strength.

Psalm 14:5

There they are in great terror,
　for God is with the generation of the righteous.

Psalm 22:27-31

All the ends of the earth shall remember
　and turn to the LORD,
and all the families of the nations
　shall worship before you.
For kingship belongs to the LORD,
　and he rules over the nations.
All the prosperous of the earth eat and worship;
　before him shall bow all who go down to the dust,
　even the one who could not keep himself alive.
Posterity shall serve him;
　it shall be told of the Lord to the coming generation;
　they shall come and proclaim his righteousness to a people yet
　　unborn,
　that he has done it.

Psalm 24:6

Such is the generation of those who seek him,
　who seek the face of the God of Jacob.

Psalm 33:11

The counsel of the LORD stands forever,
　the plans of his heart to all generations.

Psalm 48:12-14

Walk about Zion, go around her,
  number her towers,
consider well her ramparts,
  go through her citadels,
that you may tell the next generation
  that this is God,
our God forever and ever.
  He will guide us forever.

Psalm 71:18

So even to old age and gray hairs,
  O God, do not forsake me,
until I proclaim your might to another generation,
  your power to all those to come.

Psalm 78:1-8

Give ear, O my people, to my teaching;
  incline your ears to the words of my mouth!
I will open my mouth in a parable;
  I will utter dark sayings from of old,
things that we have heard and known,
  that our fathers have told us.
We will not hide them from their children,
  but tell to the coming generation
the glorious deeds of the LORD, and his might,
  and the wonders that he has done.
He established a testimony in Jacob
  and appointed a law in Israel,
which he commanded our fathers
  to teach to their children,
that the next generation might know them,
  the children yet unborn,
and arise and tell them to their children,
  so that they should set their hope in God
and not forget the works of God,

but keep his commandments;
and that they should not be like their fathers,
    a stubborn and rebellious generation,
a generation whose heart was not steadfast,
    whose spirit was not faithful to God.

Psalm 79:13

But we your people, the sheep of your pasture,
    will give thanks to you forever;
    from generation to generation we will recount your praise.

Psalm 89:1

I will sing of the steadfast love of the LORD, forever;
    with my mouth I will make known your faithfulness to all generations.

Psalm 89:4

I will establish your [David's] offspring forever,
    and build your throne for all generations.

Psalm 100:5

For the LORD is good;
    his steadfast love endures forever,
    and his faithfulness to all generations.

Psalm 102:18

Let this be recorded for a generation to come,
    so that a people yet to be created may praise the LORD.

Psalm 119:90

Your faithfulness endures to all generations;
    you have established the earth, and it stands fast.

Psalm 145:4

One generation shall commend your works to another,
    and shall declare your mighty acts.

Proverbs 22:6

Train up a child in the way he should go;
    even when he is old he will not depart from it.

Ecclesiastes 1:4

A generation goes, and a generation comes,
   but the earth remains forever.

Isaiah 41:4

"Who has performed and done this,
   calling the generations from the beginning?
I, the LORD, the first,
   and with the last; I am he."

Isaiah 51:7-8

"Listen to me, you who know righteousness,
   the people in whose heart is my law;
fear not the reproach of man,
   nor be dismayed at their revilings. . . .
but my righteousness will be forever,
   and my salvation to all generations."

Jeremiah 1:5-8

   "Before I formed you in the womb I knew you,
   and before you were born I consecrated you;
   I appointed you a prophet to the nations."
Then I said, "Ah, Lord GOD! Behold, I do not know how to speak, for
      I am only a youth." But the LORD said to me,
   "Do not say, 'I am only a youth';
   for to all to whom I send you, you shall go,
   and whatever I command you, you shall speak.
   Do not be afraid of them,
   for I am with you to deliver you,
   declares the LORD."

Lamentations 5:19

But you, O LORD, reign forever;
   your throne endures to all generations.

Daniel 4:3

How great are his signs,

how mighty his wonders!

His kingdom is an everlasting kingdom;

and his dominion endures from generation to generation.

Joel 1:3

Tell your children of it,

and let your children tell their children,

and their children to another generation.

Joel 2:15-16

Blow the trumpet in Zion;

consecrate a fast;

call a solemn assembly;

gather the people.

Consecrate the congregation;

assemble the elders;

gather the children,

even nursing infants.

Let the bridegroom leave his room,

and the bride her chamber.

Joel 2:28 & Acts 2:17

"And it shall come to pass afterward,

that I will pour out my Spirit on all flesh,

your sons and your daughters shall prophesy,

your old men shall dream dreams,

and your young men shall see visions."

Matthew 18:1-6 At that time the disciples came to Jesus, saying, "Who is the greatest in the kingdom of heaven?" And calling to him a child, he put him in the midst of them and said, "Truly, I say to you, unless you turn and become like children, you will never enter the kingdom of heaven. Whoever humbles himself like this child is the greatest in the kingdom of heaven. Whoever receives one such child in my name receives me, but whoever causes one of these little ones who believe in me to sin, it would be better for him to have a great millstone fastened around his neck and to be drowned in the depth of the sea."

Matthew 19:13-15 Then children were brought to him that he might lay his hands on them and pray. The disciples rebuked the people, but Jesus said, "Let the little children come to me and do not hinder them, for to such belongs the kingdom of heaven." And he laid his hands on them and went away.

Mark 9:35-37 And he sat down and called the twelve. And he said to them, "If anyone would be first, he must be last of all and servant of all." And he took a child and put him in the midst of them, and taking him in his arms, he said to them, "Whoever receives one such child in my name receives me, and whoever receives me, receives not me but him who sent me."

Mark 10:13-16 And they were bringing children to him that he might touch them, and the disciples rebuked them. But when Jesus saw it, he was indignant and said to them, "Let the children come to me; do not hinder them, for to such belongs the kingdom of God. Truly, I say to you, whoever does not receive the kingdom of God like a child shall not enter it." And he took them in his arms and blessed them, laying his hands on them.

Luke 1:48-50
For he has looked on the humble estate of his servant.
    For behold, from now on all generations will call me blessed;
for he who is mighty has done great things for me,
    and holy is his name.
And his mercy is for those who fear him
    from generation to generation.

Luke 9:46-48 An argument arose among them as to which of them was the greatest. But Jesus, knowing the reasoning of their hearts, took a child and put him by his side and said to them, "Whoever receives this child in my name receives me, and whoever receives me receives him who sent me. For he who is least among you all is the one who is great."

Luke 18:15-17 Now they were bringing even infants to him that he might touch them. And when the disciples saw it, they rebuked them. But Jesus called them to him, saying, "Let the children come to me, and do not hinder them, for to such belongs the kingdom of God. Truly, I say to you, whoever does not receive the kingdom of God like a child shall not enter it."

John 1:12-13 But to all who did receive him, who believed in his name, he gave the right to become children of God, who were born, not of blood nor of the will of the flesh nor of the will of man, but of God.

John 13:33-35 Little children, yet a little while I am with you. . . . A new commandment I give to you, that you love one another: just as I have loved you, you also are to love one another. By this all people will know that you are my disciples, if you have love for one another.

John 17:20-21 I [Jesus] do not ask for these [disciples] only, but also for those who will believe in me through their word, that they may all be one, just as you, Father, are in me and I in you, that they also may be in us, so that the world may believe that you have sent me.

Acts 16:14-15 One who heard us was a woman named Lydia, from the city of Thyatira, a seller of purple goods, who was a worshiper of God. The Lord opened her heart to pay attention to what was said by Paul. And after she was baptized, and her household as well, she urged us, saying, "If you have judged me to be faithful to the Lord, come to my house and stay." And she prevailed upon us.

Acts 16:30-33 Then he [the jailer] brought them [Paul and Silas] out and said, "Sirs, what must I do to be saved?" And they said, "Believe in the Lord Jesus, and you will be saved, you and your household." And they spoke the word of the Lord to him and to all who were in his house. And he took them the same hour of the night and washed their wounds; and he was baptized at once, he and all his family. Then he brought them up into his house and set food before them. And he rejoiced along with his entire household that he had believed in God.

Acts 20:7-12 On the first day of the week, when we were gathered together to break bread, Paul talked with them, intending to depart on the next day, and he prolonged his speech until midnight. There were many lamps in the upper room where we were gathered. And a young man named Eutychus, sitting at the window, sank into a deep sleep as Paul talked still longer. And being overcome by sleep, he fell down from the third story and was taken up dead. But Paul went down and bent over him, and taking him in his arms, said, "Do not be alarmed, for his life is in him." And when Paul had gone up and had broken bread and eaten, he conversed with them a long while, until daybreak, and so departed. And they took the youth away alive, and were not a little comforted.

Acts 21:5-6 When our days there were ended, we departed and went on our journey, and they all, with wives and children, accompanied us until we were outside the city. And kneeling down on the beach, we prayed and said farewell to one another. Then we went on board the ship, and they returned home.

Romans 8:14-17 For all who are led by the Spirit of God are sons of God. For you did not receive the spirit of slavery to fall back into fear, but you have received the Spirit of adoption as sons, by whom we cry, "Abba! Father!" The Spirit himself bears witness with our spirit that we are children of God, and if children, then heirs—heirs of God and fellow heirs with Christ, provided we suffer with him in order that we may also be glorified with him.

Romans 12:4-5 For as in one body we have many members, and the members do not all have the same function, so we, though many, are one body in Christ, and individually members one of another.

1 Corinthians 1:10 I appeal to you, brothers, by the name of our Lord Jesus Christ, that all of you agree and that there be no divisions among you, but that you be united in the same mind and the same judgment.

1 Corinthians 12:12-27 For just as the body is one and has many members, and all the members of the body, though many, are one body, so it is with Christ. For in one Spirit we were all baptized into one body—Jews or Greeks, slaves or free—and all were made to drink of one Spirit.

For the body does not consist of one member but of many. If the foot should say, "Because I am not a hand, I do not belong to the body," that would not make it any less a part of the body. And if the ear should say,

"Because I am not an eye, I do not belong to the body," that would not make it any less a part of the body. If the whole body were an eye, where would be the sense of hearing? If the whole body were an ear, where would be the sense of smell? But as it is, God arranged the members in the body, each one of them, as he chose. If all were a single member, where would the body be? As it is, there are many parts, yet one body.

The eye cannot say to the hand, "I have no need of you," nor again the head to the feet, "I have no need of you." On the contrary, the parts of the body that seem to be weaker are indispensable, and on those parts of the body that we think less honorable we bestow the greater honor, and our unpresentable parts are treated with greater modesty, which our more presentable parts do not require. But God has so composed the body, giving greater honor to the part that lacked it, that there may be no division in the body, but that the members may have the same care for one another. If one member suffers, all suffer together; if one member is honored, all rejoice together.

Now you are the body of Christ and individually members of it.

2 Corinthians 6:18
And I will be a father to you,
   and you shall be sons and daughters to me,
says the Lord Almighty.

Galatians 3:26-29 For in Christ Jesus you are all sons of God, through faith. For as many of you as were baptized into Christ have put on Christ. There is neither Jew nor Greek, there is neither slave nor free, there is neither male nor female, for you are all one in Christ Jesus. And if you are Christ's, then you are Abraham's offspring, heirs according to promise (see also 4:1-7).

Galatians 6:10 So then, as we have opportunity, let us do good to everyone, and especially to those who are of the household of faith.

Ephesians 2:19-22 So then you are no longer strangers and aliens, but you are fellow citizens with the saints and members of the household of God, built on the foundation of the apostles and prophets, Christ Jesus himself being the cornerstone, in whom the whole structure, being joined together, grows into a holy temple in the Lord. In him you also are being built together into a dwelling place for God by the Spirit.

Ephesians 3:20-21 Now to him who is able to do far more abundantly than all that we ask or think, according to the power at work within us, to him be glory in the church and in Christ Jesus throughout all generations, forever and ever. Amen.

Ephesians 4:15-16 Rather, speaking the truth in love, we are to grow up in every way into him who is the head, into Christ, from whom the whole body, joined and held together by every joint with which it is equipped, when each part is working properly, makes the body grow so that it builds itself up in love.

Ephesians 6:4 Fathers, do not provoke your children to anger, but bring them up in the discipline and instruction of the Lord.

Philippians 2:14-15 Do all things without grumbling or questioning, that you may be blameless and innocent, children of God without blemish in the midst of a crooked and twisted generation, among whom you shine as lights in the world.

Colossians 3:14-16 And above all these put on love, which binds everything together in perfect harmony. And let the peace of Christ rule in your hearts, to which indeed you were called in one body. And be thankful. Let the word of Christ dwell in you richly, teaching and admonishing one another in all wisdom, singing psalms and hymns and spiritual songs, with thankfulness in your hearts to God.

1 Timothy 3:15 If I (Paul) delay, you may know how one ought to behave in the household of God, which is the church of the living God, a pillar and buttress of truth.

1 Timothy 4:12 Let no one despise you for your youth, but set the believers an example in speech, in conduct, in love, in faith, in purity.

1 Timothy 5:1-4 Do not rebuke an older man but encourage him as you would a father. Treat younger men like brothers, older women like mothers, younger women like sisters, in all purity.

Honor widows who are truly widows. But if a widow has children or grandchildren, let them first learn to show godliness to their own household and to make some return to their parents, for this is pleasing in the sight of God.

Titus 2:2-4 Older men are to be sober-minded, dignified, self-controlled, sound in faith, in love, and in steadfastness. Older women likewise are to be reverent in behavior, not slanderers or slaves to much wine. They are to teach what is good, and so train the young women to love their husbands and children.

Hebrews 10:23-25 Let us hold fast the confession of our hope without wavering, for he who promised is faithful. And let us consider how to stir up one another to love and good works, not neglecting to meet together, as is the habit of some, but encouraging one another, and all the more as you see the Day drawing near.

1 Peter 2:9 But you [plural] are a chosen race, a royal priesthood, a holy nation, a people for his own possession, that you may proclaim the excellencies of him who called you out of darkness into his marvelous light.

1 Peter 4:9 Show hospitality to one another without grumbling.

1 John 1:7 But if we walk in the light, as he is in the light, we have fellowship with one another, and the blood of Jesus his Son cleanses us from all sin.

Intergenerational Biblical Relationships
Samuel and Eli
Elijah and Elisha
David and King Saul
Ruth and Naomi
Twelve-year-old Jesus teaching the elders in the synagogue
Barnabas and John Mark
Timothy and Paul

BIBLIOGRAPHY

AARP. *Intergenerational Projects Ideas Book*. Washington, DC: American Association of Retired Persons, 1993.

Allen, Holly C. "Bringing the Generations Back Together: Introduction to Intergenerationality." *Christian Education Journal* (series 3) 9, no. 1 (Spring 2012): 101-5.

———. "Bringing the Generations Together: Support from Learning Theory." *Christian Education Journal* (series 3) 2, no. 2 (Fall 2005): 319-33.

———. "Bringing the Generations Together: Support from Learning Theory." *Lifelong Faith: The Theory and Practice of Lifelong Faith Formation* 3 (Spring 2009): 3-11.

———. "No Better Place: Fostering Intergenerational Christian Community." In *Shaped by God: 12 Essentials for Nurturing Faith in Children, Youth, and Adults,* edited by Robert Keeley, pp. 109-25. Grand Rapids: Faith Alive Christian Resources, 2010.

———. "Nurturing Children's Spirituality in Intergenerational Christian Settings." In *Children's Spirituality: Christian Perspectives, Research, and Applications,* edited by Don Ratcliff, pp. 266-83. Eugene, OR: Cascade, 2004.

———. "Nurturing Children's Spirituality in Intergenerational Settings." *Lutheran Educational Journal* 139 (Winter 2003): 111-124.

———. "A Qualitative Study Exploring the Similarities and Differences of the Spirituality of Children in Intergenerational and Non-Intergenerational Christian Contexts." Doctoral dissertation, Talbot School of Theology, Biola University, La Mirada, CA, 2002.

Armstrong, Lance. *Children in Worship: The Road to Faith*. Melbourne, Australia: Joint Board of Christian Education, 1988.

Bandura, Albert. "On the Psychosocial Impact and Mechanisms of Spiritual Modeling." *International Journal for the Psychology of Religion* 13, no. 3 (2003): 167-73.

―――. "Social Cognitive Theory: An Agentic Perspective." *Annual Review of Psychology* 52 (2001): 1-26.

―――. "A Social Cognitive Theory of Personality." In *Handbook of Personality: Theory and Research,* edited by Lawrence A. Pervin and Oliver P. John, pp. 154-96. 2nd ed. New York: Guilford, 1999.

―――. *Social Foundations of Thought and Action: A Social Cognitive Theory.* Englewood Cliffs, NJ: Prentice Hall, 1986.

Banks, Robert. *Paul's Idea of Community.* Rev. ed. Peabody, MA: Hendrickson, 1994.

Barker, Jeff. "The Power of Telling a Story." In *The Church of All Ages: Generations Worshiping Together,* edited by Howard Vanderwell, pp. 95-111. Herndon, VA: Alban Institute, 2008.

Barna, George. *Marketing the Church.* Colorado Springs, CO: NavPress, 1988.

―――. *Real Teens: A Contemporary Snapshot of Youth Culture.* Ventura, CA: Regal Books, 2001.

Bartholomew, Craig G., and Michael W. Goheen. *The Drama of Scripture: Finding Our Place in the Biblical Story.* Grand Rapids: Baker, 2004.

Beckwith, Ivy. *Postmodern Children's Ministry: Ministry to Children in the 21st Century.* Grand Rapids: Zondervan, 2004.

Behling, Karen Rask, and Carol Rask. "Ordinary Time: Intergenerational Ministry." In *Ordinary Ministry, Extraordinary Challenge: Women and the Roles of Ministry,* edited by Norma Cook Everis, pp. 73-79. Nashville: Abingdon Press, 2000.

Benson, Peter. *All Kids Are Our Kids.* San Francisco: Jossey-Bass, 1997.

Berger, Peter. *The Sacred Canopy.* New York: Anchor, 1967.

Berryman, Jerome W. "Teaching As Presence and the Existential Curriculum." *Religious Education* 85: 509-34.

Bickel, Kurt. *Funtastic Family Nights.* St. Louis: Concordia Publishing House, 1998.

Boice, James Montgomery. *Foundations of the Christian Faith: A Comprehensive and Readable Theology.* Downers Grove, IL: InterVarsity Press, 1986.

Bolinder, Garth, and James Emery White. "Two Pastors in a Demographic Debate: Should the Church Target Generations?" *Leadership Journal* 20 (Spring 1999): 104-6.

Bonhoeffer, Dietrich. *The Communion of Saints: A Dogmatic Inquiry into the Sociology of the Church.* Translated by R. Gregor Smith. New York: Harper and Row, 1963.

Brabazon, Kevin, and Robert Disch, eds. *Intergenerational Approaches in Aging: Implications for Education, Policy, and Practice.* New York: Haworth Press, 1997.

Breaux, Mike. "A Mad, Multi-Gen Strategy That Works, Dude." *Leadership* 26 (Spring 2005): 44-46.

Bronfenbrenner, Urie. *The Ecology of Human Development: Experiments by Nature and Design.* Boston: Harvard University Press, 1979.

———. *Two Worlds of Childhood: U.S. and U.S.S.R.* New York: Simon and Schuster, 1970.

Brown, Diane R., and Lawrence E. Gary. "Religious Socialization and Educational Attainment among African Americans: An Empirical Assessment." *Journal of Negro Education* 60 (1991): 411-26.

Brown, Raymond E. *The Gospel According to John.* Anchor Bible Commentary 29a. Garden City, NY: Doubleday, 1966.

Bytheway, Bill. "Ageism and Age Categorization." *Journal of Social Issues* 61, no. 2 (2005): 361-74.

Callahan, Kennon. *Twelve Keys to an Effective Church.* New York: Harper & Row, 1983.

Carroll, Jackson W., and Wade Clark Roof. *Bridging Divided Worlds: Congregational Cultures in Congregations.* San Francisco: Jossey-Bass, 2002.

Carter, Elizabeth A., and Monica McGoldrick. *The Changing Family Life Cycle: A Framework for Family Therapy.* New York: Allyn & Bacon, 1989.

Castleman, Robbie. *Parenting in the Pew: Guiding Your Children into the Joy of Worship.* Expanded ed. Downers Grove, IL: InterVarsity Press, 2002.

———. *The Story of Scripture.* LifeGuide Bible Study. Downers Grove, IL: InterVarsity Press, 2008.

Cha, Peter. T. "Constructing New Intergenerational Ties, Cultures, and Identities among Korean American Christians: A Congregational Case Study." In *This Side of Heaven: Race, Ethnicity, and Christian Faith,* edited by Robert A. Priest and Alvaro L. Nieves, pp. 259-73. Oxford: Oxford University Press, 2007.

———, Paul Kim and Dihan Lee. "Multigenerational Households." In *Growing Healthy Asian American Churches: Ministry Insights from Groundbreaking Congregations.* Downers Grove, IL: InterVarsity Press, 2006.

Chechowich, Faye. "Intergenerational Ministry: A Review of Selected Publications Since 2001." *Christian Education Journal* (series 3) 9, no. 1 (Spring 2012): 182-93.

Chesto, Kathleen O'Connell. *Family-Centered Intergenerational Religious Education: Director's Guide.* Kansas City, MO: Sheed & Ward, 1988.

————. FIRE (Family-Centered Intergenerational Religious Education): An Alternative Model of Religious Education. *Dissertation Abstracts International,* 48, 2034, D.Min. Dissertation, Hartford Seminary, 1987.

Clark, Chap. *Hurt: Inside the World of Today's Teenagers.* Grand Rapids: Baker Academic, 2004.

Cornwall, Marie. "The Determinants of Religious Behavior: A Theoretical Model and Empirical Test." *Social Forces* 68 (1989): 572-92.

Crouch, Andy. "For People Like Me: The Myth of Generations." *Culture Making* (blog), 2012. <www.culture-making.com/articles/for_people_like_me>.

Davis, Russell Haden. "The Middle Years." In *Human Development and Faith: Life-Cycle Stages of Body, Mind, and Soul,* edited by Felicity B. Kelcourse, pp. 251-58. St. Louis: Chalice Press, 2004.

DeVries, Mark. *Family-Based Youth Ministry.* Rev. ed. Downers Grove, IL: InterVarsity Press, 2004.

De Waal Malefyt, Norma, and Howard Vanderwell. "Worship Planning in a Church of All Ages." In *The Church of All Ages: Generations Worshiping Together,* edited by Howard Vanderwell. Herndon, VA: Alban Institute, 2008.

Dinges, William. "Faith, Hope, and (Excessive) Individualism." In *Handing on the Faith: The Church's Mission and Challenge,* edited by Robert P. Imbelli, pp. 30-43. New York: Crossroad Publishing Company, 2006.

Dittmer, Terry. "Ministry Among the Generations: Challenges and Opportunities." *Issues in Christian Education* 41 (Fall 2007): 10-13.

Eliot, T. S. *Complete Poems and Plays.* New York: Harcourt and Brace, 1952.

Elmore, Tim. *Generation iY: Our Last Chance to Save Their Future.* Atlanta: Poet Gardener Publishing, 2010.

Erikson, Erik H. *Childhood and Society.* 2nd ed. New York: Norton, 1963.

Estep, Jr., James R. "Spiritual Formation as Social: Toward a Vygotskyan Developmental Perspective." Paper presented at North American Professors of Christian Education Annual Conference, San Diego, CA, October 1999.

Foster, Charles R. "Intergenerational Religious Education." In *Changing Patterns of Religious Education,* edited by Marvin J. Taylor, pp. 278-89. Nashville: Abingdon, 1984.

Fowler, James W. "Stages of Faith and Selfhood." Paper delivered at Abilene Christian University, Abilene, Texas, March 1998.

————. *Stages of Faith: The Psychology of Human Development and the Quest for Meaning.* San Francisco: Harper, 1981.

————. *Weaving the New Creation: Stages of Faith and the Public Church.* New

York: HarperCollins, 1991.

Fraze, David. "Something Is Not Right: Revisiting our Definition of Family." Fuller Youth Institute, 2009. <fulleryouthinstitute.org/2009/01/something-is-not-right/>.

Frazier, James. "All Generations of Saints at Worship." In *Across the Generations: Incorporating All Ages in Ministry: The Why and How,* edited by Vicky Goplin, Jeffrey Nelson, Mark Gardner and Eileen Zahn, pp. 56-63. Minneapolis: Augsburg, 2001.

Fretheim, Terence E. "Yada." In *New International Dictionary of Old Testament Theology and Exegesis,* edited by Willem A. VanGemeren, 2:409-14. Grand Rapids: Zondervan, 1997.

Freudenburg, Ben, and Rick Lawrence. *The Family Friendly Church.* Loveland, CO: Group Publishing, 1998.

Fried, Linda P., Michelle C. Carlson, Marc Freedman, Kevin D. Frick, Thomas A. Glass, Joel Hill, Sylvia McGill, George W. Rebok, Teresa Seeman, James Tielsch, Barbara A. Wasik and Scott Zeger. "The Experience Corps: A Social Model for Health Promotion, Generativity, and Decreasing Structural Lag for Older Adults." Symposium presented at the 53rd Annual Meeting of the Gerontological Society of America, Washington, DC, November 17-21, 2000.

Gaede, Stan. "A Causal Model of Belief-Orthodoxy: Proposal and Empirical Test." *Sociological Analysis* 37 (1976): 205-17.

Gambone, James V. *All Are Welcome: A Primer for Intentional Intergenerational Ministry and Dialogue.* Crystal Bay, MN: Elder Eye Press, 1998.

———. *Together for Tomorrow: Building Community Through Intergenerational Dialogue.* Crystal Bay, MN: Elder Eye Press, 1997.

Gardner, Jason. *Mend the Gap: Can the Church Reconnect the Generations?* Nottingham, UK: Inter-Varsity Press, 2008.

Gentzler, Richard. *Designing an Older Adult Ministry.* Nashville, TN: Discipleship Resources, 1999.

Giles, Howard, Kimberly A. Noels, Angie Williams, Hiroshi Ota, Tae-Seop Lim, Sik Hung Ng, Ellen B. Ryan and Lilnabeth Somera. "Intergenerational Communication across Cultures: Young People's Perceptions of Conversations with Family Elders, Non-Family Elders and Same-Age Peers." *Journal of Cross-Cultural Gerontology* 18 (2003): 1-32.

Gilligan, Carol. *In a Different Voice: Psychological Theory and Women's Development.* Cambridge, MA: Harvard University Press, 1982.

Ginsburg, Herbert P., and Sylvia Opper. *Piaget's Theory of Intellectual Development.* 3rd ed. Englewood Cliffs, NJ: Prentice Hall, 1988.

Glassford, Darwin. "Fostering an Intergenerational Culture." In *The Church of All Ages: Generations Worshiping Together,* edited by Howard Vanderwell, pp. 71-88. Herndon, VA: Alban Institute, 2008.

————, and Lynn Barger-Elliot. "Toward Intergenerational Ministry in a Post-Christian Era." *Christian Education Journal* (series 3) 8, no. 2 (Fall 2011): 364-78.

Gobbel, Roger, and Philip Huber. *Creative Designs with Children at Worship.* Atlanta: John Knox Press, 1981.

Goplin, Vicky, Jeffrey Nelson, Mark Gardner and Eileen Zahn, eds. *Across the Generations: Incorporating All Ages in Ministry: The Why and How.* Minneapolis: Augsburg Fortress, 2001.

Gorman, Julie. "Christian Formation." In *Evangelical Dictionary of Christian Education,* edited by Michael Anthony, pp. 134-36. Grand Rapids: Baker Academic, 2001.

Gray, Robert M., and Josephine M. Kasterler. "An Evaluation of the Effectiveness of a Foster Grandparent Project." *Sociology and Social Research* 54 (1970): 181-89.

Greeno, James G., Allan M. Collins and Lauren B. Resnick. "Cognition and Learning." In *Handbook of Educational Psychology,* edited by David C. Berliner and Robert C. Calfee, pp. 15-46. New York: Macmillan, 1996.

Grefe, Dagmar. "Combating Ageism with Narrative and Intergroup Contact: Possibilities of Intergenerational Connections." *Pastoral Psychology* 60 (February 2011): 99-105.

Grenz, Stanley. *Theology for the Community of God.* Nashville: Broadman & Holman, 1994.

Gruenler, Royce G. "John 17:20-26." *Interpretation* 43, no. 2 (1989): 178-83.

Hagestad, Gunhild O., and Peter Uhlenberg. "The Social Separation of Old and Young: A Root of Ageism." *Journal of Social Issues* 61, no. 2 (2005): 343-60.

Hall, Chad. *"All in the Family* Is Now *Grey's Anatomy:* Today's Segregation Is by Age." *Leadership* 27 (Fall 2006): 33.

Han, Key Young. *Implementation of Multigenerational Ministry Activities and Worship for a Korean-American Church.* Abstract. Doctor of Ministry project, Golden Gate Baptist Theological Seminary, San Francisco, CA, 2009.

Harkness, Allan G. "Intergenerational and Homogeneous-Age Education: Mutually Exclusive Strategies for Faith Communities?" *Religious Education* 95 (2000): 51-63.

———. "Intergenerational Christian Education: An Imperative for Effective Education in Local Churches (Part 1)." *Journal of Christian Education* 41, no. 2 (1998b): 5-14.

———. "Intergenerational Christian Education: An Imperative for Effective Education in Local Churches (Part 2)." *Journal of Christian Education* 42, no. 1 (1998c): 37-50.

———. "Intergenerational Christian Education: Reclaiming a Significant Educational Strategy in Christian Faith Communities." Doctoral dissertation, Murdoch University, Perth, Australia, 1996.

———. "Intergenerational Corporate Worship as a Significant Educational Activity." *Christian Education Journal* 7NS (Spring 2003): 5-21.

———. "Intergenerational Education for an Intergenerational Church?" *Religious Education* 93 (1998a): 431-47.

———. "Intergenerationality: Biblical and Theological Foundations." *Christian Education Journal* (series 3) 9, no. 1 (Spring 2012): 121-34.

Harrison, John E. "Forming Connections: A Study of Adolescent Faith Development as Perceived by Adult Christians." Doctoral dissertation, Princeton Theological Seminary, *Dissertation Abstracts International*, 60, 07A, 1999.

Harrison, Matthew C. *Christ Have Mercy: How to Put Your Faith into Action.* St. Louis: Concordia, 2008.

Hauck, Friedrich. "Koinonia." In *Theological Dictionary of the New Testament*, edited by Gerhard Kittel and Gerhard Friedrich, 3:786-809. Grand Rapids: Eerdmans, 1965.

Hellerman, Joseph H. *When the Church Was a Family: Recapturing Jesus' Vision for Authentic Christian Community.* Nashville: B & H Academic, 2009.

Hilborn, David, and Matthew Bird. *God and the Generations: Youth, Age and the Church Today,* Carlisle, UK: Paternoster Press, 2003.

Icenogle, Gareth Weldon. *Biblical Foundations for Small Group Ministry: An Integrative Approach.* Downers Grove, IL: InterVarsity Press, 1994.

"Intergenerational Teams: How One Ministry Shows They Can Work." Interview with Jay Pasavant, Dan Chaverin and J. R. Kerr. *Christian Management Report* 30 (August 2006): 17-20.

Johnson, Erik. "Stepping Over the Gap." *Leadership Journal* 20 (Spring 1999): 107-8.

Joiner, Reggie, Chuck Bomar and Abbie Smith. *The Slow Fade.* Colorado Springs: David C. Cook, 2010.

Kang, Young-Shin. "The Role of Religious Socialization in Asian Families for Children's Self-Perceived Early Academic Success and Social Competence."

Doctoral dissertation, Counseling Psychology Dissertations. Paper 12. Northeastern University, Boston, MA, 2010.

Kegan, Robert. *The Evolving Self: Problem and Process in Human Development.* Cambridge, MA: Harvard University Press, 1982.

Kinnaman, David, with Aly Hawkins. *You Lost Me: Why Young Christians Are Leaving the Church . . . and Rethinking Faith.* Grand Rapids: Baker Books, 2011.

Kirk, Daphne. *Reconnecting the Generations: Empowering God's People, Young and Old, to Live, Worship, and Serve Together.* Buxhall, Suffolk, UK: Kevin Mayhew LTD, 2001.

Kline, Kathleen Kovner. *Authoritative Communities: The Scientific Case for Nurturing the Whole Child.* New York: Springer Verlag, 2008.

Ko, Min Ho. "Recognizing and Bridging Common Intergenerational Differences in a Korean American Congregation." Doctor of Ministry project, Drew University, Madison, NJ, 2010.

Kocarnik, Rosanne R., and James J. Ponzetti. "The Influence of Intergenerational Contact on Child Care Participants." *Child Care Quarterly* 15 (1986): 244-50.

Koehler, George. *Learning Together: A Guide for Intergenerational Education in the Church.* Nashville: Discipleship Resources, 1977.

Kohlberg, Lawrence. *Collected Papers on Moral Development and Moral Education.* Cambridge, MA: Center for Moral Development and Education, Harvard Graduate School of Education, 1973.

————. *Essays on Moral Development.* Vol. 2, *The Psychology of Moral Development.* San Francisco: Harper & Row, 1984.

————, and Rochelle Mayer. "Development as the Aim of Education." *Harvard Education Review* 41 (1972): 451-69.

Komonchak, Joseph A., Mary Collins and Dermot A. Lane, eds. *The New Dictionary of Theology.* Wilmington, DE: Michael Glazier, 1987.

Kuehne, Valerie S., ed. *Intergenerational Programming: Understanding What We Have Created.* Binghamton, NY: Haworth Press, 1999.

Kuhn, Margaret. "Foreword." In *Intergenerational Programs: Imperatives, Strategies, Impacts, Trends,* edited by Sally Newman and S. W. Brummel, pp. xi-xii. Binghamton, NY: Haworth Press, 1989.

Kwon, Danny. "Spiritual Formation in the Lives of Korean-American Youth." *The Journal of Youth Ministry* (Spring 2005): 81.

Lanker, Jason. "The Family of Faith: The Place of Natural Mentoring in the Church's Christian Formation of Adolescents." *Christian Education Journal* (series 3) 7, no. 2 (Fall 2010): 267-80.

————. "The Relationship Between Natural Mentoring and Spirituality in Christian Adolescents." *Journal of Youth Ministry* 9 (Fall 2010): 93-109.

Lave, Jean, and Etienne Wenger. *Situated Learning: Legitimate Peripheral Participation.* New York: Cambridge University Press, 1991.

Lee, Helen. "Age-Old Divide: How Do You Integrate the Generations and Life Stages at your Church? Five Church Leaders Respond." *Leadership* 27 (Fall 2006): 43-46.

LeFever, Marlene. *Creative Teaching Methods.* Colorado Springs: Cook Communication Ministries, 1996.

————. *Learning Styles: Reaching Everyone God Gave You to Teach.* Colorado Springs: Cook Communication Ministries, 2001.

Lenski, Gerhard. *The Religious Factor: A Sociological Study of Religion's Impact on Politics, Economics, and Family Life.* Garden City, NY: Doubleday, 1961.

Levinson, Daniel. *The Seasons of a Man's Life.* New York: Ballantine Press, 1978.

Lewis, Gordon Russell, and Bruce A. Demarest. *Integrative Theology.* Vol. 3. Grand Rapids: Zondervan, 1994.

Loder, James. "Conversations on Fowler's Stages of Faith and Loder's *The Transforming Moment:* Reflections on Fowler's 'Stages of Faith,'" *Religious Education* 77, no. 2 (1982): 133-39.

Lutheran Worship. St. Louis: Concordia Publishing Company, 1982.

MacCallum, Judith, David Palmer, Peter Wright, Wendy Cumming-Potvin, Jeremy Northcote, Michelle Brooke and Cameron Tero. *Community Building Through Intergenerational Exchange Programs.* Australia: National Youth Affairs Research Scheme, 2006.

Marr, Peter R. "Development of an Intergenerational Curriculum for Christian Education Ministry in the Church." *Dissertation Abstracts International,* 51, 1182. Doctoral dissertation, Eastern Baptist Theological Seminary, 1990.

Martineau, Mariette, Joan Weber and Lief Kehrwald. *Intergenerational Faith Formation: All Ages Learning Together.* New London, CT: Twenty-Third Publications, 2008.

Martinson, Roland, and Diane Shallue. "Foundations for Cross-Generational Ministry." In *Across the Generations: Incorporating All Ages in Ministry: The Why and How,* edited by Vicky Goplin, Jeffrey Nelson, Mark Gardner and Eileen Zahn, pp. 4-10. Minneapolis: Augsburg, 2001.

Marx, Marcia, Pamela Hubbard, Jiska Cohen-Mansfield, Maha Dakheel-Ali and Khin Thein. "Community-Service Activities Versus Traditional Activities in an Intergenerational Visiting Program." *Educational Gerontology* 31 (2004): 263-71.

Maslow, Abraham. *Motivation and Personality.* New York: Harper & Brothers, 1954.

McGavran, Donald A. *Understanding Church Growth.* Grand Rapids: Eerdmans, 1970.

———, with Win C. Arn. *How to Grow a Church.* Glendale, CA: Regal, 1973.

McIntosh, Gary. *One Church, Four Generations: Understanding and Reaching All Ages in Your Church.* Grand Rapids: Baker, 2002.

Mead, Margaret. *Culture and Commitment: The New Relationships Between the Generations in the 1970s.* Rev. ed. New York: Columbia University Press, 1978.

Menconi, Pete. *The Intergenerational Church: Understanding Congregations from WWII to www.com.* Littleton, CO: Mt. Sage Publishing, 2010.

Meyers, Patty. *Live, Learn, Pass It On!—The Practical Benefits of Generations Growing Together in Faith.* Nashville: Discipleship Resources, 2006.

Michael, Sally. *Lord, Teach Us to Pray: A Study for Children and Adults on Prayer.* Minneapolis: Children Desiring God, 2006.

———. *The Righteous Shall Live by Faith: A Study for Children and Adults on the Ten Commandments.* Minneapolis: Children Desiring God, 2005.

Miles, M. Scott. *Families Growing Together.* Wheaton, IL: Victor Books, 1990.

Minatrea, Milfred. *Shaped by God's Heart: The Passion and Practices of Missional Churches.* San Francisco: Jossey-Bass, 2004.

Moran, Gabriel. *Interplay: A Theory of Religion and Education.* Winona, MN: Saint Mary's College Press, 1981.

———. "Where Now, What Next." In *Foundations of Religious Education,* edited by Padraic O'Hare, pp. 93-110. New York: Paulist, 1978.

Morgenthaler, Shirley. *Right from the Start: A Parent's Guide to the Young Child's Faith Development.* St. Louis: Concordia Publishing House, 2001.

Mounstephen, Philip, and Kelly Martin. *Body Beautiful? Recapturing a Vision for All-Age Church.* Cambridge: Grove Books, 2004.

Nelson, C. Ellis. *How Faith Matures.* Louisville, KY: Westminster John Knox, 1989.

———. *Where Faith Begins.* Atlanta: John Knox Press, 1967.

Newman, Sally, and Barbara Larimer. *Senior Citizen School Volunteer Program: Report on Cumulative Data, 1988-1995.* Pittsburgh, PA: Generations Together, 1995.

Newman, Sally, and Steven W. Brummel, eds. *Intergenerational Programs: Imperatives, Strategies, Impacts, Trends.* New York: Haworth Press, 1989.

Newman, Sally, Christopher R. Ward, Thomas B. Smith, Janet O. Wilson and James M. McCrea, eds. *Intergenerational Programs: Past, Present and Future.* Washington, DC: Taylor & Francis, 1997.

Newman, Sally, Emin Karip and Robert B. Faux. "Everyday Memory Function of Older Adults: The Impact of Intergenerational School Volunteer Programs." *Educational Gerontology* 21 (1995): 569-80.

Ng, David, and Virginia Thomas, *Children in the Worshiping Community*. Louisville, KY: Westminster John Knox, 1985.

Nichols, Charles. "If We're a Family, Let's Learn Together!" *The Messenger* 41, no. 1 (2003): 4-5.

Nussbaum, Jon F., Margaret J. Pitts, Frances N. Huber, Janice L. R. Krieger and Jennifer E. Ohs. "Ageism and Ageist Language Across the Life Span: Intimate Relationships and Non-Intimate Interactions." *Journal of Social Issues* 61, no. 2 (2005): 287-305.

Olson, Ginny, Diane Elliot and Mike Work. *Youth Ministry Management Tools*. Grand Rapids: Youth Specialties, Zondervan, 2001.

Ortberg, John. "The Gap: The Fractured World of Multigenerational Church Leadership." *Leadership* 30 (Summer 2009): 48-52.

Osmer, Richard, R. "James W. Fowler and the Reformed Tradition: An Exercise in Theological Reflection in Religious Education." *Religious Education*, 85 (1990): 51-68.

Peterson, Eugene H. "Introduction to Exodus." In *The Message: The Bible in Contemporary Language*. Colorado Springs: NavPress, 2002.

Piaget, Jean. *Moral Judgment of the Child*. Translated by Marjorie Gabain. 3rd ed. London: Routledge & Kegan Paul, 1932.

———, and Bärbel Inhelder. *The Psychology of the Child*. Translated by Helen Weaver. New York: Basic Books, 1969.

Pinnock, Clark. *Flame of Love: A Theology of the Holy Spirit*. Downers Grove, IL: InterVarsity Press, 1996.

Pipher, Mary. "The New Generation Gap." *USA Weekend,* March 19-21, 1999, p. 12.

Post, Stephen. "Preface: Love Begets Love." In *The Best Love of the Children: Being Loved and Being Taught to Love as the First Human Right*, edited by Timothy Jackson, pp. xiii-xxiv. Grand Rapids: Eerdmans, 2011.

Powell, Kara E. "Is the Era of Age Segregation Over?" *Leadership* 30 (Summer 2009): 43-47.

———, Brad M. Griffin and Cheryl A. Crawford. *Sticky Faith: Youth Worker Edition: Practical Ideas to Nurture Long-Term Faith in Teenagers*. Grand Rapids: Zondervan, 2011.

Prest, Eddie. *From One Generation to Another*. Capetown: Training for Leadership, 1993.

Probst, Dorothy. "Worshipping God: Godly Play Joined with Intentional Inter-generational Ministry and the Ensuing Architectural Implications." M.A. Thesis, Luther Seminary, St. Paul, MN, 2003.

Rah, Soong-Chan. *The Next Evangelicalism: Freeing the Church from Western Cultural Captivity.* Downers Grove, IL: InterVarsity Press, 2009.

Rendle, Gil. *The Multigenerational Congregation: Meeting the Leadership Challenge.* Bethesda, MD: Alban Institute, 2002.

Rhodes, Jean. *Stand by Me: The Risks and Rewards of Mentoring Today's Youth.* Cambridge, MA: Harvard University Press, 2004.

Richards, Lawrence O. *A Theology of Christian Education.* Grand Rapids: Zondervan, 1975.

Richardson, Rick. "Preaching Across the Great Divide: Seven Means to Communicate when Facing Today's Ethnic, Gender, and Generational Gaps." *Leadership* 26, no. 2 (2005): 47-49.

Rieber, Robert W., and Aaron S. Carton, eds. *The Collected Works of L. S. Vygotsky.* Vol. 1. New York: Plenum Press, 1987.

Roberto, John. "Our Future Is Intergenerational." *Christian Education Journal* (series 3) 9, no. 1 (Spring 2012): 105-21.

—————, with Mariette Martineau. *Generations of Faith Resource Manual: Lifelong Faith Formation for the Whole Parish Community.* New London, CT: Twenty-Third Publications, 2005.

Rodriguez, Daniel A. *A Future for the Latino Church: Models for Multilingual and Multigenerational Hispanic Congregations.* Downers Grove, IL: InterVarsity Press, 2011.

Roehlkepartain, Eugene. "Engaging International Advisors in Creating a Shared Understanding of Spiritual Development: Seeking Common Ground in Understanding Spiritual Development: A Preliminary Theoretical Framework." Search Institute, 2012. Retrieved from <www.search-institute.org/csd/major-projects/definition-update>.

—————. *The Teaching Church: Moving Christian Education to Center Stage.* Nashville: Abingdon, 1993.

Rosencranz, Howard A., and Tony E. McNevin. "A Factor Analysis of Attitudes Toward the Aged." *The Gerontologist* 9, no. 1 (1969): 55-59.

Ross, Christine M. "Being an Intergenerational Congregation." *Issues* 41, no. 2 (2007): 24-32.

—————. "Four Congregations That Practice Intergenerationality." *Christian Education Journal* (series 3) 9, no. 1 (Spring 2012): 135-47.

————. *Intergenerational Christian Education: Opportunity for Building Community.* River Forest, IL: Lutheran Education Association Monograph Series, Spring 2003.

————. "A Qualitative Study Exploring Churches Committed to Intergenerational Ministry." Doctoral dissertation, Saint Louis University, St. Louis, MO, 2006.

Sadler, Judith. "Learning Together: All-Age Learning in the Church." In *Learning in the Way: Research and Reflection on Adult Christian Education,* edited by Jeff Astley. Leominster, Herefordshire, UK: Gracewing, 1999.

Sandage, Steven, Carol Aubrey and Tammy Ohland. "Weaving the Fabric of Faith." *Marriage and Family: A Christian Journal* 2, no. 4 (1999): 381-98.

Sawin, Margaret M. *Family Enrichment with Family Clusters.* Valley Forge, PA: Judson, 1979.

Schaller, Lyle. *Looking in the Mirror: Self-Appraisal in the Local Church.* Nashville: Abingdon Press, 1984.

Seefelt, Carol, Richard K. Jantz, Alice Galper and Kathy Serock. "Children's Attitudes Toward the Elderly: Educational Implications." *Educational Gerontology* 2 (1977): 301-10.

Smidt, Don. "Ten Principles of Intentional Intergenerational Ministry." Paper presented at Concordia University, Irvine, CA, October 2004.

Smith, Christian. *American Evangelicalism: Embattled and Thriving.* Chicago: University of Chicago Press, 1998.

————, with Kari Christoffersen, Hilary Davidson and Patricia Snell Herzog. *Lost in Transition: The Dark Side of Emerging Adulthood.* Oxford: Oxford University Press, 2011.

Smith, Christian, with Melinda Denton. *Soul Searching: The Religious and Spiritual Lives of American Teenagers.* Oxford: Oxford University Press, 2005.

Smith, Christian, with Patricia Snell. *Souls in Transition: The Religious and Spiritual Lives of Emerging Adults.* Oxford: Oxford University Press, 2009.

Snailum, Brenda. "Implementing Intergenerational Youth Ministry Within Existing Evangelical Church Congregations: What Have We Learned?" *Christian Education Journal* (series 3) 9, no. 1 (Spring 2012): 165-81.

Snyder, William, and Etienne Wenger. *Communities of Practice in Government: The Case for Sponsorship.* Report to the CIO Council of the U.S. Federal Government, 2003.

Stearns, Peter N. "Historical Trends in Intergenerational Contact." In *Intergenerational Programs: Imperatives, Strategies, Impacts, Trends,* edited by Sally Newman and Steven W. Brummel, pp. 21-31. Binghamton, NY: Haworth, 1989.

Stonehouse, Catherine. *Joining Children on the Spiritual Journey: Nurturing a Life of Faith*. Grand Rapids: Baker, 1998.

The Story: The Bible as One Continuing Story of God and His People. Grand Rapids: Zondervan, 2004.

Strauss, William, and Neil Howe. *Generations: The History of America's Future, 1584 to 2069*. New York: Quill, William Morrow Publisher, 1991.

Strommen, Merton, and Richard Hardel. *Passing on the Faith: A Radical New Model for Youth and Family Ministry*. Winona, MN: St. Mary's Press, 2000.

Struntz, Karen A., and Shari Reville, eds. *Growing Together: An Intergenerational Sourcebook*. Washington, DC: American Association of Retired Persons; Palm Springs, CA: The Elvirita Lewis Foundation, 1985.

Taylor, Andrea S., Leonard LoSciuto, Margaretta Fox, Susan Hilbert and Michael Sonkowsky. "The Mentoring Factor: Evaluation of the Across Ages' Intergenerational Approach to Drug Abuse Prevention." In *Intergenerational Programs: Understanding What We Have Created*, edited by Valerie S. Kuehne, pp. 77-99. Binghamton, NY: Haworth Press, 1999.

Vanderwell, Howard, ed. *The Church of All Ages: Generations Worshiping Together*. Herndon, VA: Alban Institute, 2008.

Vann, Jane R. "Foreword." In *The Church of All Ages: Generations Worshiping Together*, edited by Howard Vanderwell, pp. xiii-xvi. Herndon, VA: Alban Institute, 2008.

Vygotsky, Lev S. *Educational Psychology*. Translated by Robert Silverman. Boca Raton, FL: St. Lucie Press, 1997.

———. *Mind in Society: The Development of Higher Psychological Process*. Edited by Michael Cole, Vera John-Steiner, Sylvia Scribner and Ellen Souberman. Cambridge, MA: Harvard University Press, 1978.

———. *Thought and Language*. Translated by Alex Kozulin. Rev. ed. Cambridge, MA: MIT Press, 1986.

Ward, Angie. "Let the Little Children Come." *Leadership* 30 (Summer 2009): 53-57.

Ward, Ted. "Foreword." In *Nurture That Is Christian: Development Perspectives in Christian Education*, edited by James Wilhoit and John Dettoni, pp. 7-17. Grand Rapids: Baker, 2005.

Welch, W. Kevin. "An Interpersonal Influence Model of Traditional Religious Commitment." *Sociological Quarterly* 22 (1981): 81-92.

Welter, Paul. *Learning from Children*. Wheaton, IL: Tyndale House, 1984.

Wenger, Etienne. "Communities of Practice: A Brief Introduction." July 2006. <www.ewenger.com/theory/>.

———. "Communities of Practice." *Healthcare Forum Journal* 39, no. 4 (1996): 20-27.

———. "Communities of Practice: Learning as a Social System." *The Systems Newsletter* 9, no. 5 (1998): 1-5.

———. *Communities of Practice: Learning, Meaning, and Identity.* New York: Cambridge University Press, 1998.

———. *The Public Involvement Community of Practice at Health Canada: A Case Study.* Ottawa: Health Canada, Corporate Consultation Secretariat, 2003.

———, Richard A. McDermott and William Snyder. *Cultivating Communities of Practice: A Guide to Managing Knowledge.* Cambridge, MA: Harvard Business School Press, 2002.

Wertsch, James, and Barbara Rogoff. "Editors' Notes." In *Children's Learning in the "Zone of Proximal Development": New Directions for Child Development,* edited by Barbara Rogoff and James Wertsch, pp. 1-6. San Francisco: Jossey-Bass, 1984.

Westerhoff, John H., III. *Will Our Children Have Faith?* Rev. ed. Toronto: Morehouse, 2000.

———, and Gwen K. Neville. *Generation to Generation: Conversations on Religious Education and Culture.* Philadelphia: United Church Press, 1974.

White, James W. *Intergenerational Religious Education: Models, Theories, and Prescription for Interage Life and Learning in the Faith Community.* Birmingham, AL: Religious Education Press, 1988.

Wilhoit, James C. *Spiritual Formation As If the Church Mattered: Growing in Christ Through Community.* Grand Rapids: Baker Academic, 2008.

Willard, Dallas. *Renovation of the Heart: Putting on the Character of Christ.* Colorado Springs: NavPress, 2002.

Williams, John T. "If You Build It, They Will Come: Using Storytelling as an Intergenerational Bridge." D.Min. thesis, Wesley Theological Seminary, Washington, DC, 2006.

Wright, N. T. *The New Testament and the People of God.* London: SPCK, 1992.

Wuthnow, Robert. *After the Baby Boomers: How Twenty- and Thirty-Somethings Are Shaping the Future of American Religion.* Princeton, NJ: Princeton University Press, 2007.

Zahn, Drew. "Connecting the Generations: How Churches Are Building and Sustaining Age-Integrated, Multigenerational Ministry." *Leadership* 23 (Spring 2002): 37-42.

Author Index

Subject Index

Scripture Index

Genesis
1, *201, 273*
1:1-2, *111*
1:26, *111*
5, *144*
9:12, *294*
17:7, *294*
22, *244*
29:31-35, *277*

Exodus
3:15, *294*
12, *80*
12:26-27, *80, 294*
23:15, *80*
23:16, *80*
34:18, *80*
34:22, *80*
34:25, *80*

Leviticus
13–15, *86*
23:5-8, *80*
23:15-21, *80*
23:23-25, *80*
23:33–36, *80*

Numbers
9:1-14, *80*
28:16-25, *80*
28:26-31, *80*
29:1-6, *80*
29:12-39, *80*

Deuteronomy
6:6-9, *81, 184, 294*
7:9, *295*
12:12, *295*
16:1-8, *80*
16:9-10, *80*
16:13-18, *80*
29:10-12, *78, 295*

31:11, *296*
31:12-13, *80, 295*

Joshua
4:1-7, *278*
4:21-24, *220*
8:34-35, *78, 295*
22:26-27, *295*

Judges
2:10, *144, 295*

Ruth
1–4, *81*

1 Samuel
2:11, *81, 296*
3, *81*
17:37, *224*
18:18-27, *81*

1 Kings
19:19-21, *81*

2 Kings
2:1-18, *81*
22–23, *81*
22:1-2, *296*
22:2, *81*

1 Chronicles
9:23, *296*
16:15, *296*

2 Chronicles
20:3, *78*
20:12, *79*
20:13, *78, 296*
20:15, *79*
20:32, *78*

Nehemiah
8:2, *296*
8:2-3, *79, 296*

12:43, *79, 296*

Esther
3, *167*
9:26-28, *296*

Job
12:12, *133*

Psalms
23, *201*
78:4, *219*
79:13, *144*
95:1, *274*
139:14, *242*

Proverbs
22:6, *299*

Ecclesiastes
1:4, *300*

Song of Solomon
1, *276*

Isaiah
41:4, *300*
51:7-8, *300*
61:1, *109*
61:1-2, *278*
61:1-4, *209*
61:3, *109*
61:3-4, *278*

Jeremiah
1:5-8, *300*

Lamentations
5:19, *300*

Ezekiel
45:21-24, *80*

Daniel
4:3, *142, 154, 300*